SHAPING THE BAR

SHAPING THE BAR

The Future of Attorney Licensing

Joan W. Howarth

STANFORD UNIVERSITY PRESS
Stanford, California

Stanford University Press
Stanford, California

Printed in the United States of America on acid-free, archival-quality paper

ISBN 9781503613560 (cloth)
ISBN 9781503633698 (electronic)

Library of Congress Control Number: 2022011081

Library of Congress Cataloging-in-Publication Data available upon request.

Cover Design and Art: Derek Thornton/ Notch Design
Typeset by Elliott Beard in Minion 11/14

For Carmen

CONTENTS

Part Three
CHARACTER AND FITNESS
The Right Stuff

Part Four
THE FUTURE
*Competence-Based Alignment of
Experience, Education, and Exams*

PREFACE

MY MEMORIES OF TAKING THE bar exam are spotty. After law school graduation I spent June and July 1980 with hundreds of others listening to lectures about legal rules in bar review classes in the Los Angeles Convention Center. When not at the convention center, I was at my kitchen table memorizing thick books of rules. I used a highlighter to try to stay focused; eventually the pages were solid yellow and soggy. Aside from the tedium, it was not a bad time. I had a job lined up and only one thing to do. Sympathy and kindness surrounded me. Studying for the bar was such a recognized ordeal that my ex-husband gave me a car to free me from the bus. Even the woman behind the counter at the convenience store wished me good luck and told me how smart I was each time I visited. The stress and boredom of bar preparation were enough to escalate my junk food cravings and visits to the sympathetic 7-11 clerk but were not bad enough to drive me back to cigarettes. My experience was okay.

One close friend was not as lucky. Her focus disappeared when her walking companion collapsed and died on an early morning walk the week of the test. That shock derailed my friend's bar exam and her career, for a time.

For the nights of the test, another friend and I shared a motel room by the Long Beach Convention Center where we took the exam. I had never heard of Rémy Martin, but I remember that was the cognac my friend pulled out of his suitcase our first jittery night in the motel. The next morning, I found my seat in an ocean of card tables, four to a table, on the floor of an arena in the vast convention center. Elbow room increased when one test-taker left the first morning and never returned.

That July, California bar examiners conducted an experiment in which test-takers were randomly assigned to take one of several new types of tests designed to be more like law practice. The experimental section would not count in our score, but we were unsettled by this random note in an exam that otherwise featured lockstep uniformity. I was a bit disappointed and a lot relieved to be selected for a relatively tame and straightforward version of the performance test experiment. Within a week I had forgotten most of the rules highlighted yellow in my bar books.

The results were released on a Friday late in November. Too impatient to wait for Monday's mail, I trekked to the state bar office early Saturday morning to look for my name. The scene was bizarre and scary. Local television crews filmed the shouts, tears, and raucous champagne celebrations. A wild crush of candidates pushed forward to read the tiny type of the alphabetized lists of names on sheets of computer paper taped inside the wall of the giant plate-glass windows. I found my name, pushed slowly back through the throng, and was delighted to never again have to think about the bar.

Bar exams became important to me again years later. I have been teaching law students in the shadow of the bar exam for thirty years. The more students I taught, the more disturbed I became about attorney licensing. It is not just that the bar exam does a poor job of testing minimum competence. Plenty of annoying and thoughtless hurdles exist, and law school supplies its share. The inequity and harm to the public are more troubling. I have known elite students at fancy law schools who should not be lawyers; they can cruise through a bar exam but not look a client in the eye or treat her with respect. I have also taught wonderful students at less elite law schools whom I would trust to represent me, except they never passed a bar exam. I have seen up close and personal the disparities inflicted by our current licensing traditions, both law school and bar exams. I can see the faces of too many highly competent former students who are not practicing law because they did not pass the bar. Too many are African American or Latinx.

The loss of that legal talent saddens and angers me. Improving attorney licensing became a personal goal.

To try to puzzle out how we should be licensing new attorneys, I have studied and written about legal education and bar exams, taught courses aimed at helping students pass bar exams, and, most recently, had the privilege of serving as a bar examiner in Nevada. I am ready to share what I have learned.

This book is for two groups of clients who deserve better from our profession: the people currently being represented by licensed attorneys who do not know what they are doing, and the grateful future clients of excellent lawyers who would have been lost to the profession without attorney licensing reform.

In 1980 California undertook the most ambitious bar exam experiment in United States history, using me and the other 7,438 applicants for its July bar exam as guinea pigs. The experiment was a bold response to two pressing problems. One big problem was that the bar exam, as gatekeeper to the legal profession, opened wide or slammed shut in predictable ways, depending on who was knocking at the gate to be admitted. In the 1970s law schools had begun enrolling and graduating greater numbers of people of color, but examiners saw that white applicants consistently passed the bar exam at higher rates than African Americans, Asian Americans, and Hispanics.

These troubling disparate impacts helped to focus bar examiners' attention on another fundamental issue: the wide gap between the skills of actual law practice and the ability to succeed on the paper-and-pencil bar exam. Were the two problems related? The massive California experiment was undertaken to test the possibility that closing the gap between actual law practice and the bar exam might also reduce the disparities in pass rates. But how to bring the bar exam closer to actual law practice?

California bar examiners designed several different versions of tests designed to simulate law practice. Most were paper-and-pencil tests conducted for a few hours. But foreshadowing *The Truman Show*, a 1998 film about a man whose whole life was an elaborately produced television show, California also set up fake law offices in which about 500 candidates spent two days each pretending to practice law under the watchful eye of fake supervisors.

The results were disappointing. Performance tests would change who passed the bar exam, advantaging those with clinical experience, but racial disparities were not significantly reduced.[1] Bar examiners—concluding that the results of all versions of the performance tests were sufficiently similar so the simplest version was good enough—added a relatively short paper-and-pencil performance test to the California bar exam. By now, similar performance tests are used by most states, the only new component since the multiple-choice Multistate Bar Exam was launched by the National Conference of Bar Examiners in 1972. Performance tests are widely and properly praised as the components of today's bar exams that come closest to law practice, but they are weighted less than multiple-choice and essay questions. Ambition for more fundamental reform burned out and disappeared for decades. Until now.

Part One

THE ATTORNEY LICENSING CRISIS AND HOW WE GOT HERE

1

THE CRISIS IN ATTORNEY LICENSING

ATTORNEY LICENSING SUFFERS FROM PROBLEMS that start deep in the culture of the legal profession. Practicing law is difficult, so obtaining a license to practice law should be hard. But demanding and misguided requirements protect lawyers more than the public. Licensing standards should protect the public by attempting to ensure that newly licensed attorneys are at least minimally competent. Our current system does not do this well. At the same time, bar exams, the signature feature of licensing, help to keep the legal profession overwhelmingly white—and largely untouched by the profession's background rhetoric of diversity, equity, and inclusion. Trouble flowing from these two problems—the disparate impact of requirements that are themselves too loosely connected to minimum competence—has erupted into a full-blown attorney licensing crisis.

High barriers to entry. Many professions wrap themselves in the rhetoric of public protection but build barriers to entry as high as possible to enhance the prestige of the profession and stifle competition.[1] The legal profession in the United States has succeeded in this project.[2] Becoming an attorney takes a good deal of time and money. Most U.S. jurisdictions require anyone seeking to practice law to obtain a bachelor's degree, graduate from an accredited law school, pass a standardized multiple-choice test on rules of professional responsibility, successfully navigate an extensive character and fitness inquiry, and pass a standardized bar exam. Deborah Rhode has summarized the problem: "In theory, these requirements serve to protect the public from incompetent or unethical attorneys. In practice, they are highly imperfect means of accomplishing either."[3]

Unlike in many other countries, the U.S. law degree typically requires three years of expensive full-time study following an undergraduate degree.[4] The tuition at this writing is already over $70,000 at Ivy League law schools like Cornell and Columbia, and over $50,000 at less famous schools like New England and Southwestern.[5] The average graduate has over $160,000 in debt at graduation, an amount that will mushroom over decades of payments; Hispanic and Black law graduates have the highest law school debt.[6]

Requirements for licensure should be laser focused on readiness to practice law with the minimum competence of a new attorney. But after seven years of education, hundreds of thousands of dollars of law school debt, two months of cramming legal knowledge, and success on a bar exam, a candidate can be licensed to practice law without having been in a law office or a courthouse and perhaps without ever having been in the presence of a lawyer with a client. How is this possible?

Law schools and bar exams are both disconnected from legal practice. The combination of three years of post-graduate law school and passing a bar exam do not adequately protect the public because law schools and bar exams share the same whopping weakness. For 150 years, law schools in the United States have been largely aligned with the "scientific" approach of Christopher Columbus Langdell, focused on dissection of appellate decisions in a university setting, the so-called case method.[7] For this and other reasons, lawyering abilities beyond core analytic skills are relatively recent additions and are still peripheral at too many law schools. Completing a legal education requires substantially less clinical experience than what is required in other professions.[8] Bar passage correlates well with law school grades in part because bar exams test some of the traditional academic skills of law school rather than the professional proficiencies required for minimum competence in practice.[9] In combination, this system permits new lawyers to be licensed without demonstrating that they can practice law at a minimum level of competence.

Bar exams are both too difficult and too easy.[10] The exams are too easy for people who excel at multiple-choice questions. Wizards at standardized tests can pass the bar with little difficulty, perhaps with a few weeks spent memorizing legal rules,[11] without showing competence in a greater range of lawyering skills or any practice in assuming professional responsibility.

And, bar exams are too difficult for candidates who do not excel at memorizing huge books of legal rules. An attorney would be committing malpractice by attempting to answer most new legal questions from memory without checking the statute, rules, or case law. Leon Green, the dean of Northwestern Law in 1939, observed that "there is not a single similarity between the bar examination process and what a lawyer is called upon to do in his practice, unless it be to give a curbstone opinion."[12] The focus on memorization of books of rules was silly in 1939, but today it is shockingly anachronistic, as attorneys asked for "curbstone opinions" would be carrying a complete law library on their phones. Extensive rule memorization makes bar exams less valid, meaning that they test attributes not associated with competence to practice law. Law graduates who would be great lawyers—too many of whom are people of color—are failing bar exams because they cannot drop everything else for two months to devote themselves to memorizing thick books of rules.[13]

Excellent reliability, weak validity and fairness. High-stakes tests should be reliable, valid, and fair.[14] Because of the ever-increasing and impressive psychometric expertise of the National Conference of Bar Examiners (NCBE), bar exams today are highly reliable, in that the same score means the same thing over different administrations.[15] But, bar exams suffer from significant problems of validity and fairness.

Validity means that the test assesses what it purports to assess. Bar exams are used validly to the extent that they measure minimum competence to practice law. In the vocabulary of testing experts, the bar exam should assess knowledge, skills, and abilities used by competent lawyers[16] and enable distinctions between candidates who are *not* minimally competent and those who are *barely* minimally competent. None of this is easy, and criticisms of the validity of bar exams are widespread and longstanding.[17]

Bar exams *do* test critical reading, legal writing, and legal analysis—all crucial legal skills. But bar exams do not yet test—and law school graduation does not guarantee—a wider range of lawyering skills long-identified as critical, including interviewing, negotiation, strategic thinking, client relationships, client communications, and case management.[18] And the kind of legal analysis tested on bar exams—artificially static rules applied to artificially stable fact scenarios—is elementary: the legal analysis of a first-year law student. Competence in practicing law requires an understanding of the malleability of the law and the ability to manipulate both rules and facts within the norms of legal analysis.[19]

The "knowledge" component of bar exams consists mainly of recall of a large swath of detailed common law rules thought to be likely to be used by new lawyers. But specialization makes it impossible to find a common denominator of legal doctrine used by most lawyers. And being a competent lawyer today does not involve the memorization of minutiae of legal rules. Capable lawyers need to be familiar with foundational concepts from a range of legal subjects to recognize the areas of law implicated by a new factual scenario, or "issue spot." Rather than memorizing the details of legal rules, good lawyers need to know how to find what they do not already know.[20]

Perhaps the most difficult aspect of validity is setting the pass-fail line, or the "cut score," so that it reasonably distinguishes between the *almost* minimally competent and the *barely* minimally competent.[21] The science of testing has led professional licensers—of nurses, engineers, dentists, and others—to use a single professionally developed multiple-choice test as the anchor for the professions' assessment of minimum competence.[22] For the legal profession in the United States, this function has been performed by the NCBE's Multistate Bar Exam (MBE).[23] Other professions have established a uniform national cut score for their multiple-choice tests used to establish the basic level of competence in the field.[24] By contrast, in law, each jurisdiction has held onto its authority to set its own MBE cut score.[25] This preference for strong local control has resulted in wide disparities in how states use the same test to assess the same thing: minimum competence to practice law. Our patchwork quilt of different cut scores operates as if crossing a state line makes someone competent to practice law, which is especially questionable now that bar exams test "general law," not the law of any one state. The wide range of cut scores used on bar exams undermines confidence that any one of them accurately reflects an attorney's minimum competence.

High-stakes tests need to be fair,[26] and professional standards for such exams require that fairness for all test-takers be built into the design of the tests and not just an afterthought.[27] Bar exam accommodations for disabled candidates are true afterthoughts, a relatively recent and contested area of bar administration left to individual jurisdictions to handle.[28] Since jurisdictions are inconsistent, disabled candidates must shop for accommodations.[29] During the pandemic, some states required only disabled applicants to test in person, forcing them to choose between receiving the accommodations for which they were legally entitled or protecting themselves from the health risk of testing in person.[30] The persistent, undisputed racial and ethnic disparities in bar passage rates also raise profound fairness concerns, especially considering the weak connection between bar exams and practice.[31]

Persistent, well-known, terrible racial disparities. The legal profession is 86 percent white,[32] making it less inclusive and less diverse than many other elite professions, including medicine,[33] engineering,[34] dentistry,[35] and accounting.[36] This well-known and widely decried lack of diversity of the legal profession[37] has many causes, chief among them admissions practices for law schools and the bar.[38]

Evidence of the disparate impact of bar exams is overwhelming. The American Bar Association (ABA) statistics for first-time passers in 2020 show white candidates passing at 88 percent compared to Black candidates (66 percent), with Asians and Hispanics in the middle (80 and 76 percent, respectively).[39] California publishes the most complete demographic information, which reveals ethnic and racial disparities for every category of test-taker for every administration of its bar exam.[40] NCBE researchers undertook a national study of racial and ethnic disparities that showed that the average 2006 MBE score for whites was 149.3, for Asians 146.1, for Hispanics 143.3, and for Blacks 137.9.[41] Racial disparities are persistent and consistent across other states that have conducted studies, like New York,[42] Texas,[43] and New Mexico.[44] Of the 345 graduates of ABA-accredited law schools who took the California bar exam in February 2020, 20 identified as Black. One passed.[45]

Bar examiners defend unequal results on bar exams by arguing that bar passage differences reflect prior differences, such as gaps in educational background, in standardized tests from PSAT to SAT to LSAT to bar exams, and in law school grades.[46] Although bar examiners cannot be expected to eliminate all preexisting inequalities, we should be expected to eliminate *unnecessary* disparities in test results. Bar examiners have enjoyed immunity from the scrutiny of discriminatory employment tests required by Title VII, but our professional responsibility requires us to weed out any unjustified licensing practices that disproportionately keep people of color out of the profession.[47] There are real and appalling educational disparities that precede bar exams. Instead of using those circumstances as an excuse for the unequal results, we are obligated to ensure that the exams are all the more valid and nondiscriminatory.

The responsibility of addressing these longstanding disparities falls squarely on the state supreme court justices and bar examiners who have a formal, professional duty to ensure that the admissions process they oversee is nondiscriminatory.[48] The persistent racial gaps in bar exam pass rates, combined with the exams' untested validity, could be unlawful if Title VII applied. Having fought to immunize ourselves from the oversight that Title VII imposes on employers who use tests with such disparate impact, state courts and bar examiners have rested on our good faith as justification. Racial gaps and unproven validity both reduce the protection the public receives from licensing.

Although even fair tests may not eliminate all disparities in results, the most authoritative source of testing standards reminds test designers that "group differences in testing outcomes should trigger heightened scrutiny for possible sources of bias."[49] In the world of bar exams, that scrutiny has focused on efforts to improve item selection and question drafting.[50] What has been much more difficult, and what has largely been missing, is an ambitious focus on job relatedness or validity.

High cut scores exacerbate racial disparities and reduce bar exam validity. Cut score decisions are a significant source of avoidable racial and ethnic disparities. Selecting a lower cut score, or passing score, is the easiest way for bar examiners and state courts to reduce the disparate impact of their exams without sacrificing public protection or changing much.[51] Choosing a higher cut score within the range currently used by states widens the disparate racial impact of bar exams.[52] If bar exams were treated like employment tests, a jurisdiction's decision to maintain a high cut score with known increased disparate impact would require evidence that the high cut score is needed to assess minimum competence to practice law.[53] No such evidence exists.

High law school debt plus low bar passage equals financial ruin for too many, especially from underrepresented groups. Record numbers of recent law graduates have failed bar exams after racking up massive law school debt. The highest mean MBE score and highest recent pass rates occurred in 2008, when 71 percent of candidates and 82 percent of first-time takers passed nationally.[54] In 2019 only 58 percent of candidates and 73 percent of first-time takers passed.[55] Racial disparities in bar passage rates mean that the worst return from the financial investment of attending law school—hundreds of thousands in debt with no law license to show for it—is a burden that falls disproportionately on people of color. Plus, students of color pay more for law school and go deeper into debt than white students.[56] This would be bad enough if we had confidence that people who have not passed the bar were not likely to be competent attorneys. But we can have no such confidence. Passing bar exams has become a test of financial security; even after controlling for LSAT scores, candidates with more financial resources are significantly more likely to pass, and candidates who work for pay are significantly more likely to fail.[57]

Declining bar pass rates have increased the pressure on law schools. Attention to bar exams is a simple but accurate measure of the prestige of a U.S. law school: The less the school focuses on bar exam preparation, the "better" the law school. But recent declines in bar pass rates have imposed pressure on many law schools for the first time and put survival of the least elite law schools at risk. Several schools with unsustainably low bar passage rates have shut down.[58]

The unsustainable mismatch between the high cost of law school and the terrible market for new lawyers during the Great Recession caused the bottom to drop out of the law school applicant pool, which shrank by 36 percent between 2010 and 2016.[59] Law schools enrolled fewer students, but the reductions were not enough to avoid admitting new students with lesser credentials. Strong LSAT takers are strong MBE-takers, so the relaxed requirements for new students explained some of the steep declines in bar passage rates that began in 2014 and continued for several years.[60] Indeed, the then-head of the NCBE famously blamed law schools for admitting "less able" students.[61]

But entering credentials explain only part of the bar pass problem. California studied its precipitous decline in bar passage and found that lower entering credentials only accounted for 20 to 50 percent of the drop.[62] Perhaps the issues were (and are) generational, due to changed reading habits or lower quality public school education, or even the bad fit between outdated testing methods and candidates born to the internet. Theories abound, but serious research to explain the drop in bar passage rates is largely absent.

The less elite law schools often have strong opportunity missions that include accepting students with lower LSAT scores. Some law schools with a history of educating people of color are at risk of losing accreditation because of the new, stringent bar passage accreditation standards enacted in response to the falling pass rates.[63] The sharp decline in bar passage rates made bar passage more of a pressing issue for the many middle-tier law schools[64] that had previously been somewhat immune from that concern. Such schools have invested in academic support and bar preparation programs, including partnering with commercial vendors of bar prep materials.[65] Many academic success professors are among the best educators at their law schools, but the pressure to prepare students for bar exams leads to teaching to the flawed test, lowering the quality of education offered.

Bar exams are making legal education worse. Poorly designed bar exams push law schools backwards.[66] Elite law schools pay virtually no attention to bar exams. Students at the most elite law schools are exceptionally good multiple-choice test-takers who can pass current bar exams without taking many courses on subjects covered on bar exams. For example, neither Yale nor Michigan requires JD students to take corporations, evidence, property, or any UCC course beyond introductory contracts.[67] JD students at Harvard are required to take property, but not constitutional law, evidence, or corporations.[68] Beyond the obvious lesson that admission to the "best" law schools and to the profession turns on multiple-choice testing expertise, we might think about what it means that the "top" law schools are the least wedded to the knowledge base considered crucial by bar examiners.

But the middle-range and less elite law schools who do not enroll the superstar test-takers face pressure to redirect curricula toward bar exam preparation and away from experiential learning courses that would prepare students to practice law. Indeed, NCBE officials blamed the increase in experiential courses for decreases in bar passage rates.[69] Law school students are now taking law school courses that drill them on quickly answering multiple-choice questions (1.8 minutes per question), as required for the MBE. Preparing for the test takes law students away from preparing to practice law. This diminishes legal education and hurts future clients. Why persist in such faulty licensing mechanisms? Perhaps attorneys prefer to keep entry barriers high[70] to maintain the astonishing benefits that come from our licenses to practice law.

Breadth, longevity, and monopoly. Because of self-interest protected by self-regulation,[71] admission to the bar in the United States, once obtained, brings three structural privileges of great value to lawyers: breadth, longevity, and monopoly. However, each imposes costs on the public.

A law license in the United States is a general license of unlimited breadth. Unlike the differential training and licensure of solicitors and barristers in Great Britain[72] or the board-certified specializations in medicine, a law license in the United States is a general one, meaning that it is neither specialized nor limited, other than geographically. My law license authorizes me to defend someone in a murder trial on Monday, finalize an adoption on Tuesday, take a start-up business public on Wednesday, argue a civil rights case in the Supreme Court on Thursday, and finalize a corporate merger on Friday. I would not take on all these lawyering roles, or even any two of them, however, because law is now a profession of specialists, not generalists. But we are still licensed through a one-size-fits-all process.

A law license also features longevity. Like federal judges, lawyers enjoy what amounts to a lifetime appointment. Passing a licensing test two months after graduation from law school gives me a license to practice law—without reexamination—until death. In this way the legal profession is like an elite college: It is hard to be accepted into the profession, but it is almost impossible to be thrown out. Very few lawyers face disbarment,[73] and no U.S. jurisdiction requires retesting after initial licensure.[74]

The only significant limitation on a law license in the United States is geography, and that limitation is disappearing. Lawyers are licensed by the states, whose authority stops at the state line. Historically each state tested on its own law, which can differ markedly. But the state courts charged with oversight of licensing have more pressing problems—judicial systems overrun by litigants not represented by counsel, for example—and precious few resources to devote to high-quality licensing exams. Thus, control over attorney licensing is increasingly consolidated with the National Conference of Bar Examiners (NCBE), a well-resourced nonprofit located in Madison, Wisconsin.[75] The NCBE produces test components for all jurisdictions and has successfully promoted the Uniform Bar Exam (UBE) with portable scores now used by about forty jurisdictions. Greater NCBE consolidation is ahead.[76] Passing a bar exam already allows an attorney to practice any kind of law for a lifetime, and soon it will permit that practice almost anywhere in the United States.

Attorney licensing is also a monopolistic system. Law is everywhere, and lawyers have the field to themselves.[77] This all-or-nothing system—a licensed attorney or nobody—results in a shockingly high number of "nobody" for legal representation. Only licensed attorneys are permitted to represent clients in court, and the shortage of affordable representation has left state courts overwhelmed by unrepresented litigants.[78] Law is everywhere, but lawyers are not, with 71 percent of state court cases being handled with at least one party unrepresented.[79] Lawyers are too expensive for too many people. The legal equivalents of physician assistants or nurse practitioners do not exist because most jurisdictions permit only one category of legal licensure.[80] Breaking up this monopoly on the provision of legal services is the most important reform to address the crisis in access to justice.[81]

Large companies do not need new forms of licensed legal service providers because they use unlicensed employees. Human resources,

compliance, contract drafting, and many other legal functions are routinely done in corporate offices without direct attorney oversight,[82] but
prohibitions on the unauthorized practice of law are not meaningful
restrictions in those arenas. Individuals do not have the same access to
less expensive legal professionals. Rethinking and reforming the lawyer's monopoly on the provision of legal services is necessary to address
the crisis in access to justice.

The current system of bar admissions also limits access to justice.
High barriers to entry—expensive educational requirements and low
bar passage rates—limit the number of lawyers and accelerate fees.
Law school graduates who never pass a bar exam are not available
to provide legal services. Graduates of less elite law schools are more
likely than graduates of elite law schools to represent people, rather
than entities.[83] The correlations between success on the standardized
tests that control admissions to law school and to the bar means that
the law graduates who do not pass a bar exam are disproportionately
likely to have been in the fraction of lawyers who represent people, not
entities. The racial and ethnic disparities in bar passage, and the fact
that lawyers of color are more likely than white lawyers to represent
clients of color,[84] means that people of color suffer a disproportionate
lack of lawyers in their communities. Candidates who do not pass a
bar exam currently have no other pathway to become a licensed provider of legal services.[85]

The stakes. The United States is awash in occupational licensing requirements, from exterminator to beautician to embalmer.[86] What
makes the licensing of attorneys so critical? A license to practice law
stands out in any economy, in any democracy committed to the rule of
law, and in any society aspiring to justice.

Law is everywhere and growing. The longstanding practice areas—
traffic accidents, business deals, keeping people out of jail—have been
eclipsed by the twentieth-century rise of the administrative state. Mush-
rooming regulations at the local, state, and federal level are drafted,
interpreted, enforced, and defended against by lawyers, as are local
ordinances and state and federal statutes. A lawyer probably drafted
the latest embalming licensing statute, and another lawyer would help
an exterminator regain her license. Lawyers routinely lead government
from small towns to the Oval Office. Decisions about who is permitted

to join and who is excluded from the legal profession are vital measures of democratic values and aspirations for justice.

The pandemic crisis of 2020 revealed that our imperfect licensing practices are held almost sacred by much of the profession. Jurisdictions across the country scrambled to attempt to administer their bar exam as usual, even when the pandemic made that impossible. The Virginia bar examiners made an illuminating accommodation to the pandemic: They relaxed their dress code for the two-day bar exam by suspending the requirement that men wear ties. To those of us unaccustomed to the professional culture of Virginia, this gesture invited a disturbing metaphor: Is the legal profession still operating too much like an exclusive club? People without financial resources, people of color, and people with disabilities are too often excluded from the club—the profession— through requirements that do not serve the public well. How attorney licensing got here and what to do about it are the subjects of the chapters that follow.

2

BECOMING A LAWYER IN
THE YOUNG NATION

LAWYERS IN THE UNITED STATES make up a powerful profession. As Richard Abel has explained, "The primary challenge for any occupation seeking to become a profession is to control supply."[1] Attorneys have shaped the profession through highly contested and changing educational requirements and licensing tests (bar exams) to determine who can practice law. Licensing systems—the mechanisms of belonging and exclusion—are key to understanding the profession.

Shaky beginnings. The legal profession's start in the American colonies was surprisingly shaky. Subjected to widespread hostility, lawyers were outlawed in some colonies, and the fees lawyers could charge were limited in others.[2] But the profession thrived with economic development and soon, like other professions, was able to define and elevate itself in part by whom it excluded, both informally and formally. Wealthy sons of the North and South were sent to England in the 1700s to study at the Inns of Court,[3] responding to Blackstone's invitation that law was an ideal calling for young gentlemen.[4] Delaware administered the first bar exam in 1737,[5] two generations before the Declaration of Independence. Earlier hostility dissipated, and the profession grew in stature. Twenty-five of the fifty-six signers of the Declaration of Independence were lawyers, as were thirty-one of the fifty-five members of the Constitutional Convention.[6]

After independence was won, American lawyers no longer looked to London for training and credentials. New lawyers typically studied on their own or in law offices. Alexander Hamilton read for three months to become a lawyer, a typical path.[7] Formal admission was lax and was handled by and limited to individual courts. The more established and accomplished courts began to impose distinctions related to number of years of apprenticeships and of formal education in deciding which candidates could appear, a home-grown version of a stratified bar.[8] In this highly decentralized way, the profession advanced with the new country. Lawyers propelled growth as the "technicians of change"[9] for the expanding nation.

Nineteenth-century transformations. Admission to the profession changed profoundly in the nineteenth century, moving from disparate local control to comprehensive systems and institutions remarkably like those of today. Attorney licensing in the first half of the eighteenth century was highly disorganized because of the expansion of the nation and the democratization of the Jacksonian era. Throughout the nineteenth century, lawyers became lawyers by working in law offices and reading. Abraham Lincoln recommended five books to read as "the best way" to enter the profession but was said to have added that "no serious damage would be done if one were to continue reading after having begun practicing."[10]

Every [white, male] person of good moral character . . . Jacksonian democratization led many states to enact laws allowing all citizens who were eligible to vote to practice law,[11] but prestige and exclusion mattered to lawyers even in the chaotic times of open admissions. For example, perhaps because farmers outnumbered lawyers sixty-two to thirty-nine at the 1850–51 Indiana Constitutional Convention, that new Indiana Constitution extended admission to the practice of law to "Every person of good moral character, being a voter," a provision that remained in Indiana's Constitution until 1932.[12] But lawyers ostracized the "untrained interlopers"[13] who tried to enter the profession through the open admission laws enacted by the anti-elitist citizenry.

The man thought to be the first Native American to practice law in the U.S. system, Choctaw citizen James McDonald, entered the profession in 1820.[14] Noteworthy exceptions like McDonald notwithstanding, the law was overwhelmingly a profession of white Protestant men of means even during periods of relatively low barriers to entry.[15] De Tocqueville's famous 1835 description of lawyers as the aristocracy of the country accurately suggested that the open admissions movement—although widespread—was relatively short-lived, at least outside of Indiana. Even metaphorical aristocracies require limitations on who is permitted to join. By the 1850s, shortly after Indiana first changed its constitution to create open admissions, the legal profession had outlasted the democratization efforts elsewhere and generally regained its reputation as a "learned profession."[16]

Graduates of law schools and office-trained lawyers practiced side by side until the early twentieth century, although not necessarily with equal status. Abraham Lincoln bemoaned the growing status of educated lawyers from the East, whom he thought looked down on lawyers like him, those who had entered the profession without formal legal education.[17] Law schools proliferated, especially after the 1870s. About 22 law schools enrolled 1,200 law students in 1860; by 1890, 61 law schools had 4,500 students.[18]

Oral bar exams. Attorney licensing was ad hoc and local until the late 1800s.[19] For most of the nineteenth century, the formal mechanism of admission—or exclusion—was the oral bar exam.[20] These oral exams were essentially interviews, with an emphasis on who you knew. In the era before consolidation of judicial systems at the state level, lawyers were admitted to practice in local districts or before individual local courts,[21] and candidates were questioned by local judges or attorneys who practiced in that court.[22] For those who seemed a good fit, the oral interviews were perfunctory, "more concerned with the applicant's good fellowship than with his or her legal prowess."[23] Oral bar exams continued well into the twentieth century in many jurisdictions.

Bar examiners are unheralded, behind-the-scenes players whose efforts are hidden unless they become famous for something else. The best-known bar examiner, Abraham Lincoln, conducted at least one bar exam while taking a bath. After offering some easy questions, including the definition of a contract, Lincoln found the candidate "smarter than he looks to be" and therefore ready for admission.[24] Presumably bathtub examinations were rare, but many exams lasted only five or ten minutes, and their rigor was questionable.[25]

Other accounts of oral bar exams survive because the candidate was a historic figure. Huey Long was admitted to practice in Louisiana in 1915 after an oral bar exam conducted by George H. Terriberry, an admiralty lawyer. After Long admitted to Terriberry that he knew nothing about admiralty law, Terriberry continued to quiz him on the subject and asked Long to explain how he would handle an admiralty matter. Long answered that he would "associate Mr. Terriberry with me and divide the fee with him," an answer that reputedly earned Long his bar license.[26]

Exceptional outsiders. The oral exams were very different for outsiders, including men of color and women of any race. These outsiders had to push their way in and met with mixed success. African Americans understood that racism was as likely to determine their results as qualifications.[27] Classically educated Macon Bolling Allen became the first Black person licensed in the United States when he passed a bar exam given to him in Maine in 1844.[28] The second African American licensed was probably Robert Morris, who passed the exam in Massachusetts in 1847 shortly after turning twenty-one.[29] In 1857 the Maryland bar denied the application of Edward Garrison Draper, a free Black man, although he was found to be qualified in every way other than race. Draper left to practice law in Liberia.[30] James Weldon Johnson, one of the first African American lawyers in Florida, was examined in Duval County, Florida. When he finished, one examiner exclaimed that he had "passed a good examination." But another examiner "blurted out in [Johnson's] face 'Well, I can't forget he's a [n-word] and I'll be damned if I'll stay here to see him admitted.'"[31]

Clara Foltz a white woman who later founded the first public defender's office, became the first female lawyer "on the Pacific coast" on September 5, 1878, the day after she passed her oral bar exam.[32] Her unusually long three-hour exam was conducted by a San Jose judge and three other men—her mentor, a friend, and a person who had refused to have her apprentice with him because she was a woman. Foltz passed with "many 'highly colored compliments' on her legal acumen and the readiness of her responses."[33]

Charlotte E. Ray, an 1872 graduate of Howard University Law School, was the first African American woman lawyer in the United States.[34] Hong Yen Chang became the first Asian American lawyer when he passed a bar exam in New York in 1888, but he was rebuffed a few years later when he attempted to become licensed in California where anti-Chinese prejudice was more virulent.[35]

Educational requirements and written bar exams. The legal profession in late nineteenth-century America was consciously striving to make itself more exclusive and rarified. The *Albany Law Journal* proclaimed in 1870 that "in every age of civilized man, the lawyers have been an important instrument in the work of refining and elevating the race."[36] Buoyed by self-congratulations and the stated mission of public protection, increasingly organized local bar associations sought more stringent, formal statewide admissions requirements to serve both prestige and anti-competitive purposes.[37] The American Bar Association joined this campaign after 1878,[38] pushing for higher standards at a time when only a few jurisdictions required formal apprenticeships or education before licensure.[39]

As the country and the profession grew, oral exams gradually gave way to written ones, thought to be more "technocratic" and "egalitarian."[40] The era of written bar exams began in the Massachusetts Court of Common Pleas, which from 1855 to 1859 required candidates who could not show three years of legal study to pass a written test.[41] In 1877 the New York Supreme Court began to require a test that included both oral and written components.[42] Idaho and Nevada started using written tests soon after.[43] Some jurisdictions used both oral and written exams in the decades-long transition to written bar exams.[44] Advocates for written tests denounced the prior oral tests as "largely meaningless."[45]

Written bar exams required more effort from examiners. A law review article from 1897 praised the "proper form" of this question from Suffolk County, Massachusetts:

> A was the owner of a stable situated on a public highway, in which he kept several horses. A had placed a sign extending from this stable over

the highway, in violation of a city ordinance. With negligence on A's part, a horse escaped from the stable and damaged B's garden. In a severe tempest the sign blew down and fell on C, then lawfully traveling on the highway. Can B recover against A for the injury to his garden? Can C against A for his personal injury?[46]

The form and subject of questions from that era would seem familiar to lawyers today, and to Leon Green, the dean of Northwestern Law School in 1939, who criticized bar exams as "a long drawn out hectic process of reviewing the Mother Goose rhymes of the law."[47]

Silly Mother Goose rhymes or not, written bar exams were widespread by 1890,[48] requiring the creation of a new bureaucracy to write and administer the tests. New Hampshire had created the first board of bar examiners in the late 1870s, a system that took off after New York became the fifth state with a board of bar examiners in 1894.[49] Attorney licensing authority was typically delegated by legislatures to supreme courts that then delegated to these new boards of bar examiners, usually controlled by the organized bar associations.[50] By 1917 thirty-seven jurisdictions had established boards of bar examiners,[51] with the same purpose as the licensing boards or committees that oversee attorney licensing in every U.S. jurisdiction today.

The move from oral to written bar exams was an indirect and perhaps surprising response to the increasing proportion of new lawyers who were law school graduates. Written bar exams became prevalent by the end of the nineteenth century in reaction to the earlier widespread diploma privileges that accompanied the shift to formal legal education and the prominence of Harvard's Langdellian model of legal education introduced in 1870. The diploma privilege and Langdell's methods of legal education have long been stubborn points of contention between the practicing bar and the legal academy, often distrustful rivals in shaping the profession.

Diploma privilege. Diploma privilege—admission to the bar based on graduation from law school without further examination—was widespread by the late 1800s. The logic of the diploma privilege was simple: Compared to office training, a law degree was the more prestigious pathway to becoming a lawyer so it should have certain privileges. Virginia was an early but temporary adopter in 1842, and Louisiana started in 1855.[52] By the 1870s, organized bars were actively opposing the diploma privilege because it shifted control from lawyers to law schools.[53] By 1890, only a fifth of new lawyers each year were law school graduates,[54] but the graduates of twenty-six law schools in sixteen states were entitled to a diploma privilege.[55]

In for the long haul, the ABA went on record opposing the privilege in 1892, 1908, 1918, and 1921. Siding with the ABA (from which it came the year before and with which it was still affiliated)[56] instead of law schools, the Association of American Law Schools (AALS) condemned the diploma privilege for the first time in 1901.[57] The privilege survived in thirteen states until 1928[58] and slowly dwindled throughout the twentieth century. It persists today in Wisconsin.[59] The organized profession's efforts to stop diploma privilege required it to take its own licensing tests more seriously, propelling the shift from oral to written exams and to more rigorous and systematic written exams overall.[60]

Law schools as we know them. The late 1800s trend to formal education[61] had its critics. "Who would think of committing a ship in the ocean to the guidance of a youth who had only studied navigation in his closets?"[62] The increased number of law school graduates provoked calls for required apprenticeships, which could be conducted in a law school.[63] Law schools, however, eventually chose the entirely different direction famously set by Harvard's first law school dean, Christopher Columbus Langdell.

Langdell and his acolytes rejected the idea that law professors should have experience practicing law. Langdell was clear:

> What qualifies a person . . . to teach law, is not experience in the work of a lawyer's office, not experience in dealing with men, not experience in the trial or argument of cases, not experience, in short, in using law, but experience in learning law.[64]

Langdell's conception of the scientific study of appellate judicial decisions meant that "the hand of a practitioner was not to sully its purity."[65] Members of the bar understood the insult and pushed back. The Baltimore lawyer's complaint in 1881 that law school education "resembles too much the scheme of education of priests and monks"[66] was echoed thirty years later when Roscoe Pound described law professors as "legal monks."[67] Current preferences for hiring entry-level law professors with PhDs instead of law practice suggests the continuing power of this profile, if not the critique.[68]

Langdell's university-based case method of legal education—in which professors question law students about the appellate decisions they have read—also helped to justify a more elite group of students. The method used previously, the lecture, was said to suit more diverse students. But with the case method, according to Charles Eliot, the Harvard president who hired Langdell, "the presence in the recitation room of a considerable proportion of persons whose minds were rude and unformed became at once a serious impediment."[69]

The case method, ubiquitous in law schools today, was vigorously opposed by the ABA in the 1890s because it would teach lawyers to become "mere hired guns" by emphasizing the adversarial system instead of teaching rules of law.[70] But the ABA soon abandoned that position. With ABA and AALS support, the case method of targeted questioning of students instead of lectures became a dominant marker of law school status throughout the twentieth century. Eventually the case method came to dominate all law schools, with lectures relegated to the commercial bar prep courses that filled the gulf between the goals of legal education and the demands of bar examiners.

3

SHAPING THE BAR IN THE
TWENTIETH CENTURY

THE PRACTICING BAR, BAR EXAMINERS, and law schools
formed a triangle of shifting internal and external tensions and alliances throughout the twentieth century. Each played several different
roles in enabling the legal profession to be "extraordinarily successful"[1]
in creating barriers to entry.

Early twentieth-century fights for prestige and exclusion. At the beginning of the century, newly established institutional players began
taking the profession's battles over prestige and exclusion to the national
level.[2] Corporate law firms took shape and built enduring alliances with
the more elite law schools. This convergence of interests between the
corporate law firms and most exclusive law schools helped them both
take leadership of the profession, which would continue for many decades to be, in fact, largely a "cottage industry of single practitioners."[3]

The number of law schools doubled between 1890 and 1920, and enrollment increased almost fivefold.[4] Law schools were not uniform; they
required different levels of prior education, not just different test scores
or grades, as they do today. By 1905 Harvard Law School required graduation from college to be considered for admission, eliminating from
consideration 96 percent of the otherwise eligible population.[5] The

middle-range law schools eliminated 80 percent.[6] Those law schools that constituted the elite in the 1920s are generally still the top ranked a century later.[7]

The new, fanciest corporate law firms did not care about the lack of practical training in law school because they preferred to train their own attorneys.[8] Increasing numbers of jurisdictions required new lawyers to have graduated from law school, but concerns that neither law students not law professors had any practical experience[9] also led to more serious and organized bar exams.[10] Beginning in 1915 the American Bar Association urged states to elevate their standards by requiring graduation from law school and passage of an examination for licensure.[11]

Distrust continued between the two gatekeepers to the profession, law schools and licensers, until it was lessened by the emergence of a new common enemy: less elite law schools, often night schools, that proliferated. Night schools, including the nineteen YMCA law schools that existed by 1927, created a pathway for ambitious immigrants and other outsiders to enter the profession.[12] This was an attractive option for those without a lot of financial resources. Leaders of the profession raised the alarm against "uneducated foreigners"[13] or "Russian jew boys"[14] becoming lawyers. Higher educational standards were used to solve the problem.[15] Through much of the twentieth century, changes in educational requirements for licensure were directed at various racial and ethnic groups who were not white, northern European, and Protestant.

Many called for the part-time law schools to be shut down entirely, but the ABA and AALS brokered a compromise in the early 1920s. The formal ABA position became that for admission to the bar, law school, preceded by at least two years of college, should be required and that part-time law school must take at least four years. Bar examiners confirmed the ABA's formal repudiation of the diploma privilege.[16] The compromise permitted the night schools to survive but entrenched the requirement of at least five years of higher education and passage of a bar exam to enter the profession.[17]

By the 1920s and 30s, status among law schools was already determined in part by the degree of focus on bar exams: The elite academic law schools used the case dialogue method instead of lectures; the next tier academic law schools like state schools and less exclusive privates used the case method but to a lesser extent; and the many practice-oriented law schools, where "legal education consisted, at most, of preparation for the local bar examination," used "a lecture-and-text" method.[18] The ABA pursued its mission of elevating legal education and the profession by enforcing this hierarchy, deliberately setting out to remove bar preparation from the law school experience .

The ABA issued its first list of "approved" law schools in 1921.[19] By 1926–27 the ABA standards explicitly prohibited law schools from providing instruction to prepare for bar exams.[20] This eagerness of the leading bar association to enforce a hierarchy of "better" law schools through disdaining bar exam preparation may have been Langdell's biggest triumph. Versions of this prohibition endured in the ABA accreditation standards into the twenty-first century. Law professors understand this, but almost anyone else might find the accreditors' contempt for the requirements of licensing quite odd, even troubling.

Meanwhile, in 1930 the ABA sponsored a new organization, the National Conference of Bar Examiners (NCBE), to promote standardization of legal education and bar admissions.[21] Prior efforts to create such an entity had failed in 1898, 1904, 1914, and 1916, but the NCBE was successfully launched in 1931.[22] By 1932 all states but Indiana had boards of bar examiners.[23] The NCBE tried to persuade bar examiners to use exam questions like those used in the "better" law schools that had embraced Langdell's case method.[24] The president of Yale University explained in 1924 that "The old way bred great lawyers, but like the caste mark of the Brahmin, the case system is the cachet of the crack law school of today."[25]

Escalating licensing and educational standards. The great compromise of the ABA and AALS in the 1920s had permitted night schools to survive. But states increasingly limited licensure to those who passed a bar exam after graduating from an ABA-accredited law school. This licensing requirement gave ABA accreditors new powers to set escalating and expensive standards designed for research-oriented, university-based law schools of the Langdellian model. The raised standards made it harder for "poorer" students to succeed and pushed out many less elite law schools, as intended.[26]

The ABA and the more elite law schools worried about the quality of bar exams, in part because the examiners were typically older members of the bar not using current methods[27] and in part because bar exams were not filtering out graduates of night schools.[28] The AALS Proceedings of 1937 reported "apparent hostility" with the bar examiners, but that was said to have been replaced by cooperation by 1939 based on the "unity of interest in reducing the number of lawyers and getting rid of the 'poorer' lawyers and law schools."[29] Racist jokes peppered the 1939 speech of the NCBE chair commending the NCBE's effectiveness, in cooperation with the AALS and the ABA, in raising bar admissions standards.[30] Some bar examiners devised steps beyond the educational and bar examination requirements. Pennsylvania, for example, hatched a plan to require each applicant to find a supervisor for a six-month clerkship with the stated purpose of keeping out Jewish candidates, who would have trouble finding lawyers willing to supervise them.[31]

Jim Crow played a part as well, with legal racial discrimination effectively keeping African Americans out of many law schools. The ABA, by endorsing ever-more rigorous admissions standards, targeted racial, ethnic, and religious outsiders and determined which law schools to approve or accredit, while staying committed to racial discrimination.[32] In 1912 the ABA Executive Committee mistakenly admitted three African American men and then quickly voted to rescind their admission. Although the three were ultimately admitted, the ABA began requiring racial identification on future applications so the mistake would not be repeated.[33] The ABA did not adopt a nondiscrimination policy until 1943.[34]

For African Americans aspiring to be lawyers, the obstacles were massive. They faced discrimination from law schools and bar examiners, and escalating accreditation standards shut down alternative paths to a law school degree. Most law schools admitted no or very few Black students. Some bar exams were still oral interviews, and some bar examiners found ways to identify Black candidates who took written exams, including by separate seating with sequential exam numbers or photographs.[35] Louisiana rejected every Black applicant between 1927 and 1947.[36]

With some public and private law schools closed to African Americans, separate Black law schools were established.[37] But the new accreditation standards implemented by the ABA closed many night schools that had served working people of all races, as well as the law schools founded to educate Blacks.[38] African Americans were barred from some public and elite law schools until the 1960s.[39] Between 1900 and 1940, the percentage of licensed attorneys who were Black was between 0.6 and 0.8 percent.[40]

This sequence of expanding educational requirements—starting with office training and ending with formal requirements of an under-graduate degree and graduation from a three-year degree program at an accredited law school—was complete by the years following World War II.[41] The profession pushed for and enforced these changes with-out much attention to whether the public needed lawyers to have this amount—or type—of education and without concern about the impact of these requirements on access to the profession of racial and ethnic minorities.[42] For some, such exclusions had been precisely the point.[43] Robert Stevens, a leading authority on the history of American legal education, acknowledged that

> some members of the ABA and many State bars used an extended period of education not to produce a broadly based, technically com-petent, ethical, socially responsible bar, but rather as an opportunity to ensure the maintenance of the Anglo-Saxon male hegemony.[44]

Distance and disdain for bar exams indicate law school prestige. Direct and indirect exclusion based on wealth, race, ethnicity, gender, and religion was a status-related theme that animated access to the pro-fession throughout the twentieth century. Another aspect of prestige that took hold in the early twentieth century and continues today is the powerful and still generally accurate message that the higher the law school's status, the lower that law school's interest in state law and procedure and bar exams. An ABA survey of the legal profession in the late 1940s included an inspection of most of the nation's law schools. The resulting ABA report used the familiar distinction between the few "national" law schools and the greater number that are "local or re-gional." The report reflected disdain for the latter category and for bar examiners' focus on readiness for practice in their jurisdictions:

> [T]he law students have pressed for the "bread and butter" courses and the subjects specified in the rules for admission to practice. The law schools have tended, because of limited funds, inadequate facilities, and lethargy, to yield to the pressures.[45]

Market forces, public protection, and status. Prestige and prejudice were not the only drivers of exclusion; economic self-protection also played its role. Evidence suggests that the anti-competitive role of licensing requirements was directly at work in states' manipulation of overall bar exam pass rates.[46] Richard Abel found that pass rates were consistently high in rural states that needed attorneys and low in urban ones where lawyers faced more competition.[47] The greater economy mattered too. In both England and the United States, "pass rates rose when the profession feared there were too few lawyers (after the two world wars) and fell when it felt there were too many (during the Depression and after the dot.com and subprime mortgage bubbles burst)."[48] In other words, the difficulty of bar exams could be changed to reflect factors other than protection of the public. For example, patriotism and a strong economy supported the decision of some jurisdictions to extend diploma privilege to veterans following World War II.[49]

We should not be surprised at the exclusionary theme of the advance of the profession. Lawyers, like those in many other professions and trades, seek economic protectionism through elevated educational requirements in the name of public protection.[50] Lawyers and law professors also use the rhetoric of public protection to promote our own prestige and status.[51] In his classic 1930 introduction to legal education, *The Bramble Bush*, Karl Llewellyn reminded his readers that "the best talent of the bar will always muster to keep Ins in and to man the barricade against the Outs."[52]

Mid-century explosion: lawyers, law schools, and standardized tests. The legal profession and legal education boomed along with the post–World War II economy. Public and private law schools thrived in an era of public investment in higher education.[53] Not surprisingly, given the legal profession's culture of stratification and legal education's tradition of basing prestige in part on admissions standards,[54] the era's newly burgeoning standardized tests quickly became ingrained into law school admissions.

The College Board and its reincarnation the Educational Testing Service played the central role in developing standardized tests to deal out differing educational opportunities, starting with its Scholastic Aptitude Test, or SAT, built from IQ tests used by the U.S. Army.[55] The Law

School Admissions Test (LSAT) began with a suggestion from Columbia Law School's admissions officer to the College Board in 1945. Representatives from the law schools at Columbia, Harvard, and Yale met with the College Board in 1947 to plan for a new standardized test. The project blossomed quickly, and the first LSAT— a full-day, ten-section test—was given in 1948.[56] The move away from proprietary (for profit) law schools, the increased numbers of college-educated applicants to law schools, and the development of the LSAT enabled a shift from competition *to survive* law school ("look to the left, look to the right, only one of you . . .") to competition *to be admitted* to law school.[57] The LSAT and bar exams became the sequenced admissions tests for law school and licensing.

The new standardized test path to becoming a lawyer did not seriously disrupt the patterns of exclusion that preexisted the LSAT. Standardized tests, in general, had a complicated history, having served both as mechanisms of "color-blind" opportunity and as a tool, sometimes explicitly, of discriminatory and racist exclusion. As Richard Abel summarized, "parental income, social status, and education correlate strongly with college attended, college grades, LSAT scores, law school attended, law school performance, and bar passage."[58] Test scores are attractive in part because the numbers seem authoritative and make hierarchical sorting very simple, what Robert Steinberg calls the "pseudo-quantitative precision heuristic."[59] The LSAT was a particularly powerful addition for a profession—including the legal academy—strongly attracted to sorting and hierarchy.[60] The limitations and social constructions of merit as defined by test scores are hard to recognize in a society that has organized itself so profoundly around them, perhaps especially for those of us in professional positions obtained in part through standardized test success.[61] Richard Delgado reminds us, "Those in power always make that which they do best the standard of merit."[62]

Racial integration, diploma privilege, and standardized tests. Some southern states adopted the LSAT for admissions to their law schools as part of an effort to maintain educational and professional racial segregation.[63] In 1949 the University of Florida Law School denied admission to six African Americans, including Virgil Hawkins, because they were Black. Hawkins sued on equal protection grounds but lost in the Florida Supreme Court before succeeding in the United States Supreme Court in 1956.[64] The Florida governor's response included convening a committee of leading lawyers to identify "lawful means" to prevent or slow down school integration.[65] The committee established the new requirement that applicants to Florida's graduate and professional schools take standardized admissions tests.[66] Hawkins had been academically qualified when he originally applied but was rejected following the additional test requirement.[67] Reflecting on this and subsequent history, Richard Delgado suggested that the emphasis on merit became serious in 1964:

> Formal racism was phased out, veiled or nonformal racism came in— racism under the guise of excellence, fairness, equal opportunity, all the things that make up the constellation of attitudes and standards we call "merit."[68]

Bar examiners also actively excluded from the profession African Americans who had been admitted and then graduated from law school. For example, the presence of Black law graduates caused bar examiners to rethink the diploma privilege in several states. Alabama, South Carolina, Georgia, and Mississippi "established new barriers to the legal profession after African Americans began graduating from separate law schools."[69] Graduates of the law school at the University of South Carolina enjoyed the diploma privilege until the first group of African Americans became eligible in 1950, at which time passing a bar exam became required.[70] Denied admission to their state law schools, some Black students received tuition money from their states to attend elsewhere. Upon return, students from Alabama found they were not eligible for the diploma privilege, which was limited to the students who had graduated from the University of Alabama's law school, all of whom were white.[71] Mississippi followed a similar pattern, having granted diploma privilege to graduates of Mississippi's law school until 1960.[72]

4

THE 1970S LEGACY OF ACTIVISM,
PSYCHOMETRICS, AND GOOD FAITH

THE 1970S WERE A MOMENTOUS time for attorney licensing. Bar examiners faced civil rights criticism that did not arise again with such force until the anti-racism activism launched by the diploma privilege movement in the 2020 pandemic. Meanwhile, the introduction of the Multistate Bar Exam (MBE) in 1972 enabled psychometric advances that still frame bar exam scoring and design and that launched the NCBE's current role as supplier of bar exams. And the 70s also produced a series of federal court decisions that gave bar examiners impenetrable protection from judicial scrutiny, entrenching assertions of good faith as respectable and sufficient justification for all bar exam problems, including racial scoring inequities.

Activism, research, and media focus on racial disparities. The racial and ethnic disparities in bar passage rates in the 1970s provoked attention from activists, coverage in popular media, inquiries in legal academies, and lawsuits. One such discriminatory policy was that Black candidates faced unusually lengthy and tough character and fitness interviews scheduled (for them only) the day before they took the bar exam.[1] The *New York Times* and *Ebony* published prominent stories about the stark racial disparities in bar exams.[2]

A Philadelphia Bar Association study released in 1970 concluded that "the only group 'weeded out by the bar examination' was blacks," who were seated together and given adjacent exam numbers."[3] The *New York Times* reported in 1974 that three-quarters of white applicants nationally passed bar examinations, but only half of that percentage of Black applicants did.[4] The same story provided figures of whites passing the Ohio bar exam at percentages between 75 and 88 with the rates for Blacks between 27 and 43 percent.[5] Only fifteen percent of the African American candidates passed the South Carolina bar exam between 1950 and 1973, compared to 90 percent of white candidates.[6] Those numbers were better than Delaware's, where no Black applicant passed the bar exam between 1957 and 1974.[7] In South Carolina, between 1969 and 1974, 2 percent of white applicants and 50 percent of Black applicants failed.[8] None of the forty Black candidates who took the summer administration of the 1972 Georgia bar exam passed, a group that included two graduates from Yale, one from Harvard, and three from Columbia.[9] California counted "one white lawyer for every 450 whites, ... one black lawyer for every 3,000 blacks (and one Chicano lawyer for every 16,000 Chicanos)."[10]

As a result of these atrocious numbers, racial bias lawsuits were brought against bar examiners in at least ten states.[11] This civil rights litigation achieved little success because plaintiffs could not prove intentional discrimination as required by the courts. Every available report shows that significant racial and ethnic bar passage disparities persist across the country without serious challenge since the failed efforts of the 1970s.

The MBE, general principles, and reliability. The NCBE's introduction in 1972 of its multiple-choice test, the Multistate Bar Exam (MBE), enabled big changes in attorney licensing. As a national test, the MBE uses "general principles" of law rather than the law of the jurisdiction doing the licensing. The addition of the MBE aligned bar exams more with the "national" law schools, where faculty ignorance of the local law has been honorable and purposeful since the early days of Langdell's case method.[12] Prestige in the legal academy had been built in part on distance from night schools known for preparing students to pass the bar exam. Before the MBE, that lack of attention to bar exams could cause problems for graduates of elite law schools, starting with Harvard grads during Dean Langdell's time.[13] The MBE focus on "national" law and the correlation between high scores on the LSAT and high scores on the MBE made post-MBE bar exams very friendly to graduates of the most elite law schools, who tended to be superb multiple-choice test-takers.

The MBE introduced a new element of difficulty for more average test-takers. Candidates were now required to prepare for bar exams by learning the legal doctrine tested in the essays, predominantly based on state law, plus the doctrine tested on the MBE, based on "general principles" that sometimes conflicted with state law. Critics have called this the "law of nowhere," but the NCBE calls it the "law of everywhere." Testing both general and state-specific rules multiplies the number of rules that must be memorized and means that the correct answer can depend on which component of the exam—essay or MBE—the question appears. These problems persist today.

The MBE also shifted the role of the NCBE from cheerleader and technical advisor to test designer and supplier. Jurisdictions' reliance on the MBE created the opportunity for the NCBE's current role as the producer of the entire bar exam and administrator of the character and fitness processes for most jurisdictions. The MBE is the anchor for the NCBE because jurisdictions cannot replicate it for themselves, unlike essays and performance tests. The MBE also plays a pivotal role in scoring all components of bar exams, including the essays and performance tests.

The MBE and psychometrics. Lawyers know what it is like to take a bar exam, but very few understand how bar exams are scored. Important policy questions are hidden within the technicalities of psychometrics, or the science of testing. Reliability means that a score reflects the ability of a test-taker and does not go up or down based on the changing specifics of a test administration, such as the content of that test, the identity of the graders, or the strength of the cohort taking the test. If reliability is strong, an applicant gets no advantage from taking the bar exam in a weaker pool in February, for example, because the applicant's score and the pass-fail decision would be the same in a different pool of applicants or different graders in July.

The MBE ushered in the new era of psychometricians and more reliable bar exam scoring. The oral exams early in our history were not reliable because the result depended on who did the interview. Written bar exams are more reliable, at the least, because all candidates taking the same exam at the same time and place receive the same questions. But written bar exams can be highly subjective and may permit cronyism and potential bias, especially when everything is done behind closed doors. Even without mischief, essays raise reliability challenges because they are new for each exam administration and, at least for now, are graded by humans with some degree of subjectivity. Inevitably essay questions vary in difficulty from the other questions given on the same exam and on earlier and subsequent exams. Multiple-choice tests have been bar examiners' chief solution to these reliability problems.

Psychometricians currently use multiple-choice tests like the MBE to enhance reliability of the entire exam, including essays and performance tests.[14] High-stakes multiple-choice tests like the MBE typically include some repeat questions whose degree of difficulty is already known. Scores on the new questions are compared and *equated* to scores on the repeat questions using sophisticated statistical psychometric processes that convert raw multiple-choice scores to equated scores for the entire MBE.[15] The use of repeat questions makes MBE test security critical and explains why MBE questions are to the NCBE what gold is to Fort Knox.

A second statistical step, *scaling*, uses the greater reliability of the equated multiple-choice scores to improve the reliability of scores from less stable parts of the test, such as essays. Psychometricians use sophisticated statistical scaling processes to match, in a way, the raw essay scores to the equated multiple-choice scores.[16] The highest essay score is adjusted based on the highest MBE score, and so on, from top to bottom. Currently, almost all jurisdictions scale their essay and performance test scores to the MBE.[17] Scaling means that the jurisdiction's MBE cut score or passing score will determine not only how many candidates pass the MBE, but also how many pass the entire exam, although the individuals are not necessarily the same.

Using repeat questions for equating and multiple-choice questions for scaling are psychometric methods that can be used to enhance reliability of exams in any field. The measurement science developed in medicine and engineering, for example, can be borrowed to improve reliability of bar exams. Since introducing the MBE fifty years ago, the

NCBE has become an expert testing organization with increasingly sophisticated psychometric resources, committed to making the bar exams very reliable with these methods. This impressive advance may be the NCBE's greatest achievement.

Validity and fairness breakdowns. Reliability is crucial, but it is only one of three touchstones for high-stakes tests. Validity and fairness are the others. Validity means that the test measures what it purports to measure. For a bar exam, validity means the extent to which the bar exam measures minimum competence to practice law, which is the purpose of the test. Perhaps because the answers are harder to find because they are specific to the law, testing experts and psychometricians at the NCBE have not yet brought the same relentless ambition they brought to reliability to the challenges of validity and fairness. Establishing that bar exams are valid and fair assessments of minimum competence to practice law requires serious research on the legal profession that has been absent until very recently. Leading scholars of the profession—including Richard Abel,[18] Gillian Hadfield,[19] Deborah Rhode, and Geoffrey Hazard[20]—have decried the lack of validity studies for bar exams. Why hasn't the legal profession moved much beyond the "we know it when we see it" approach to assessing minimum competence to practice law?

Courts sided with bar examiners in civil rights cases. One powerful explanation for persistent weaknesses related to validity and fairness in the exam is a series of 1970s federal court victories for bar examiners. These decisions established that bar examiners, unlike employers, face no legal pressure to demonstrate the validity of tests that have racially disparate results. In the decades since the 1964 Civil Rights Act, Title VII has remade the workplace by requiring countless employers to stop using discriminatory tests unless the tests' job relatedness, or validity, can be shown. Women became firefighters and people of color became police officers based on these laws. But bar examiners have been immune from Title VII challenges, as a result of a collection of cases that upheld highly questionable practices of bar examiners from Georgia, Alabama, South Carolina, and Virginia against Title VII and equal protection challenges by African American applicants.[21] These cases provided bar examiners with immunity, but they should not offer any of us much comfort.

In *Tyler v. Vickery*, for example, the Fifth Circuit rejected the claims of African Americans who challenged the Georgia bar exam on equal protection and due process grounds.[22] Over half of the African American applicants who took the Georgia bar exam in 1973 were unsuccessful compared to between one-fourth and one-third of white applicants.[23] All forty African Americans who took the July 1972 Georgia bar exam had failed.[24] The court recognized that

> [s]ince it is undisputed that the Georgia bar examination has a greater adverse impact on black applicants than on whites and has never been the subject of a professional validation study, acceptance of appellants' suggested standard of review would inexorably compel the conclusion that the examination is unconstitutional.[25]

But the court rejected the plaintiffs' challenge because the bar examiners designed the test for the purpose for which it was used and set the passing score ("70") for that same purpose: to determine minimum competence.[26] By this deferential rational basis standard, bar exams are lawful so long as bar examiners are well intentioned and do not borrow tests originally used for some other purpose (such as to license doctors).[27]

The Fifth Circuit returned to similar issues in *Parrish v. Board of Commissioners of the Alabama State Bar*.[28] Once again, African American plaintiffs showed evidence of disparate impact (over ten administrations, African Americans passed the Alabama bar exam at 32 percent while whites passed at 70 percent[29]) of a bar exam that had not been validated.[30] *Parrish* generally followed *Vickery*,[31] but the plaintiffs won a narrow victory on a discovery issue. Over a partial dissent, the court determined that the trial court incorrectly granted summary judgment without ruling on the plaintiff's motion to compel disclosure of the score sheets and grading notes for the February 1973 exam.[32] The Fifth Circuit rejected the bold claim by the bar examiners that their own good faith and credibility in denying any wrongdoing made the scoring documents irrelevant.[33]

In *Richardson v. McFadden*, African American applicants argued that their equal protection challenge to the South Carolina bar exam should incorporate Title VII's framework regarding disparate impact and job relatedness.[34] The *Richardson* plaintiffs were unsuccessful, not because the Fourth Circuit was impressed by the validity of the exams, but because the court held that Title VII standards did not apply: "[I]f we were to determine that Title VII standards were applicable, it would be necessary to reverse and declare the South Carolina Bar Examination constitutionally invalid."[35]

Without Title VII's disparate impact theory to prove discrimination, the plaintiffs tried to prove intentional race discrimination with a timeline showing that South Carolina bar examiners changed policies just as Black applicants were in a position to use them.[36] Plaintiffs produced evidence that South Carolina eliminated its diploma privilege "in 1950, three years (the normal law school term) after a 'separate but equal' law school was started at South Carolina State College, a black school."[37] "Reading law" (apprenticeship instead of law school) was "eliminated in 1957, 'coincidentally' shortly after a black applicant used this method."[38] Reciprocity was "abolished in January 1972, not long after a black member of the Oklahoma Bar applied under the reciprocity rule."[39] The court declared this evidence insufficient.[40]

Plaintiffs next sought to prove that the licensing test did not bear "a fair and substantial relationship" to the determination of minimum competence as a lawyer.[41] Witheringly, the Fourth Circuit described the evidence introduced to validate the cut score as "very subjective and general in nature and hardly acclaimed by the educational testing experts who testified."[42]

The court was even less impressed by methods used to score bar exams, acknowledging that "it would be almost a matter of pure luck if the '70' thereby derived corresponded with anybody's judgment of minimal competency."[43] But the court's deference to the examiners was so great that "almost a matter of pure luck" was deemed sufficient.[44] After having noted that the examiners were not trained in test design, the Fourth Circuit upheld the tests because the bar exams were designed and scored by the bar examiners for the right purpose.[45] Again, good faith controlled.

Richardson also revealed the shocking length to which the federal court would back the bar examiners. Two African American applicants proved at trial that they had scored 70.5 and 69.6 respectively when the required score was 70, and bar examiners' standard practice was "rounding up."[46] The more the examiners attempted to describe their methods, the more arbitrary they appeared.[47] Bar examiners tried to justify having passed one applicant and failed another with an identical score.[48] The trial court had concluded that "the correspondence of a score of 70 with even their own judgment of minimal competency was little more than fortuitous" and found in favor of the two individual plaintiffs on the basis of arbitrary and capricious scoring that violated due process and equal protection.[49] In its first consideration of this case, the Fourth Circuit agreed and ordered remand to the district court to certify the admission to the South Carolina bar of the two African American men who had scored 70.5 and 69.6.[50]

The bar examiners kept fighting. On rehearing *en banc*, the court reversed.[51] The court found that evidence of discrimination against these two men was not sufficient to provide them with a remedy: "over a four-year period, *only these two examples of alleged discrimination were proved*, and [. . .] Spain and Kelly continued to fail on subsequent reexaminations."[52] *Richardson v. McFadden* stands for the principle that claims of racial bias in bar exams require proof of intentional discrimination.[53] It should be remembered as a Fourth Circuit decision that prevented two African American men from being admitted to practice because each had passed the bar exam only once.

In these cases, the federal courts deferred to bar examiners' good faith instead of holding them accountable for shoddy practices and even blatant scoring discrepancies used to prevent African Americans from getting licenses to practice law. These civil rights losses from the 1970s left the validity and fairness of bar exams safe from scrutiny and challenge for another half century. Perhaps bar examiners have not been ambitious about validity and fairness because they have not had to be. Professional responsibility principles arguably require the profession itself to bring the same level of scrutiny of racially disparate bar exams that Title VII requires of employers, meaning that state courts and bar examiners should work as hard to achieve validity and fairness as they have labored to achieve reliability.[54] Otherwise, good faith will continue to excuse questionable scoring, lack of validity, racial and ethnic bar passage disparities, and problematic public protection.

5

PRESSURE POINTS IN CONTEMPORARY LICENSING

THE CURRENT ERA IN ATTORNEY licensing, the most volatile since the 1970s, is marked by five notable pressure points. First, the affordability of law school is increasingly stratified, with Black and Latinx students paying much of the bill to promote law schools' prestige goals. Second, ABA accreditors have executed a quick about-face on rules for how law schools relate to bar exams. Third, that accreditation reversal invited a significant incursion of commercial bar prep providers into law schools, and not just following graduation. Fourth, during the same time the NCBE has consolidated its control of bar exams, with most bar exams now coming from Madison, Wisconsin. And, finally, perhaps most profoundly, this previously somewhat stagnant field has been shaken by the pandemic disruption and advocacy started in 2020 when licensing as usual became impossible.

Good faith, prestige, and law schools. Admission to law school is the first formal stage in attorney licensing, and arguably the highest barrier.[1] Legal educators should not simply decry the practices of bar examiners, past or present, without acknowledging past and current inequities in how law schools shape the profession that are justified in good faith and fueled by our rarely questioned quest for prestige. Racial disparities in law school admissions and financial aid decisions continue to shape access to the legal profession.

Law schools allow *U.S. News* rankings to drive law school admissions and financial aid, dramatically exacerbating the overuse and misuse of the LSAT in law school admissions[2] and scholarship priorities.[3] A higher percentage of African American applicants than other racial groups is not admitted to any law school, and Blacks are admitted at lower rates than others in the same LSAT band.[4] In part as a reaction to the severe downturn in law school applications following the Great Recession of 2008, many law schools have chosen to invest sizable portions—sometimes substantially more than half—of their potential tuition income to attract students with desirable numerical indicators. These tuition discounts, which make law school inexpensive or even tuition-free plus a living stipend, are awarded based on the rankings goals of the schools, not the financial need of the students who receive the big scholarships. Other students are paying sticker price and going deeply into debt. Since 2009 student debt for white students has decreased, while it has increased for African American and Latinx students, who "have the highest rates of borrowing and the highest expected student loan balances."[5] These admissions and financial aid policies that diminish the availability of needs-based scholarships are significant barriers to access to the profession.[6]

ABA accreditation reversal regarding bar exams. By the last decades of the twentieth century, the Langdellian model of legal education had achieved decisive victory in the United States. Every accredited law school, not just the elite, featured pedagogy based on the case method, a curriculum focused on "thinking like a lawyer," and a professoriate, other than faculty teaching in clinics, contentedly or proudly removed from practice. The task of educating future lawyers for a lifetime of practice was understood to be very different from preparing future lawyers to pass a bar exam, work that was relegated to commercial bar preparation companies that offered two months of intensive cramming following law school graduation. This purposeful distancing between legal education and bar prep was more than an attitude; it had been enforced in the ABA accreditation standards since their first iteration in the 1920s.

When the precursor of today's *ABA Standards* was updated in 1973 the longstanding prohibition on instruction designed to "coach students for bar examination"[7] became ABA Standard 302(b): "The law school may not offer to its students, for academic credit or as a condition to graduation, instruction that is designed as a bar examination review course."[8] The prohibition remained until 2005,[9] when a series of modifications to weaken the restriction began.[10] Any restriction on bar prep courses for credit, whether elective or required, was gone by 2008.[11] The ABA and the NCBE have been intertwined since the ABA launched the NCBE, so the fact that the ABA accreditation prohibition on coursework to prepare for the bar examination lasted so long is a testament to the distance between the legal academy and the profession and to the deep disdain for bar exams shared by academic and professional elites.

ABA accreditors swung the pendulum in the opposite direction with the adoption of the first numbers-based bar passage accreditation requirement in 2008.[12] *Standard 316* requires law schools to have their graduates achieve a 75 percent pass rate within two years. Most law schools achieve this without difficulty unless: they are in a state using a very high cut score, they have so few graduates that wide fluctuations occur, or they have a defining mission of access to the profession. A few schools will be sanctioned and will face loss of accreditation. More law schools will change their curriculum to eliminate any threat under *Standard 316*. This new standard has accelerated the preexisting trend of law schools creating new staff or faculty positions to help prepare students for bar passage.[13]

The ABA House of Delegates resoundingly rejected current *Standard 316* because of the impact that the rule could have on access to the profession for people of color.[14] As predicted and feared, the lists of law schools at risk of losing accreditation have included two historically Black college and university (HBCU) law schools, two law schools in Puerto Rico, and one law school that leads or comes close to leading the field in enrollment of students of color.[15] The ABA Council's enactment of specific numerical goals for bar passage contrasts with the longtime lack of specificity or apparent enforcement of Standard 205, requiring nondiscrimination and equality of opportunity.[16]

The relatively quick reversal in bar exam accreditation standards— from forbidding law schools from giving any credits for preparing for bar exams to requiring law schools to meet numerical bar passage standards—was due to new ABA accreditation focus on consumer protection and on outcomes, not inputs. The about-face may also have been related to leadership patterns. During the years of these quick and dramatic changes in ABA accreditation standards, several people served simultaneously on both the ABA Council and on the board of the NCBE—including as chair, as executive committee members, or as other officers. These are distinguished leaders of high integrity. The underlying structural question, though, is whether the interests of the ABA Council are identical to the interests of the NCBE, as the multiple and routine dual roles seem to assume. Recognizing the difference in roles and creating more separation between the law school accreditation body and the NCBE would lead to less groupthink and better attorney licensing policy.

Bar prep industry infiltration of legal education. By the mid-twentieth century, the gulf between the goals of law professors and the demands of bar examiners had created a massive market for the commercial bar prep companies operating cram schools to prepare recent law graduates for bar exams.[17] The sequence of bar prep courses following law school graduation was enforced by the ABA accreditation prohibition against bar review courses for credit in law school. Each recent change in ABA accreditation standards invited the bar prep industry further into the law school curriculum, especially because many law faculties continue to emulate Langdellian ideals in curriculum, pedagogy, and culture and therefore were poorly equipped for bar preparation.

The ABA repeal of prohibitions on bar prep courses for credit and the adoption of specific numerical bar pass requirements in Standard 316 created a new market for the commercial bar prep companies: that of providing services to law schools themselves, not just law students. Law schools flocked to bar prep companies especially after bar pass rates dropped in 2014. Commercial bar prep companies now offer data analytics, formative assessments, and bar courses and faculty for those courses, blurring the traditional line between legal education and bar prep.

BARBRI, the giant of the bar prep industry, epitomizes this development. BARBRI describes itself as offering a "suite of curriculum, faculty training, and assessment solutions" to law schools.[18] BARBRI acquired iLaw in 2017. At least until the sudden pandemic conversion of U.S. law schools to remote learning in the spring of 2020, iLaw was the biggest platform for online legal education in the United States, offering JD and non-JD courses and working with about a quarter of ABA-accredited law schools.[19] The looming clout of the bar prep industry reached a new milestone in early 2022 when BARBRI, the self-described "world's premier legal education provider," acquired West Academic, the leading U.S. legal publisher.[20] In some ways these moves indicate that for-profit legal education has returned in the twenty-first century to an extent not seen since proprietary law schools flourished in the early twentieth century. This change is largely driven by heightened bar exam pressure.

Consolidation of NCBE control. The idea of a national bar exam has been floated at least since 1941.[21] Under Erica Moeser's strong leadership, the NCBE introduced the Uniform Bar Exam (UBE) in 2011 when it was used by two states: Missouri and North Dakota. By 2022, the UBE had been adopted in forty-one jurisdictions, including two of the three most populous, New York and Texas.[22]

The UBE offers candidates portability, the valuable power to circumvent many of the anachronisms of state licensure in our mobile age. A law graduate taking the UBE could take a job in Denver, Seattle, Chicago, Philadelphia, Houston, New York, or any other location in forty-one jurisdictions.

The other significant benefit from the UBE is professional development of questions. Bar exams for UBE jurisdictions consist entirely of NCBE products: the MBE, the Multistate Essay Exam (MEE), and the Multistate Performance Test (MPT). These questions benefit from being written and developed by full-time testing experts. The questions drafted (not just graded) by jurisdictional bar examiners and staff do not always have the same consistency and are more likely to reflect a single examiner's judgment about what is important.

The UBE also has its disadvantages. Jurisdictions that use the UBE are choosing to give a bar exam that does not test the law of that jurisdiction. The NCBE's "general principles" may or may not be consistent with a particular jurisdiction's rules. On the other hand, if the chief value of current licensing tests is to determine whether a candidate has fundamental legal reasoning skills, those skills can be demonstrated whatever body of law provides the "knowledge" platform for the test.[23] Jurisdictions can create a variety of mechanisms—including online interactive lessons and tests—to ensure that new lawyers learn jurisdiction-specific doctrine and procedure.[24]

A potentially more significant negative of the UBE is that consolidation of control by the NCBE can inhibit innovation and further magnify the weaknesses of the NCBE. Current UBE and non-UBE tests have a dramatic disparate impact based on race and ethnicity, without sufficient connection to the qualities and skills that lawyers need. Although the diffusion of authority with each state court leads to problems of lack of expertise, engagement, and resources, there are potential advantages, largely unrealized so far, to not using the UBE; namely, the state courts and the bar leaders in each jurisdiction could be experimenting, using their roles to improve the exam. To the extent that they depend on the NCBE to do their thinking for them, the promise of experimentation is lost.

Consolidation in Madison also risks losing crucial connections between bar exams and the changing profession. Bar exams today are nostalgic throwbacks to a mythical Main Street lawyer of the past, probably a white male, who needed to memorize the law and who handled all manner of common law subjects on behalf of people in his town. Deference to even an excellent testing organization in Madison, Wisconsin—a state that famously retains a diploma privilege for graduates of its two law schools—is not a recipe for the kind of progress that relies on deep understanding of the changing law practice of today and the future. Because the NCBE's *NextGen Bar Exam*, planned for 2026, is being designed to be an integrated exam without component parts,[25] it is likely to further consolidate NCBE control over bar exams by requiring jurisdictions to use the entire exam, eliminating the current ability of non-UBE jurisdictions like California and Florida, for example, to combine the MBE with state essays and performance tests.

Pandemic bar exams of 2020: disruption, entrenchment, and change. Until 2020, the bar exam ran like a well-oiled, expensive machine known for its exceptional stability and predictability. Convention space was booked years in advance for the last weeks in February and July. Tens of thousands of candidates were fingerprinted and then prepared with two months of intensive study. Bar study meant relentless drilling to become proficient at answering hundreds of multiple-choice questions (1.8 minutes each) and writing essays in the jurisdiction's allotted time. Candidates would arrive at an arena or a hotel with nothing beyond whatever was permitted in the small, clear plastic bag with identification and authorized writing utensils. But the pandemic caused havoc with bar exams in 2020.

The likelihood of serious disruption and the resulting need to quickly consider alternatives (such as diploma privilege, supervised practice, or remote testing) was apparent four months before the July exam date.[26] Proceeding as usual in massive, crowded gatherings risked the health of candidates, staff, their families, and communities. In some states bar exams as usual would have been unlawful because of emergency social distancing orders.

One alternative was remote examinations, but bar examiners were not ready to deliver bar exams remotely. Security was the big problem, both making sure that the correct person took the exam and keeping the test questions, particularly the MBE questions, secure. The current elaborate psychometric system to achieve reliable scores starts with re-using old MBE questions for equating, so MBE questions need to be kept secret. Bar examiners faced a conflict between the safety of candidates and the security of test questions.

Jurisdictions scrambled, and the July 2020 examinations turned into July, August, September, and October exams, with cascading delays and changing plans and instructions.[27] The NCBE initially insisted that its exam components and typical scoring services would only be available for in-person exams. Facing this squeeze, some jurisdictions offered the bar exam as usual in July with NCBE test components and scoring support as usual. Instead of the typical 45,344 test-takers in 54 jurisdictions who had taken the July bar exam in 2019, there were 5,678 examinees in 23 jurisdictions sitting for July 2020 in-person bar exams.[28] Some jurisdictions required candidates to sign waivers of serious injury or death; Mississippi provided on-site nurses. Texas housed candidates in hotel rooms, with elaborate procedures to prevent test-takers from getting into their closets during the test. Some candidates with compromised health situations opted not to take the in-person exam. Disabled students with accommodations were required to take their exams in person, even in states that otherwise offered their exams remotely because of pandemic health concerns.

Facing these bad choices, several jurisdictions adopted some version of emergency diploma privilege with supervised practice requirements. Utah moved first, with a diploma privilege for graduates of law schools with high bar pass rates who also successfully completed a period of 360 hours of supervised practice, followed by Washington, Oregon, Louisiana, and Washington, DC.[29] The Washington Supreme Court explicitly rested its emergency order on the health and racial justice challenges faced by candidates. The order for Washington, DC, was late in coming; it required three years of supervised practice as an alternative to taking a bar exam. Seventeen states denied petitions that sought emergency diploma privilege.[30]

The outlier non-UBE states had greater flexibility in the pandemic because they did not use NCBE products for their entire exams. Bar examiners accustomed to writing their own questions, for example, could do that more easily in the emergency. Michigan, Indiana, and Nevada gave remote exams online in July and August, none of which included NCBE components. Nevada's exam was noteworthy both because it included a performance test based on actual Nevada cases interpreting an actual statute and because it had an open-book format. Richard Trachok, chair of the Nevada Board of Bar Examiners with decades of experience, explained that an open-book bar exam "incorporates what we as lawyers do every day: look up the applicable law."[31] Making the exam open book also eliminated the need to monitor the test-takers' access to reference materials, reducing some of the privacy and equity problems from surveillance of remote test-takers. Michigan's exam suffered a cyberattack that delayed one portion, and both Indiana and Nevada postponed their original dates and chose to deliver the tests via email because of technical problems with the platforms that had been planned.

The NCBE ultimately provided exam materials for in-person administrations in July and twice in September and for a remote exam in October. The remote October exam used abbreviated versions of NCBE test components and was not a UBE with portable scores or scaled by the NCBE as usual. Approximately 30,000 candidates took the October remote exam, including in two large jurisdictions: California and New York.[32]

One profound but discouraging message from the 2020 pandemic #barpocalypse[33] was that the current testing methods were sacrosanct. Walter Lippman was one of the first to warn in the 1920s that the simplicity and apparent authority of test scores could be intoxicating and lead people to give them too much weight. Faced with conditions that made traditional bar exams impossible, a large part of the profession, led by the NCBE, insisted that the only way to adequately protect the public was to test as usual, whenever that might become possible. This unwavering belief in the necessity of the usual bar exam is especially striking because of the well-known limitations of bar exams. The resistance to emergency accommodations shown by many bar examiners, courts, and other leaders of the profession demonstrated the grip of the testing culture that has taken hold in the United States since the 1950s.[34]

But the louder message from the pandemic's disruption of bar exams was widespread readiness to rethink attorney licensing. One visible change in the 2020 bar exam season was the arrival of an energetic national diploma privilege movement led by recent graduates.[35] These bar candidates mobilized lawyers, law professors, law deans, judges, and legislators through advocacy and litigation across the country. Organizing through social media, #DiplomaPrivilege4All[36] pushed for the decisions of Washington, Oregon, Louisiana, and Washington, DC, each of which provided some version of diploma privilege. They had more modest victories, too, such as Georgia's decision to make its essay questions open book[37] and California's to permit scratch paper for the October online performance test.[38] The advocacy involved legislators in New York and California, challenging elected officials' longstanding deference to the judiciary in matters relating to regulation of the legal profession, including admissions.

Like tax collectors or night club bouncers, bar examiners are accustomed to a steady backdrop of complaints about their work. But the quiet world of bar examiners was shaken by the intensity of the advocacy and scrutiny generated by social media organizing for diploma privilege, well covered by the legal press, that gained traction with every misstep by scrambling bar examiners.[39] Some bar examiners responded by reminding diploma privilege activists about character and fitness requirements, which activists understood to be threats to misuse the power of character and fitness inquiries to silence legitimate criticism.[40]

How much will the new visibility of licensing—and its problems— translate into ongoing engagement and change? Speculation is cheap, but some predictions are sound. Pandemic conditions have hastened bar examiners' move to remote testing. The platforms were shaky in 2020, but the need will not disappear. Also, the states with flexibility in 2020 were the non-UBE jurisdictions. The initial resistance of the NCBE to delivering an online UBE may have slowed the NCBE consolidation juggernaut.

The pandemic revealed that jurisdictions had very different levels of commitment to the traditional bar exam. Some flatly equated any deviation from their traditional test with abandoning their responsibility to public protection. Other states were willing to be more flexible, and a few jurisdictions appeared almost to welcome the shake-up. The Utah Supreme Court, known for innovation in other aspects of attorney regulation, acted quickly to adopt a diploma privilege with supervised practice.[41] The Nevada Board of Bar Examiners embraced the opportunity to provide an open-book test and a performance test based on Nevada law.

The upheaval of the pandemic has spurred ongoing reconsideration of licensing in several states, including Kentucky, Minnesota, Oregon, New York, Nevada, and Washington. The Oregon Supreme Court is pursuing proposals for two pathways to licensure that do not require a traditional bar exam: one based on a structured law school curriculum and the other using a post-graduation period of supervised practice.[42] The California Supreme Court also has appointed a Blue Ribbon Commission to consider the future of the California bar exam and possible additional pathways to licensure.[43]

At least in some jurisdictions, the pandemic-driven experience with supervised practice, essay-only bar exams, online tests, and diploma privilege appears to be spurring more long-lasting reforms. These advances are benefiting from research on minimum competence to practice law that had been missing until very recently.

Part Two

SLOUCHING TOWARDS MINIMUM COMPETENCE

6

DECADES LOST WITHOUT RESEARCH

PROFESSIONAL LICENSING REQUIREMENTS should protect the public by attempting to ensure that the newest members of the profession are at least minimally competent to practice their profession.[1] Thus understanding minimum competence in a lawyer is a primary task of bar examiners (and law professors) as the gatekeepers of a licensed profession. Until disrupted by the pandemic, our bar exams rituals have been as settled as concrete. But the necessary underpinnings to establish the validity of the tests—an evidence-based understanding of minimum competence—has been missing. We have sometimes asked but largely failed to answer this question for at least half a century.

The 2007 *Carnegie Report* on legal education described three apprenticeships of thinking like a lawyer, undertaking the tasks of a lawyer, and having the identity of a lawyer.[2] Similarly, although less elegantly, licensing regulators assume that minimum competence in any profession requires certain fundamental knowledge, skills, and abilities, known as KSAs.[3] Thus bar examiners must first determine what knowledge, skills, and abilities are necessary for minimum competence as an attorney and then establish the requirements to attempt to align licensure with that competency level.[4] Neither step is easy. Figuring out what it takes to practice law with minimum competence is so difficult that law schools rarely try, and bar examiners have skipped to perfecting the reliability of bar exams (so scores have stable meanings) without a solid foundation about the "minimum competence" that the tests should assess.

Validity means that the test assesses what it purports to assess. Validity requires serious attention to first identifying minimum competence and then fixing the line between not minimally competent and barely minimally competent.[5] Criticism that bar exams lack sufficient evidence of validity is widespread, longstanding, and true.[6] Is defining minimum competence to practice law even possible?

My three lawyers. Some of what I understand about attorney competence comes from having been a client three times: for arrests as a college student; to handle my divorce a few years later; and, most recently, for estate planning. All three lawyers were expert in their work. The criminal charges were dismissed, my divorce became final, and I am confident that my wishes for my estate will be carried out when I am dead. None of the three lawyers would have known how to handle either of the other two problems. But, having seen them work, I am confident that, with enough time, each could have figured out the other two matters and taken care of them well.

What would give a criminal defense attorney in Northampton, Massachusetts, the ability to handle a divorce in Los Angeles or a complex estate planning problem in Las Vegas? When we strip away a lawyer's experience and expertise in any practice area or location, we should be left with minimum competence, the foundation or building blocks of legal practice that translate from one legal setting to another. What are those common threads? What competencies would permit my criminal defense attorney to figure out how to handle my divorce or write trusts and a will, using entirely different law in a completely different jurisdiction?

Imagining experienced lawyers being thrown into entirely novel legal matters is not realistic in our age of hyper-specialization. But the thought experiment gives me confidence that such minimum attorney competence exists, is important, and can be defined.

Competence is a core, commonplace concept for lawyers. We understand attorney competence at a general level. Competence is the first duty owed by a lawyer to the client under the *Model Rules of Professional Conduct*.[7] The *Model Rules* do not tell us much about what competence looks like, beyond the general description of "reasonably necessary" knowledge and skills. But hints exist. Perhaps oddly in a profession of specialists, the *comment to Rule 1.1* suggests that competence requires the "proficiency of a general practitioner."[8] This mythical general practitioner, perhaps with an office on Main Street, is also the imaginary creature at whom current bar exams are aimed.

The *comment to Rule 1.1* also identifies "some important legal skills" including "the analysis of precedent, the evaluation of evidence and legal drafting" that are "required in all legal problems."[9] These are indeed central competencies. The *comment* identifies issue spotting ("determining what kind of legal problems a situation may involve") as "[p]erhaps the most fundamental legal skill," a "skill that necessarily transcends any particular specialized knowledge."[10]

This is a good start. The law school accreditor, the ABA Council of Legal Education and Admissions to the Bar, adds a bit more. To maintain ABA accreditation, law schools are now required to establish learning outcomes that include competency in the following:

- Knowledge and understanding of substantive and procedural law

- Legal analysis and reasoning, legal research, problem solving, and written and oral communication in the legal context

- Exercise of proper professional and ethical responsibilities to clients and the legal system

- Other professional skills needed for *competent* and ethical participation as a member of the legal profession[11]

These descriptions are sound, but they do not offer specificity about competence, let alone minimum competence. Knowledge and understanding of *what* substantive and procedural law? *Which* other professional skills? The rules of professional responsibility and the standards for law school accreditation leave the question of minimum competence, and how to assess it, largely unanswered.

Challenges of time, space, and specialization. Unfortunately, some of the difficulties in defining minimum competence are as fundamental as time and space. Lawyers' work evolves.[12] Some aspects of competence change over time, and others are stable. Which is which? Written bar exams started when legal practice was local, and most lawyers represented people, not corporations. But in the twentieth century, there was an explosion of case law, statutes, and regulations. What portion of that law is fundamental now? In earlier ages, the requirement that legal knowledge be memorized made good sense. But how should knowledge be tested today when lawyers carry a law library in their pocket?

Place matters too. Unlike human anatomy, law changes at state lines. Local priorities might not make sense in a test of minimum competence, whether it is oil and gas law on the Texas bar exam or poverty law as has been tested in Massachusetts. As a long-time Californian, I appreciate that California requires that structural engineers pass a supplemental test on seismic soundness in addition to their national licensing tests. Do similar jurisdiction-specific features of minimum competence exist for lawyers? What are the universal aspects of minimum competence applicable to every jurisdiction?

Specialization may be the most difficult challenge. Minimum competence is hard to identify in part because knowing that someone is a lawyer does not tell you much about what that person does. Lawyers handle all manner of matters in countless settings, and almost all specialize.[13] Medical professionals share knowledge of basic science and an understanding of the human body no matter where or what they practice. What is to law as the human body is to medicine, or gravity is to structural engineering? What are the foundational competencies that are necessary for minimum competence in any setting? What is relevant to a lawyer's basic ability as an "officer of the court"? Understanding minimum competence requires more than the intuition, tradition, and good faith that bar examiners and law professors have brought to the task.

Where are the practice studies? Despite the challenges of understanding the minimum competence required to practice law, the legal profession has largely ignored the need for research.[14] Testing experts understand that licensing exams start with practice studies, followed by reverse-engineering to create a documented nexus between job-related tasks and questions on the exams.[15] Licensing tests rely on job analyses for validity: "The standard and most useful device for representing the construct of professional competence is a *job* or *practice analysis*."[16] Until very recently, job analysis research for bar exams has been almost nonexistent. What happened?

False starts in California and New Mexico. California and New Mexico made noteworthy but unsuccessful attempts to understand minimum competence about fifty years ago. The Mexican American Legal Defense and Education Fund (MALDEF) was a leader in both efforts in an era when bar exam inequities were a focus of civil rights advocacy groups in the Southeast and the West.

The California push started with *Espinoza v. Bar Examiners of the State Bar of California*, a lawsuit filed by public interest law offices directly in the California Supreme Court in 1972. Plaintiffs were three people of color, recent graduates of the law schools at Berkeley and UCLA, who had failed California bar exams, and several advocacy groups, including the Western Region and San Francisco branches of the NAACP, the Mexican American Political Association, the Northern California Confederation of Black Law Student Associations, and the Chicano Law Students Association of California. The court rejected the plaintiffs' claims in a one-line order.[17] Although unsuccessful for its plaintiffs, *Espinoza* provoked study of the problems it highlighted.[18] The State Bar of California created the Commission to Study the Bar Examination Process with two very important charges: investigate bias *and* determine "if the bar exam [is] related to the practice of law."[19]

Lawyers are not surprised by commissions and task forces that work hard to generate reports that gather dust. This commission was worse. Their 1975 report explained that identifying minimum competence was so hard that the commission decided not to try. "[I]t was practically impossible to arrive at an acceptable measure of one's effectiveness as an attorney."[20] A commission member admitted why they "did not attempt to determine whether the bar [exam] is job related": "We just didn't know how to do it."[21]

Critics noticed. The lack of evidence of the validity of bar exams—combined with racial and ethnic disparities in pass rates—were the two themes of a landmark 1976 UCLA *Black Law Journal* symposium. An

Illinois bar examiner who also served on the NCBE board acknowledged at that program that he was "not familiar with any extensive studies on validity as such."[22] "There is quite a problem in trying to quantify some measure of competence," admitted the person in charge of administering the California bar exam. "[I]f you are talking about validation, we don't know."[23]

Testing experts were appalled:

"So far as I know, no bar examination is based on . . . a description of the work of lawyers."[24]

"If the Bar cannot tell good lawyers from bad, why screen them at all?"[25]

"Since the purpose of the examination is to protect the public from lawyers who will perform poorly because they do not know enough law, and the Bar cannot tell who is performing poorly there is no legitimate purpose being served by the examination."[26]

Temple University's law dean summarized the validity issue:

The real problem seems to be with the Bar Examiners and their failure to reply to this simple question: what, according to them, constitutes the minimum competence to practice law, and how does a score of 100, 120, 130, or 140 (70% of 200%) on the MBE portion of the Bar exam rationally relate to such "minimum competence?"[27]

A 1970 report in Pennsylvania had found that "the Bar examination was invalid because the Bar Examiners did not know whether their exam was an 'achievement test' or an 'aptitude test.'"[28]

New Mexico's efforts to address minimum competence a few years later also sputtered initially. But following litigation and advocacy by civil rights attorneys from MALDEF and others, in December 1980, following the filing of a writ of mandate, the New Mexico Supreme Court became the first to hold public proceedings on how to professionalize bar exams and address disparate outcomes.[29]

Understanding minimum competence is a precondition for assessing it, and it is certainly required for drawing a line between *not* minimally competent and *barely* minimally competent, as a bar exam must. But none of the expert witnesses in the New Mexico proceeding could define minimum competence.[30] A nationally prominent bar examiner testified, "I don't think if you really looked at the question of what lawyers do, that there's a high correlation in many states, between actual practice and subject matters on the bar exam."[31] The New Mexico Supreme Court learned from the experts that "no one has ever performed a true validity study to determine if the bar examination is related to what lawyers actually do in practice and to the sorts of skills needed to practice law competently."[32]

A member of the failed California commission had recognized in 1976 that minimum competence needed to be defined, and with apparent regret suggested, "Hopefully one of these days somebody will come up with the answer to that."[33] In the absence of any good litigation avenues to press the issue, "one of these days" turned into decades.

Recent recognition of the need for practice analysis. The NCBE conducted a job analysis in 2012.[34] The study suffered from a low response rate and relatively small pool of survey respondents. Other than the addition of civil procedure to the subjects covered by the MBE, which may or may not have been in the works before that study,[35] little in the bar exam appears to have changed in response to this research. The focus on testing for memorized legal rules continued, although the practice study found twenty-five skills to be more important than the most important knowledge domain, civil procedure.[36]

In 2017, the California bar requested that Dr. Tracy Montez, an expert in how licensing tests should protect the public, review their standard setting (cut score) study. Dr. Montez condemned the lack of a job study for the bar exam: "Given that a state-specific occupational analysis does not appear to have been conducted, it is critical to have this baseline for making high-stakes decisions."[37] Professor Deborah Merritt made the same criticism: "California's bar exam—like the exams in other states—has never been validated. This means that no job analysis or other scientific study links the exam's content to the skills and knowledge needed by new attorneys."[38] The California bar's separate 2017 Content Validation Study also identified the need for a job analysis.[39] These critics probably did not realize that the California task force created to address the same issue had walked away from the assignment a half century before.

Understanding and assessing minimum competence is the core purpose of licensing tests. Our tradition since the nineteenth century has been to identify one part of minimal competence—the ability to apply set legal rules to new fact scenarios—and let that aspect of competence, using memorized rules, stand in for the whole. In the absence of research, bar examiners have relied on generalized notions of competence, tradition and habit, and legal education when designing and evaluating exams. However, legal education is a surprisingly weak source for connecting bar exams to minimum competence.

7

DOUBLING DOWN ON THE ERRORS
OF LEGAL EDUCATION

LAW PROFESSORS AND BAR EXAMINERS are typically wary of each other at best, and sometimes dismissive or even antagonistic. This culture of mutual disdain obscures the reality that, in the absence of more meaningful inquiries about the practice of law, licensers have had to look almost entirely to legal education for bar exam content. This explains the high correlation between law school grades and bar exam passage. Rather than bolstering confidence in the bar exam, the correlation could suggest that bar exams are not adding much to the law degree.[1] More importantly, bar exams should replicate law school grades only if law schools are doing a good job of assessing competence in practicing law. Licensers should be able to use the academic programs of professional schools as evidence of what knowledge, skills, and abilities are required for professional competence.[2] But the law school curriculum continues to emphasize thinking about the law outside of the context of learning to practice the law. And doubling down on the traditions of legal education has been a profound error.

Gap between legal education and legal practice. Much to the surprise of generations of law students, preparing for competent practice has not been the historic mission of most U.S. law schools. Law schools are famously—and shamefully—distant from the practice of law. Law-yering competencies beyond core analytic skills are relatively recent concerns in law school programs and are still peripheral at too many law schools. Compared to other professional schools, legal education requires substantially less clinical experience, and nothing guarantees that law school graduates have ever set foot in a law office.[3] In these circumstances, licensing tests that replicate the most traditional aspects of law school are not closely connected to legal practice and do not adequately protect the public.

Most law school professors know little about practicing law. For 150 years, law schools in the United States have been largely aligned with the "scientific" approach of Langdell that focused on dissection of appellate decisions in a university setting, most properly taught by academics with little or no experience practicing law.[4] My eight years of practice were six too many for the mentors urging me to join them in legal academia. The new tenure system law professor today is more likely to have a PhD than to have practiced law for more than a minute. Although the most highly acclaimed medical school professors also treat patients, law school faculty who practice law—in law school clinics—are often relegated to non-tenure system positions with more work, less money, less status, weak job security, and limited voting rights.

False hierarchy of knowledge over skills. Bar exams replicate legal education's false distinction between knowledge and skills and the culture of putting "skills" in the back seat.[5] The skill or ability to do anything requires knowledge about how to do it. The cook learns the properties of food and language of recipes to produce an excellent meal. The quarter-back knows the vocabulary of football and the names and descriptions of plays in the playbook to complete a pass. Competent client counseling, typically understood as a "skill," requires knowing the client's goals and many other aspects of the context of the matter, knowing about duties to clients, knowing about active listening, and knowing about whatever legal doctrine may be relevant to the client's concerns.

Borrowing from legal education, bar examiners also work within a culture that *assumes* that knowledge is separate from and more import-ant than skills. Bar examiners add more assumptions, including that the most important knowledge is that of the legal rules (doctrine) and that the most important rules are common law, or judge made. These assumptions have become cascading fallacies of bar exams, each step taking us further from what lawyers do.

Misleading course titles: Law professors use doctrine to teach analytical methods. Bar examiners reasonably point to the uniformity and stability of law school curricula, especially in the first year, as evidence of the importance of those doctrinal subjects to attorney competence— civil procedure, constitutional law, contracts, criminal law, property, torts. A closer look reveals cracks. The remarkable staying power of the Langdellian first-year curriculum rests on the usefulness of these doctrinal subjects as platforms for teaching and learning methods of analysis, not the necessity for, or even likelihood of, using the doctrinal knowledge in practice.

The longstanding practice of naming courses after their doctrinal subject matter hides the truth that these courses may have methodological goals—skills being taught—that are at least as important as the goals related to doctrinal knowledge. Recognizing this, one of our newest law schools, the University of California Irvine School of Law, renamed its first-year courses: civil procedure is now procedural analysis; contracts is common law analysis: contracts; criminal law is statutory analysis; and torts became common law analysis: torts.[6]

Consider torts. Law schools require students to take torts, typically in the first semester of law school. We should be neither surprised nor troubled that torts survives in the required curriculum untouched by the steep drop in the percentage of attorneys who handle tort matters, which "declined from 16% of civil filings in state courts in 1993 to about 4% in 2015."[7] Like other core first-year courses, the torts course uses doctrine as a platform for students to learn common law legal analysis. As a torts professor, I believe that the torts course includes some knowledge that every lawyer must understand, no matter their area of practice. This necessary knowledge base includes differences between civil and criminal law; stare decisis and common law development; burdens of proof; standards of review; differences between standards and rules; distinctions between elements and factors; differing roles of judges and juries, and of courts and legislatures; burdens of production and proof; the impact of procedural context on doctrinal analysis; the purposes and limitations of systems for allocating the costs of accidents; and the fault continuum of intentional, reckless, negligent conduct and strict liability. Law students should learn to use the elements of negligence and of some intentional torts; causation principles; common defenses and privileges; theories of liability for injuries from products; and types of damages. The doctrinal knowledge portion of this foundational inventory is relatively limited.

Ignoring most lawyering skills and abilities. Bar examiners and legal educators alike understand that legal analysis and the communication skills of critical reading and lawyerly writing are foundational lawyering skills. Law students are introduced in the first year to the basic critical thinking skills of legal reading, legal research, legal writing, and application of legal doctrine to new fact patterns.[8] Similarly shallow legal reasoning—applying uncontested facts to artificially stable (and memorized) rules—has been the hallmark of bar examinations for over a century. Ohio bar examiners asked candidates in 1909 to consider whether the dawn of the automobile age created a duty of a shopkeeper to tie up his team of horses:

> A grocer leaves his delivery team, as was his custom, untied in front of his place of business. B., in passing with his automobile, frightened the team and caused it to run away, and in so doing it ran into the carriage of C. and injured his minor son. Against whom, if anyone, can C. recover for the injury?[9]

With a few changes in historic details, the same question would fit a bar exam today. Mechanical application of legal rules to new facts is a crucial and fundamental aspect of attorney competence. But this is the skill of a novice law student, not a novice lawyer, and it is just one of many legal methods that a minimally competent lawyer needs to be able to use.

Studies about attorney competence have been largely ignored. Numerous reports and studies have presented a consistent message over decades about what skills or abilities are necessary for competence in practicing law. The ABA's 1992 *MacCrate Report*[10] sought to identify the "skills and values" essential to members of the legal profession—highlighting the "skills" of problem solving, legal analysis, legal research, factual investigation, communication, counseling, negotiation, familiarity with litigation and alternative dispute resolution methods, ability to organize and manage legal work, and ability to recognize and resolve ethical dilemmas, and the "values" of commitment to maintaining competence and representing clients competently; promoting justice, fairness, and morality; improving the profession and remedying bias; and continuing to develop professionally.[11]

University of California Berkeley scholars Marjorie Shultz and Sheldon Zedeck began publishing results of their significant empirical work on attorney competence in 2008.[12] Using social psychology methodologies in which Zedeck was expert, the pair undertook empirical studies to determine what knowledge, skills, and values supervisors and clients expected junior lawyers to possess. Shultz and Zedeck developed eight clusters of twenty-six abilities that are necessary to be effective in legal practice:

- *Intellectual and cognitive:* analysis and reasoning, creativity and innovation, problem solving, practical judgment
- *Research and information gathering:* researching the law, fact gathering, questioning and interviewing
- *Communication:* influencing and advocating, writing, speaking, listening
- *Conflict resolution:* negotiation skills, ability to see the world through the eyes of others
- *Character:* Passion and engagement, diligence, integrity and honesty, stress management, community involvement and service, self-development
- *Working with others:* developing relationships within legal profession; evaluation, development, mentoring
- *Planning and organizing:* strategic planning, organizing one's own work, organizing and managing others
- *Client and business relationships:* networking and business development, providing advice and counsel and building relationships with clients[13]

Shultz and Zedeck undertook this work to improve law school admissions, but their findings have had little impact. Today's law school admissions are probably even more driven by test scores than when Shultz and Zedeck began this project to make the admissions process more focused on eventual lawyering competence.

More recently, Professor Neil Hamilton and colleagues associated with St. Thomas's Holloran Center have intensively examined the development of professional identity as students transition from law school into the profession. Summarizing empirical studies, Hamilton identifies these "very important/critically important competencies":

- *Integrity, honesty, trustworthiness:* good judgment, common sense, and problem solving
- *Analytical skills:* identification of legal issues from facts, application of the law, and drawing conclusions
- *Initiative, ambition, drive, strong work ethic*
- *Effective written and oral communication skills*
- *Dedication to client service, responsiveness to client*
- *Commitment to firm, department, office and its goals and values*
- *Initiative and maintenance of strong work and team relationships*

Professor Hamilton found "important to very important" competencies to be: project management, including high quality, efficiency, and timeliness; legal competency, expertise, and knowledge of the law; ability to work independently; commitment to professional development toward excellence; strategic and creative thinking; research skills; inspiring confidence; seeking feedback and responsive to feedback; stress and crisis management; leadership; negotiation skills.[14]

Alli Gerkman and Logan Cornett with the Institute for the Advancement of the American Legal System studied employer expectations about the competence and skills of entry-level attorneys. Their research found that employers particularly valued attributes that fell within the categories of communications, emotional and interpersonal intelligence, legal thinking and application, litigation practice, passion and ambition, professional development, professionalism, stress and crisis management, technology and innovation, working with others, and workload management.[15]

These consistent results from multiple studies show that we *can* identify important lawyering competencies. But both legal education and bar exams have remained notably untouched by this research. Legal research is covered well in law schools, but not on bar exams. And although the core competencies of communication (legal reading and writing) and legal analysis (applying legal principles to facts) are well covered in law schools and bar exams, the other skills are not addressed.

Partially as a result of the *MacCrate Report*, many law schools have expanded curricular opportunities related to counseling, negotiation, and alternative dispute resolution (ADR), including clinical courses that may also reach fact investigation. Like the *MacCrate Report*, the Shultz-Zedeck factors have been used by some law schools for curricular review and development of learning outcomes as now required by ABA accreditation standards, but otherwise this research has not yet had a deep impact on law school culture and academic priorities.

The recent accreditation requirement that each graduate must have taken at least six credits of "experiential" courses—defined as simulation courses, law clinics, and field placements[16]—leaves law schools woefully behind other professional schools in the percentage of the degree (six of at least eighty-eight credits) devoted to experiential learning. And the ABA leaves the skills crucial for competency largely undefined. In addition to knowledge of substantive and procedural law and exercise of ethical responsibilities, *Standard 302* requires learning outcomes related to "Legal analysis and reasoning, legal research, problem-solving, and written and oral communication in the legal context" and the umbrella catchall: "Other professional skills needed for competent and ethical participation as a member of the legal profession."[17] Many of the competencies consistently recognized since the 1992 *MacCrate Report*—factual investigation, counseling, negotiation, ability to organize and manage legal work—are relegated to the elective curriculum of law schools.

Bar examiners need to look beyond legal education to understand minimum competence. In sum, legal education does not provide many answers related to minimum competence. The hard work that remains is to determine which abilities are necessary aspects of minimum competence; determine what level of each is required for that skill; and then align educational, experiential, and assessment requirements to ensure that each necessary understanding or ability has been covered for the level of minimum competence. The question of minimum competence has loomed too large to be solved. Until now.

8

FINALLY, RESEARCH ON
MINIMUM COMPETENCE

AFTER DECADES OF NEGLECT, 2020 was the year that serious research about minimum competence to practice law freed us to move beyond the "I know it when I see it" approach to attorney licensing. The NCBE, the State Bar of California, and the Institute for the Advancement of the American Legal System (IAALS) released studies that attempted to describe minimum competence sufficiently for it to be meaningfully assessed. The insights from the NCBE's most recent job analysis,[1] the similar but somewhat more ambitious study by the California bar,[2] and an exceptional focus group study, *Building a Better Bar*, from IAALS[3] should enable us to protect the public with well-designed licensing requirements.

NCBE's 2020 practice survey. The NCBE undertook its most recent practice study as part of a three-year effort led by its *Testing Task Force* to consider what bar exams of the future should look like.[4] The *Testing Task Force* was a serious effort, undertaken with significant resources and the stated intention of preparing for a major revision of NCBE bar exam products. A major overhaul is tricky for any testing organization, whose biggest asset is confidence in the quality and necessity of its tests, and the NCBE is trying to maintain trust in its current tests while building support to change them. The NCBE practice analysis suffers from some perhaps inevitable built-in defensiveness, as it was conducted with the announced premise that current bar exams already "test the knowledge, skills, and abilities needed for competent entry-level legal practice in a changing profession."[5] Unsurprisingly, NCBE studies presuppose the necessity of including a bar exam in every licensing system, reaffirming the NCBE's current raison d'etre.

NCBE's latest practice survey was based on usable responses from almost 15,000 lawyers across the country—one-fifth of whom had been licensed within three years (the NCBE definition of newly licensed lawyers) and almost half of whom had been licensed for sixteen or more years.[6] The structure of the study was relatively traditional: namely, an initial classification of categories of tasks; knowledge areas; skills, abilities, and other characteristics (SAOs); and technology. Survey respondents indicated frequency and importance from long lists supplied for each category.[7]

The most common lawyering tasks identified were not surprising: "Identify issues in client matter, including legal, factual, or evidentiary issues; Research case law; Interpret laws, rulings, and regulations for client; Research statutory and constitutional authority; and Evaluate strengths and weaknesses of client matter."[8] This is not new. The importance of regulations and statutes is noteworthy considering their longstanding absence in bar exams. These common tasks are used by almost everyone across most practice areas,[9] unlike any one substantive area of law.

The NCBE wisely took its list of "skills, abilities, and other characteristics" (SAOs) from the important prior research by Marjorie Shultz and Sheldon Zedeck that identified twenty-six attributes of successful lawyering.[10] The NCBE practice survey found nearly the entire Shultz and Zedeck list to be either "moderately or highly critical."[11] The most critical SAOs were: written/reading comprehension, critical/analytical thinking, written expression, identifying issues, and integrity/honesty.[12] Again, these results are not surprising.

Regarding "knowledge areas," lawyers who answered the survey picked rules of professional responsibility and ethical obligations, civil procedure, contract law, rules of evidence, and legal research methodology as most important.[13] Legal research methodology could be an important breakthrough because it constitutes knowledge of a legal method instead of the bar examiners' more traditional narrow focus on doctrinal knowledge, or substantive subject areas rules. The importance of knowledge of legal research methodology has led the NCBE to investigate how to add the skills of legal research to the next version of the bar exam, the *NextGen* Bar Exam, planned for operation by 2026.[14]

Like its 2012 predecessor, the practice analysis published by the NCBE in 2020 confirmed that many competencies classified as "skills" are more important than competencies classified as "knowledge." The 2020 study found written and oral communication to be more "critical" than the substantive knowledge area with the highest criticality rating: professional responsibility.[15] Eighteen SAOs were rated by newly licensed lawyers to be as or more critical than the top three knowledge areas (professional responsibility, civil procedure, and contracts).[16]

The NCBE's relatively traditional practice study was in some ways less ambitious than the other research NCBE used to launch its reconsideration of its bar exam products—namely, inviting stakeholders to comment about current bar exams in focus groups that reached about 400 lawyers, judges, bar examiners and administrators, and law professors. These members of the profession delivered messages consistent with longstanding critiques of bar exams, including that the Multistate Performance Test (MPT) is the bar exam component most closely aligned with law practice, that bar exams test too many subjects and require memorization of too many picky rules ("exceptions to exceptions to rules"), that the essays and performance tests are preferred over the multiple-choice questions, and that bar exams should emphasize lawyering skills or methods more than subject matter knowledge.[17]

The next stage of the NCBE project is translating these findings into a new bar exam, what the NCBE calls its *NextGen Bar Exam*.[18] The effort is daunting and critical. The NCBE already supplies the Uniform Bar Exam (UBE) to forty-one jurisdictions and wants its *NextGen* exam to be adopted in its entirety by every jurisdiction. Will any jurisdiction push back against this control by the NCBE over all U.S. bar exams? California has undertaken the most serious research for understanding and improving its bar exam and may be best positioned to proceed independently. California's 2020 job analysis was particularly impressive.

California Attorney Practice Analysis (CAPA). After decades of relative inattention, in recent years the California Supreme Court and the state bar have invested in serious study of their bar exam, far beyond any other state and rivaling the efforts of the NCBE. Multiple experts involved in California's 2017 bar exam studies identified the need for a job analysis. In response, California conducted a job analysis study based on surveys, focus groups, and task sampling. This long-overdue practice analysis study was undertaken "to gauge alignment between the content of the California Bar Exam (CBX) and the practice of law in California."[19]

California used a more ambitious and advanced survey methodology than the NCBE. CAPA includes the traditional survey of ratings based on lawyers' recollection of experience like the NCBE survey but added an experience sampling method (ESM) survey that used multiple randomly timed emails to interrupt attorneys and capture data in real time about what they were doing when interrupted.[20] Interrupting lawyers at work provides different data than recollections over time. The CAPA study combined the results of these two methods, using the traditional survey to measure criticality and the real-time interruption survey to assess frequency.[21]

California's CAPA study also outdid the NCBE by approaching the "knowledge" aspect of the research in a more sophisticated way. The randomly timed prompts asked lawyers not only what they were doing, but what level of cognitive complexity (depth of knowledge) they had been using before being interrupted: (1) recalling from memory, (2) understanding, (3) applying, (4) analyzing, or (5) synthesizing/evaluating.[22]

The average level of cognitive complexity was close to "analyzing" or 4 on this 5-point scale.[23] Indeed, of the 114 subtopics identified through the experience sampling survey, only eight resulted in an average depth of knowledge result below 3 ("applying").[24] Two survey results seem predictable: The thirty-five lawyers interrupted while working on "Human Resources Policies" gave an average "depth of knowledge" of 2.7, while the sixty-four who were busy with "Fees, Billing & Trust Accounting" gave that an average of 2.8.[25] The lowest on the scale was the 2.5 from the seven lawyers apparently not very deep into "Eminent Domain."[26]

The "depth of knowledge" data demonstrates what we all know—lawyering tasks require cognitive complexity beyond memorization. This should help push California, other states, and the NCBE to abandon the relentless memorization that characterizes bar exams today in such vivid contrast to actual practice of law.

In other ways, CAPA's design was like what had been done before. CAPA's survey categories are similar to those of the NCBE: competencies and legal topics.[27] Familiar, broad categories of competencies were identified as most important to be assessed, including drafting and writing; research and investigation; issue spotting and fact gathering; counseling and advising; litigation; and communication and client relationship.[28] These echo the *MacCrate Report*, the Shultz-Zedeck factors, Neil Hamilton's findings, the 2016 IAALS *Foundations of Practice* study, and the advice of the 2020 ABA Commission on the Future of Legal Education.

The *CAPA Report* recommends reducing the legal topics tested on the California bar exam from thirteen to eight: administrative law and procedure; civil procedure; constitutional law; contracts; criminal law and procedure; evidence; real property; and torts.[29] The addition of administrative law and procedure is important not just because so many lawyers spend their days dealing with regulations. Adding admin law could also disrupt a central design flaw in bar exams: the dominance of sometimes archaic common law rules and disregard of the administrative state that has overtaken the day-to-day work of so many attorneys. Neither constitutional law nor real property loomed large in the practice study, but the CAPA working group viewed them as "conceptually core legal topics that are required in the performance of fundamental legal skills, such as issue spotting and legal analysis."[30]

The sensible addition of constitutional law and property points to a serious limitation on the use of practice survey data in determining the knowledge base of minimum competence of a lawyer. The legal topic that a lawyer is working on may build on foundational concepts from a different area of law. For example, a lawyer working in intellectual property may be using as background core concepts from the study of real property that help her to understand copyright. Relatively few lawyers practice constitutional law, but a lawyer who is ignorant about the Constitution may fail in her role as officer of the court and defender of the rule of law. Members of the CAPA task force understood that comprehension of the Constitution is professional literacy for lawyers in the United States.

The California study also identified the importance of practice management. "Practice management" registered higher on the experience sampling part of the study, which interrupted lawyers in real time, than in the traditional study. In combination it ranked as the eleventh highest competency.[31] Everything we know about how lawyers get into trouble, whether malpractice or disciplinary actions, requires taking practice management seriously as an aspect of attorney competence.

Like the NCBE, the California Supreme Court and the State Bar of California are using their recent practice study as the foundation for a serious reconsideration of the strengths and limitations of the California bar exam.[32] California, too, is potentially poised for a major overhaul of attorney licensing.

The *Building a Better Bar* study from IAALS. The ambitious focus group research from IAALS led by Professor Deborah Merritt, *Building a Better Bar: The Twelve Building Blocks of Minimum Competence*, could transform our understanding of minimum competence and how to assess it.[33] *Building a Better Bar* analyzes transcripts of 90-minute focus groups of either new lawyers or supervisors of new lawyers exploring the work performed in the first year of licensed practice. Each of the fifty focus groups was asked the same scripted questions about the work performed, with follow-up questions about how the new lawyers had learned to do that work.[34]

Instead of repeating and refining separate lists of knowledge areas and of skills,[35] *Building a Better Bar* identifies twelve building blocks that combine both understanding and ability, together constituting minimum competence: "[N]ew lawyers who possess these building blocks are able to represent clients with little or no supervision."[36] Echoing the *MacCrate Report*'s emphasis on competence as continually evolving, *Building a Better Bar* highlights that the twelve building blocks of minimum competence ensure that a lawyer "has a basis for growth that will continuously improve the quality of their representation."[37]

Building a Better Bar identified these twelve building blocks of minimum competence:

1. The ability to act professionally and in accordance with the rules of professional conduct

2. An understanding of legal processes and sources of law

3. An understanding of "threshold concepts" in numerous practice areas

4. The ability to interpret statutes, judicial opinions, and other legal materials

5. The ability to interact with clients effectively

6. The ability to identify issues in client matters

7. The ability to research both legal rules and non-legal matters

8. The ability to communicate effectively as a lawyer

9. The ability to manage projects

10. The ability to see the "big picture" in client matters

11. The ability to cope with stress

12. The ability to learn continuously[38]

With relatively few changes, these building blocks are consistent with the principles of professional competence identified by leading researchers of medical education who found that "professional competence is the habitual and judicious use of communication, knowledge, technical skills, clinical reasoning, emotions, values, and reflection in daily practice for the benefit of the individual and community being served."[39]

Some of the twelve building blocks—professional conduct, legal processes and sources of law, interpretation of legal materials, client interaction, issue identification, research, communication, project management—are familiar from the extensive prior work on attorney competence. *Building a Better Bar* also makes a number of impressive conceptual advances:

1. Rejection of the false dichotomy and simplistic separation of lists of "knowledge" and "skills"

2. Replacing "knowledge" with "understanding"

3. Focusing on understanding of "threshold concepts" instead of practice areas, a more accurate and nuanced framing of the cognitive meaning of what lawyers must understand

4. Recognizing that managing stress is part of competence for the benefit of clients, not just the health or well-being of lawyers

5. Explicitly including aspects of metacognition, namely the "ability to learn continuously"

Moving beyond lists of knowledge areas and skills gets much closer to what lawyers do, and how they do it. Practice analyses that identify lawyers as working in contracts law, for example, hide the competencies of contract drafting or negotiation that may fill the lawyer's day. By identifying building blocks that blend understanding and ability, *A Better Bar* creates a more nuanced and accurate picture.

A Better Bar also advances the cognitive dimensions of minimum competence by replacing "knowledge" with "understanding." "Understanding" is not as easily confused with memorization, which for decades has been what bar exams meant by "knowledge."

A Better Bar's adoption of "threshold concepts" could transform the subject matter content of bar exams. Studying for the bar today means memorizing many rules and exceptions for ten or more subject areas thought by licensers to be areas of law in which many lawyers practice. The tests were originally designed for the itinerant country lawyer of yesteryear who handled a variety of legal problems for the townspeople with few law books and relatively little law to be applied, most of it stable. Today lawyers specialize and carry a complete law library on their phones. Lawyers' work is so specialized that attempting to match rules to be tested with rules to be used in practice is a fool's game. Many critics object to the detailed, sometimes arcane and picky rules that must be memorized today.

Threshold concepts, on the other hand, are the law that every lawyer needs to know. Focus group subjects "often struggled to characterize the type of 'basic knowledge' needed for entry-level practice."[40] The *Better Bar Exam* researchers drew on cognitive science to capture this aspect of minimum competence:

> A threshold concept is an insight that transforms understanding of a subject. These concepts, which are often counter-intuitive, distinguish individuals who have begun to master a subject from all others. Threshold concepts allow new learners to understand the "how" and "why" of their field rather than simply the "what."[41]

Deborah Merritt and Logan Cornett use jurisdiction as an example of a threshold concept. "Lawyers know that an aggrieved person cannot walk into any court and file a lawsuit against any defendant."[42] Further, "Lawyers also know that these jurisdictional limits arise from a mixture of constitutional provisions, statutes, and rules. This understanding is far from intuitive, and it is critical to a new lawyer's success."[43] Threshold concepts from torts might include: the fault continuum of intentional, reckless, negligence conduct and strict liability; the elements of negligence and of some intentional torts; causation principles; common defenses and privileges; theories of liability for injuries from products; and types of damages. Identifying the scope of threshold concepts for minimum competence could be one of the next big projects to improve bar exams.

Building a Better Bar makes another conceptual advance by explicitly recognizing that minimally competent lawyers have learned how to keep learning what they need to know. Critical thinking includes key abilities to know, comprehend, apply, analyze, synthesize, and evaluate,[44] plus metacognition, or the understanding of one's thinking processes and the ability to regulate them.[45] Lawyers need metacognition, a higher order skill, so that they understand what they *don't know* and what avenues they need to pursue in order to meet their obligations to clients without falling prey to blind spots.[46] Many professors—especially those who teach in first-year courses,[47] academic support,[48] legal writing,[49] or clinical education[50]—understand that metacognition and the ability to reflect are among the most important skills that students can develop both to achieve academic success and to meet their obligations to future clients. The most valuable aspect of knowledge-based competence in an attorney today is understanding what we do *not* know and then how to find it, understand it, and use it. To a greater extent than ever before, knowing when and how to find legal knowledge is more critical than the knowledge itself.

Using the IAALS building blocks to assess my lawyers. My thinking about minimum competence started with the intuition that minimum competence looks a lot like what is left after we strip away the expertise and experience from an accomplished attorney. The lawyers who handled my legal problems—antiwar arrests in Massachusetts, divorce in

Los Angeles, estate planning in Nevada—were experienced experts in the work they did for me, but I believe each had the minimum competence to be able to handle any of the three matters.

My divorce—no children, no real property, no hostility—was the simplest of the three, quite routine, really. Even so, this very simple divorce required ascertaining our history and goals; knowing (or learning) and using the legal rules for an uncontested divorce; knowing and implementing the ethical rules and procedures for the attorney to represent both spouses; knowing what court documents needed to be filed, where they needed to be filed, and on what schedule; having the ability to keep our personal life confidential; and, most importantly, demonstrating trustworthiness throughout, including by actually doing what he said he would do to make the divorce final.

Handling my arrests was only slightly more doctrinally complicated. With hundreds of others, I sat down at the gates of the Westover Air Force Base to protest the Vietnam War, and particularly the bombing escalation ordered by President Nixon that required each of the airmen to make two tours in Vietnam, instead of one. Our pro bono attorney arranged for me and the others to be released on our own recognizance and to subsequently plead nolo contendere—acknowledging responsibility without admitting guilt, with an agreement of expungement.

The crucial competencies here included understanding jurisdiction and judicial procedures and, above all, negotiating well. Jurisdiction was potentially complex because the trespasses were on a federal Air Force base. The theoretically controlling doctrinal law of say, trespass or disruption of the peace, was almost irrelevant, and no obvious defenses existed.[51] Our attorney got the charges dismissed by being a good negotiator who understood how to work in the local court system. He also drafted proposed orders and managed the individual cases of hundreds of protesters. Law office management was crucial.

The substantive law—or doctrine—of our estate plans was terribly complicated. My partner and I owned property in California, where we were domestic partners, and Nevada, which considered us legal strangers, and spent time in both states. Our goals related to health care decisions and disposition of our assets upon death were not simple to execute. Our attorney had to use her understanding of existing principles to predict how best to handle our new factual situation. She also had to get the relevant facts from us, earn our trust, communicate with us about how to proceed, and then follow through and get it all done.

Grappling with these tax, marriage, and estate planning complexities would have been a challenge (easily a solid 5 on the CAPA study depth of knowledge scale) for my LA divorce lawyer or the wonderful man who represented all the protesters in Massachusetts. But either of them could have figured it out, with time, because each would responsibly conduct relevant legal research; read and understand cases, statutes, and regulations; apply that law to new facts; explain the decisions and choices to me and my partner; and execute the documents consistent with our wishes.

My experience as a client confirms the *Building a Better Bar* building blocks of minimum competence. My attorneys each demonstrated an understanding of legal processes and sources of law, and each had the ability to interpret statutes, judicial opinions, and other legal materials. Each understood threshold concepts in many practice areas sufficiently to determine what new areas of law would have to be learned, and then researched legal rules and non-legal matters. Each had an ability to identify issues beyond doctrine, such as the possibility of future constitutional change related to same-sex marriage. Each was able to interact and communicate with me effectively. Each managed my matters well, each understood the big picture, and each made sure that my interests were taken care of despite whatever stress he or she was also dealing with. Perhaps most importantly, each could have jumped into something brand new because of an ability and desire to continuously learn.[52]

Above all, my experiences as a client confirm that the "ability to act professionally and in accordance with the rules of professional conduct," the aspect of minimum competence *Building a Better Bar* puts first, is at the heart of competence. I would trust any of my three lawyers to do whatever it took to figure out how to handle my matter competently because each had internalized his or her professional responsibilities as a lawyer. Having the character and fitness to practice law is a necessary component of competence, not the separate concern as currently conceptualized by both legal educators and bar examiners.

Part Three

CHARACTER
AND FITNESS

The Right Stuff

9

WHO FITS?

LIST EVERY ADDRESS *you have had for at least thirty days during the past ten years. Name every organization to which you have belonged in the past ten years. Have you ever sought treatment for mental illness?* For almost a century every jurisdiction has conducted some sort of character and fitness inquiry—now typically starting with a 36-page application—to determine whether the candidate is the right kind of person to become a licensed attorney.[1] A wide range of reported conduct triggers further inquiry, including any history of misconduct, criminal activity, false statements, mental or emotional instability, or drug or alcohol dependency.[2]

Most client problems are about ethical violations, not failure to understand legal analysis or even failure to know the rules of professional responsibility.[3] Sloppy office management, missing deadlines because of personal problems, and "borrowing" client funds because of gambling issues are the kinds of things that lawyers do wrong. If we are serious about public protection, character and fitness is potentially the most important aspect of attorney licensing.[4]

But the entire character and fitness project may be fundamentally misguided.[5] At its worst, the character and fitness inquiry deploys the prejudices of the day to foster an elite image of the profession by discriminating against outsiders. The more legitimate purpose is to attempt to predict future bad acts, but such prediction is more difficult than we admit.[6] Should convicted murderers be eligible for law licenses? What about white supremacists?[7] Undocumented immigrants? Alcoholics? People with mental illness? Lesbians? Do the 36 pages of background questions work?

I had a few character and fitness concerns when I filled out my questionnaire. First, I could not find any record of my antiwar arrests eight years previously and was confused about my obligation to report what I had been told had been expunged and would never have to be disclosed. Similar confusion exists today regarding whether juvenile adjudications or other sealed records must be disclosed.[8] Failure to disclose can be worse than the underlying conduct.[9]

My First Amendment class gave me confidence that my continuing political activism would not disqualify me. I was correct about my First Amendment rights, but naive about the political blinders of bar examiners. I was already successfully licensed and practicing law with the ACLU in the 1980s when 80 percent of jurisdictions surveyed by Deborah Rhode reported that they "would or might investigate conduct such as sit-ins resulting in misdemeanor convictions or membership in radical political organizations," apparently unimpressed by Supreme Court determinations that exclusion on such grounds would have violated the First Amendment.[10]

My related fear was about being openly lesbian. I had heard rumors that Florida continued to exclude openly gay or lesbian candidates for the bar, and I knew that millions of Californians had voted in 1978 to ban gay people and our advocates from teaching in the public schools.[11] I was right about Florida, and many other jurisdictions.

Although none of my character and fitness concerns materialized, the weight of being scrutinized for my political activity and sexual identity was real.[12] That experience gives me special sympathy for recent graduates advocating for diploma privilege in 2020 who were warned by bar examiners that some of their advocacy could raise character and fitness concerns.[13] And just completing the questionnaire is only manageable for young adults who have not worked much and rarely moved. One of my students spent too many hours trying to track down out-of-state traffic citations from her past.

The consensus for some sort of character and fitness inquiry and determination is hard to dispute. But current practices are equally hard to justify.

Inconsistency and inadequate procedural protections. The NCBE provides model procedures and forms and contracts with many jurisdictions to obtain letters of recommendation and review other character and fitness materials. But each jurisdiction sets its own standards and procedures. Jurisdictions treat identical information differently, and reviews range from a simple interview to elaborate hearings.[14] Procedural protections can be surprisingly minimal given that the inquiries are intrusive and may prevent an otherwise qualified applicant from being able to practice law.[15] Eleven states, for example, do not publish standards for their character and fitness inquiries.[16] Only about 1 percent of otherwise qualified future attorneys are excluded because of the character and fitness inquiry, but many more suffer delays and other stressors.[17]

Predictions of future wrongdoing are often wrong. The reassuring fantasy driving the character and fitness process is that the "bad apples" can be identified and kept out. The ABA once considered giving some sort of character test to all law students to predict future misconduct.[18] No matter how important it is to be able to predict future character and fitness problems, it may also be impossible. Our current attempts are only a bit more effective than those of the Romans, sixteen centuries ago, who preferred that their lawyers had praiseworthy past lives.[19]

The two leading scholars of character and fitness inquiries, Professor Deborah Rhode and Professor Leslie Levin, have agreed that courts and bar examiners seem to ignore the "the large volume of social science research that questions both the consistency and predictability of moral behavior."[20] Professor Levin explains that the "character and fitness questions are largely based on intuitions that certain past behavior indicates that the applicant poses a significant risk that he or she will engage in future misconduct."[21] But character is highly changeable and hard to predict.[22]

One problem with prediction is that people of good character do the wrong thing in certain circumstances. Most people are willing to inflict

severe pain when instructed to do so, and the percentage of wrongdo-
ers goes even higher when others around them seem to find the bad
behavior acceptable.[23] People are less likely to help another in need if
someone else is present and failing to offer such help. If they were in a
hurry, 90 percent of seminary students walked by a person in apparent
distress slumped in a doorway, but two-thirds of them stopped to help
if they were not rushed. Even seminarians on their way to deliver a lecture about the Good Samaritan were no more likely to stop, and some
stepped right over the slumped figure to proceed without delay.[24]

In other words, character is not fixed, and bad acts are not as predictable as intuition suggests and character and fitness inquiries pre-
sume. This legitimate purpose—predicting and therefore preventing
wrongdoing—is very difficult, perhaps impossible. And the illegitimate
purpose—discriminating against anyone perceived to undermine the
prestige of the profession—is central to our profession's tradition and
culture of character and fitness inquiries.

Excluding undesirables. Character and fitness requirements give lawyers another way to elevate our own status by excluding the disfavored.
Deborah Rhode explained that the requirement of moral fitness operates as a "cultural showpiece" that "has excommunicated a diverse
and changing community, variously defined to include not only former
felons, but women, minorities, adulterers, radicals, and bankrupts."[25]
The vagueness of "character" and "fitness" gives cover to the bigotries
and biases being deployed to protect the image of the profession.[26]

Indeed, the history of character and fitness inquiries is a summary of
exclusionary passions in American history, whether aimed at women;
immigrants; people of color; those who are poorly educated; those with
criminal convictions; lesbians, gays, transgender candidates; or people
with mental illness. James Willard Hurst summarized: "Over the years,
the bar shared the prevailing religious, racial and national prejudices of
middle-class Americans."[27]

In the second half of the eighteenth century, fitness to practice law
often meant being the son of wealthy southern plantation owners sent
to England to qualify, who returned as "the social aristocracy of the
profession."[28] The early 1800s were times of shifting sensibilities and
relative openness about who was entitled to become a lawyer, including

every citizen in some states. By the late nineteenth and early twentieth centuries, more exacting character and fitness review was enacted, fueled by prejudice and economic protectionism, as the established white, male, Protestant legal profession found itself facing competition from new lawyers from different classes and backgrounds. After failing to eliminate all night schools, the established legal community watched as the profession became more accessible to groups beyond the traditional elite.[29] The organized profession responded with new rules of conduct, including those against advertising and ambulance chasing, and stepped up character and fitness inquiries.

Character investigations before law school were used to persuade the "unworthy" to choose a different profession.[30] Deborah Rhode found that the "unworthy" rejected by one county board in 1929 included people said to be "'dull,' 'colorless,' 'subnormal,' 'unprepossessing,' 'shifty,' 'smooth,' 'keen,' 'shrewd,' 'arrogant,' 'conceited,' 'surly,' and 'slovenly.'"[31] The profession also happily attempted to exclude "radicals, religious 'fanatics,' fornicators, and adulterers."[32] The organized bars often considered people of Irish descent, Jewish people, African Americans, and women to be "morally unfit,"[33] with "evaluation of character allow[ing] for the relatively free play of social ostracism."[34] Character and fitness denials were a part of the arsenal that kept the profession as wealthy, white, and Christian as possible. For example, bar examiners in the 1960s weaponized character and fitness inquiries by subjecting Black candidates to searching interviews the day before the bar exam, in contrast to the perfunctory interviews scheduled for white candidates well before the exam.[35]

Punishing dissent. Bar examiners have followed mainstream orthodoxy in finding political dissenters lacking in moral character, especially in times of social anxiety and polarization, such as the Cold War in the 1950s, the antiwar movement later in the twentieth century, and perhaps our current era. Rhode reported that "nonconformists" paid the price "throughout the twentieth century": "Conscientious objectors, religious 'fanatics,' and student radicals were exhaustively investigated and occasionally denied admission."[36] Jerold Auerbach described how the organized bar "ostracized dissidents who challenged their political or economic values."[37]

The organized bar used character and fitness inquiries to enforce Joseph McCarthy's norms of virulent anticommunist purges and civil liberties atrocities in the 1950s.[38] In a case about whether an attorney with suspected communist sympathies could be admitted to the bar, Justice Black recognized in 1957 that "good moral character" is so ambiguous that any definition would reflect "the attitudes, experiences, and prejudices of the definer."[39] No wonder Jerome Auerbach warned that character and fitness inquiries were "a dangerous instrument for arbitrary and discriminatory denial of the right to practice law."[40]

Until schooled in the First Amendment, California bar examiners attempted to exclude an applicant who had been convicted for civil disobedience during a civil rights protest.[41] The Association of the Bar of the City of New York rushed so quickly to bring disciplinary charges against William Kunstler during the Chicago Eight trial that it violated its own rules that prohibited such action until proceedings were finished.[42] Concerns about character and fitness inquiries chilling lawful speech are very much alive in the polarized politics of recent U.S. history.[43]

Sexual minorities and gender identity. Sexual orientation and gender identity have been grounds for blanket exclusion and continue to trigger character and fitness trouble. Knowledge of a candidate's homosexuality typically meant an "automatic denial" until the 1970s.[44] In 1973, an intermediate New York court voted 3–2 to deny a license to an attorney who had been disbarred in Florida following a sodomy conviction almost twenty years before.[45] Harris Kimball, who considered himself the first openly gay attorney in the United States,[46] had been licensed first in Illinois in 1951 and then licensed in Florida from 1953 until he was disbarred in 1957. The dissenting New York judges recognized in 1973 that "the social and moral climate in New York (and probably throughout the Western world) has in recent years changed dramatically with respect to homosexuality."[47] Happily, the New York Court of Appeals adopted this dissent in reversing the lower court,[48] opening the door for the Florida Supreme Court to eventually allow Mr. Kimball's readmission in 1982.[49]

In 1978 the Florida Board of Bar Examiners requested guidance from the Florida Supreme Court about whether Robert Francis Eimers, an attorney licensed in Pennsylvania who was otherwise qualified to be admitted to the Florida bar, should be excluded for failing the "good moral character" requirement because of his "admitted homosexual orientation."[50] The court found for Mr. Eimers, holding that the "mere preference" for homosexuality was not a sufficient threat.[51] But, less encouraging, the court noted that "this opinion, then, does not address itself to the circumstance when the evidence establishes that an individual has actually engaged in homosexual acts."[52]

Three years later in 1981, the Florida Supreme Court considered how far the Florida bar examiners could go in investigating a homosexual applicant's sexual conduct.[53] The Florida court permitted questions about the candidate's sex life so the bar examiners could assure themselves that the applicant's sexual conduct was "noncommercial, private, and between consenting adults."[54] Justice Boyd dissented on grounds that anyone whose "lifestyle [is] likely to involve routine violation of a criminal statute" should be prohibited from admission, "even without evidence of actual conduct."[55] Justice Alderman also dissented, declaring that anyone with "a recent history of homosexual activity" should be denied just like anyone with a recent history of shoplifting because it "indicates that he plans to continue this activity because he sees nothing wrong with what he is doing."[56] Justice Alderman wanted the board to treat homosexual activities like "any other illegal and morally reprehensible conduct."[57]

Just as family law judges across the country have used sodomy statutes as automatic grounds to rule against gay and lesbian parents in custody battles, the Board of Bar Examiners associated homosexual orientation with felonious conduct in which the candidate would "disobey the laws of Florida which he seeks to be sworn to uphold."[58] The board also argued that "an applicant's past homosexual acts are relevant to determine whether past conduct will prevent him from achieving the social acceptance necessary to enable him to discharge his professional responsibilities."[59] This explicit concern about "social acceptance" is a thinly veiled worry about the reputation of the profession.

No wonder gays and lesbians felt trepidation about being out in the legal profession. Fordham law professor Elizabeth Cooper remembers being informed in college in the early 1980s that "as a gay person I might not satisfy the 'character and fitness' requirement for admission to the bar."[60] Her concern was well grounded. Deborah Rhode found in the mid-1980s that half the jurisdictions "would investigate sexual conduct, sexual orientation, or 'lifestyle.'"[61]

Professor Cooper persevered, and she became part of the cohort of attorneys and law professors who led one commentator to conclude that by 2000 openly gay or lesbian applicants had "little to fear" from character and fitness inquiries.[62] Along the way, the ABA became a voice for LGBTQ rights, although a resolution to condemn discrimination on the basis of sexual orientation failed in 1983 by twenty-four votes, and again in 1985 by nine votes.[63] By 2008, a California attorney experienced in character and fitness matters declared that "sexual orientation rarely, if ever, prevents an applicant from practicing law."[64]

Character and fitness struggles continue for transgender candidates, who face discrimination, overt and more subtle. The extensive documentation required—every aspect of one's employment, residences, former names—causes dire problems for many transgender candidates. A Florida attorney had to deal with former employers receiving inquiries from the Florida bar examiners that used his former and current names: "They outed me as trans."[65] A network of visible trans attorneys helps trans candidates across the country with references and other support as they make their way through the daunting character and fitness process.[66]

Prior arrests and convictions. Criminal records and juvenile adjudications are a major focus of character and fitness inquiries that provide little benefit to the public but impose a significant disparate impact on African American and Latinx applicants and those from less economically secure backgrounds.[67] In some jurisdictions anyone with a felony conviction is automatically disqualified, at least for some period.[68] The rare application from a candidate convicted of murder[69] or manslaughter[70] draws publicity, but the broader public policy issue is exclusion of the large swath of the population who have been convicted of lesser crimes. Deborah Rhode and Leslie Levin both have emphasized that the character and fitness inquiries into past criminal conduct build on the racial and class bias in the criminal justice system.[71] Racial minorities pay a "special price" for these inquiries and exclusions in light of mass incarceration and persistent racial bias in the criminal justice system.[72] Many jurisdictions make more flexible individualized consideration of criminal records rather than automatic denials.[73] Some require disclosure of convictions that were previously expunged, however.[74] Applicants in New York are currently subjected to a particularly broad inquiry:

> Have you ever, either as an adult or a juvenile, been cited, ticketed, arrested, taken into custody, charged with, indicted, convicted or tried for, or pleaded guilty to, the commission of any felony or misdemeanor or the violation of any law, or been the subject of any juvenile delinquency or youthful offender proceeding?[75]

The New York State Bar Association and the New York City Bar Association have challenged the legality, fairness, and diversity impact of this question in formal submissions to the New York Court of Appeals.[76] Using possibly illegal questions to try to weed out future lawyers on character grounds is ironic, embarrassing, and suggests that the "sordid" history of character and fitness inquiries is not yet eradicated.[77]

Immigration status. Immigration status is another area of contention and inconsistency.[78] Some states require applicants to disclose their immigration status and others do not.[79] A small number of states permit immigrants who are not fully documented to become licensed attorneys.[80] When Florida declined to admit undocumented immigrants, three former ABA presidents filed a brief with the Florida Supreme Court to urge their admission. The court was unpersuaded by the ABA leaders' concern that preventing undocumented immigrants from practicing law is a "waste of exceptional talent for our profession."[81]

Sergio Garcia embodies the justice in permitting undocumented candidates to join the profession. Garcia first came to the United States from Mexico at the age of eighteen months, but subsequently was prevented from obtaining regularized status by the backlog of applications of eligible immigrants from Mexico. He brought to his bar application exemplary personal and professional references and an unblemished record, other than his undocumented immigration status. The California Supreme Court decision affirming the state bar's petition that he be permitted to join the profession came five years after Garcia had graduated from law school and passed the bar examination.[82] Five years

later, attorney Garcia's decades-long efforts to obtain citizenship were
finally successful.[83]

Mental health. Jurisdictions have been routinely investigating candidates' mental health for about fifty years,[84] practices that have earned
greater scrutiny recently. Critics justifiably charge that requiring candidates to answer questions about whether they have sought psychological
assistance invades privacy unnecessarily and deters law students from
seeking such care to the detriment of their health and—perversely—
impairing their ability to manage the stress of practicing law.[85]

After decades of controversy,[86] bar leaders, led by various entities
associated with the ABA, are convincing jurisdictions to change their
mental health question to focus on behavior rather than diagnoses of
or treatments for mental illness.[87] These efforts are propelled in part
by claims that standard character and fitness inquiries about mental
health status violate the Americans with Disabilities Act (ADA).[88]

These arguments gained momentum from landmark litigation
brought by the Civil Rights Division of the Department of Justice
against the Louisiana Supreme Court on grounds that the mental
health questions of the character and fitness inquiry discriminated
against people with disabilities in violation of the ADA. Pursuant to a
2014 consent decree, Louisiana agreed to stop asking questions about
candidates' mental health diagnoses and treatment that had been
supplied by the NCBE.[89] In 2015 the ABA House of Delegates passed
a resolution urging all jurisdictions to eliminate "any questions that
ask about mental health history, diagnoses, or treatment and instead
use questions that focus on conduct or behavior that impairs an applicant's ability to practice law in a competent, ethical, and professional
manner."[90] In recent years, state-specific advocacy led by a coalition of
professional organizations has resulted in this reform in most jurisdictions across the country.[91]

Current character and fitness efforts do not work well. Even when not
tainted by prejudice, bias, or arguable illegality, character and fitness
inquiries are not particularly effective. Rates of discipline are so low
that prediction is close to impossible. Deborah Rhode summarized the
problem: "Much of the conduct that triggers character investigation of

applicants, such as financial mismanagement, psychiatric treatment, minor drug offenses, and political activity, almost never results in disciplinary investigations of practicing attorneys."[92]

The most authoritative study of character and fitness screening was a review of 1,300 Connecticut bar applicants and their subsequent disciplinary records conducted by Leslie Levin.[93] When all the risk factors were taken into account, only two of the candidates studied had more than an even chance of being disciplined based on the information in their applications.[94] The researchers sensibly concluded that this finding "casts serious doubt on the usefulness of the character and fitness inquiry as a predictor of lawyer misconduct."[95] As Levin explained, "the baseline probability of discipline is so low that even a factor that more than doubles this probability—say, from 2.4% to 5%—has little predictive power."[96]

Records of bankruptcy showed the opposite of what bar examiners might expect: "[N]one of the disciplined lawyers reported bankruptcy on their applications, although four of the never disciplined lawyers had previously declared bankruptcy."[97] None of the applicants who went on to receive severe discipline had reported mental health diagnosis or treatment or substance abuse dependency or treatment on their application, although the "less severely disciplined group" was "significantly more likely to reveal a higher rate of mental health issues."[98]

A prior criminal record would seem to be the most important character and fitness inquiry. But Levin's research showed that, after regression analysis, "being male was statistically significant; having a prior criminal conviction was not."[99] Levin found no evidence "that the character and fitness process protects the public from lawyer misconduct."[100] All of this suggests that current character and fitness practices—questionnaires and subsequent inquiries intended to predict future wrongdoing—are largely ineffective and not sufficient for the public protection role they are intended to play. We need to rethink character and fitness.

10

FIXING CHARACTER AND FITNESS

BETTER PUBLIC PROTECTION REQUIRES two important conceptual shifts in character and fitness efforts. First, we should focus pre-licensure character and fitness efforts on prevention, not on prediction, by requiring much more of law schools. Second, state bars should transfer some of their character and fitness scrutiny and resources away from applicants and toward lawyers already in practice.

Require law schools to educate for strong professional identities. Character and fitness are intrinsic to lawyer competence, not somehow separate. The legal profession should translate to law the emphatic message of leading medical educators Ronald Epstein and Edward Hundert that professional competence "builds on a foundation of basic clinical skills, scientific knowledge, and moral development."[1] The ability to follow ethical norms is an essential aspect of competence, the first building block of competence identified by Deborah Merritt and Logan Cornett in *Building a Better Bar.*[2] The most prevalent failures of lawyers involve falling short on ethical and professional responsibilities, not on lack of analytical ability. Thus, educating for strong professional identities, with the character and fitness to practice law, should be at the heart of law school curricula. Traditionally, it has not been.

Fifteen years ago the *Carnegie Report* warned that law schools had fallen short in educating for professional identity formation.[3] Professor Louis Bilionis pinpointed the problem as the "failure of law schools to pursue the professional formation dimension of the educational endeavor with anything like the intentionality and drive for excellence that they exhibit when helping students to think like a lawyer."[4] This breakdown flows from both the legal academy's purposeful distance from law practice and the inherent challenges of teaching character. Disbelief that ethics or character can be taught or learned—and queasiness about trying—are widespread. Teaching or learning the rules of professional responsibility is much easier than teaching or learning how to follow them. But both are possible. The insight that character is not fixed suggests that it is also teachable and learnable.

Thankfully, professional identity formation is now a substantial focus of legal education at a growing number of law schools[5] and supported by excellent resources.[6] Professor Bilionis defines the goal of professional identity education as "the acceptance and internalization of a personal responsibility to others whom one serves as a professional, including clients, colleagues, and society."[7]

We now know a great deal about what leads to success in educating law students to take responsibility for their learning and to internalize their responsibilities to clients, the public, and the profession.[8] Contrary to assumptions of earlier eras, law schools can effectively teach ethics and the internalization of professional responsibilities.[9] One-on-one relationships are crucial.[10] A law student's sense of personal responsibility for his or her learning generally, and for professional behavior specifically, is central. Instilling habits of self-regulation and reflection are key.[11] This is best accomplished with first-year coursework plus subsequent clinical practice for every student.

Require 1L coursework in professional identity. Unless the ABA accreditors beat them to it,[12] state courts and bar examiners should use their licensing authority to insist on professional identity coursework, a long-neglected aspect of legal education. Jurisdictions should consider requiring completion of an interactive professional formation course, preferably in the first year, to change the frame of legal education and capture student attention at its height.[13] Law schools are increasingly positioned and motivated to do this well.[14] About sixty law schools already have such required first-year courses.[15]

In part to reverse the unhealthy impact of law school,[16] and in part to better prepare law students for the challenges of law practice, the course should include explicit education related to building habits for successful management of stress. Legal educators are becoming more engaged and sophisticated about how law students can be taught to manage stress.[17] *Building a Better Bar* recognizes "the ability to cope with the stresses of legal practice" as one of the fundamental building blocks of minimum competence that should be included in any licensing process.[18] Attorneys are disciplined for mistakes they make when their life problems overwhelm them.[19]

The course should also require students to begin their lifelong engagement with the meaning of justice.[20] *Building a Better Bar* similarly recommends that candidates be required to have completed coursework focused on the lawyer's role as "a public citizen having special responsibility for the quality of justice."[21] This focus on the lawyer's role in improving society and the profession is consistent with the leading theories about what it means to be a professional, more broadly.[22]

Sadly, until such new requirements replace current bar exam practices, the bar exam's current overemphasis on rule memorization will continue to pull students (and faculty) away from the one-on-one, experiential, and other purposefully reflective parts of the law school curriculum that best prepare ethical attorneys.[23]

Require supervised practice as a student attorney prior to full licensure. As I discuss more fully in Chapter 12, states should require every candidate to complete a "clinical residency" of fifteen academic credits, of which at least six must be in a clinic or externship with responsibility for direct client representation under student practice rules. New lawyers in the *Building a Better Bar* study acknowledged struggling with actual ethical problems, even though they knew the rules. They found, not surprisingly, that it

> was hard to identify ethical issues in the moment, while interacting directly with clients, supervisors, or opposing counsel. "In actual practice," one new lawyer confessed, "you see how things [go] sideways really quickly, and without even realizing it."[24]

Putting public protection first means that every new lawyer should experience these ethical pressures first while being supervised so that mistakes can be corrected and avoided without harm to clients.[25] Indeed, what message do we send new lawyers about ethical responsibilities to clients by *not* requiring them to practice first under supervision?

Clinical education—in which students face ethical issues in the context of client representation—is the best way to instill habits of ethical behavior that are more likely to last. New lawyers learn how to respond to ethical dilemmas by imitating the lawyers around them.[26] The clinical residency provides strong mentorship in moral and ethical practice when novice student attorneys are most susceptible to influence.[27]

New lawyers learn that "[t]here's such a deep level of responsibility that comes with being a lawyer."[28] The first experience of that weight of responsibility should come in the context of a structured learning environment in which the professional identity formation of the student attorney is a very high priority, closely following the highest priority of competent, excellent representation of the client.[29] The supervising attorney is an experienced educator (with minimal business pressures) whose job includes guiding the ethical development of student attorneys and identifying those who do not follow ethical norms.[30] Requiring a clinical residency as the foundation for ethical practice would be a much better investment in public protection than the extensive character and fitness inquiries now undertaken.

Require law office or project management course or certificate. Attorney mistakes come from administrative lapses more than identifiable character defects or substantive knowledge gaps. States should acknowledge that ethical practice requires technical competence and therefore require every newly licensed attorney to have some training in law office management or project management.

Bar examiners worry most about new lawyers who practice by themselves or with other junior lawyers; lawyers practicing by themselves or in small law firms are most likely to be disciplined.[31] But all three recent practice studies confirm that *all* lawyers, no matter their practice settings, need the tools to manage their work responsibly. NCBE's 2020 practice analysis identified the ability to "develop specific goals and plans to prioritize, organize, and accomplish work activities" as one of the ten most important tasks for new lawyers.[32] "Practice management" was the eleventh-highest competency found in the recent California practice study.[33] *Building a Better Bar* identified the "ability to manage a law-related workload responsibly" as one of the twelve foundational building blocks of competence.[34] The new lawyers in that study understood that clients were "irrevocably harmed" by the inability to manage workload effectively, which requires "careful time management, meticulous organization, and effective collaboration."[35] Those skills—time management, meticulous organization, and effective collaboration— can and should be taught, not left to chance with the risk of harming clients. The new lawyers in the *Building a Better Bar* focus groups conveyed the problem: "When asked how they developed appropriate time management skills, most focus-group members drew a blank. Several suggested they learned these skills out of necessity, with 'feet to the fire.'"[36]

There are various ways to introduce these skills. Whether through a law school class or a continuing legal education-type training, public protection means familiarizing every future lawyer with case management software, spreadsheets, calendaring systems, and similar basic tools of competent, ethical legal practice, before clients are at risk.[37]

Continue to test the rules of professional responsibility. The most important aspects of character and fitness to practice law are not conducive to multiple-choice testing,[38] but familiarity with the rules of professional responsibility and their application is a positive baseline.[39] Therefore, passage of an improved version of the Multistate Professional Responsibility Examination (MPRE) should probably still be required. The MPRE should be open book, because finding the correct rules is the professional habit to be inculcated, not the habit of guessing or winging it. Jurisdictions should agree on a uniform cut score to facilitate portability of scores. And the MPRE should not stand alone. Any post-JD bar exam should contain a heavy dose of professional ethics problems.

Streamline the character and fitness application. Jurisdictions should drastically streamline the character and fitness questionnaire to include only information with a demonstrated connection to fitness.[40] Require candidates to disclose criminal convictions and academic discipline related to dishonesty and to provide an explanation for why they are now sufficiently trustworthy to become licensed. Eliminate all questions about mental health treatment, past substance abuse, bankruptcy, arrests or contact with police not leading to convictions, juvenile adjudications, organizational affiliations, former addresses, and many of the current 36 pages of background questions.[41]

Applicants and potential applicants to law school should be able to obtain a character and fitness review prior to matriculating in law school or at any time after they have enrolled.[42] Someone with a serious criminal conviction, for example, should be permitted to find out whether that record will be a barrier to licensing prior to making a substantial investment of time and money in law school. Some states permit such inquiries as early as the first year of law school.[43] Every jurisdiction should permit such reviews prior to enrollment. With average law school debt in six figures, plus the opportunity costs of three years of delayed employment, nobody should have to enroll in law school to obtain a preliminary character and fitness determination regarding preexisting problems.

Invest in monitoring and preventing attorney misconduct. Prevention of attorney misconduct and ethical breaches may be the hardest aspect of attorney licensing to address at the licensing stage. In addition to requiring law schools to do more to educate for professional identity, states should shift their character and fitness focus from applicants trying to enter to those already licensed. Most attorney misconduct occurs a long time after the lawyer was licensed;[44] the typical lawyer facing discipline is a middle-aged male.[45] Instead of attempting the largely undoable task of preventing the "wrong" people from joining the profession, the profession should put its efforts into preventing, knowing about, and correcting misconduct—including incompetence—of licensed attorneys. This means shifting some of their character and fitness focus from candidates trying to *get into* the profession to those *already in it*.

Our current professional culture supports disciplinary systems that touch few attorneys. An ABA Special Committee from 1970 found the lack of disciplinary enforcement to be "a scandalous situation that requires the immediate attention of the profession."[46] In 1972, 357 of the country's 380,000 practicing lawyers were disciplined, about 0.09 percent.[47] The likelihood of discipline rose over the next fifty years; by 2018, complaints were filed against 7 percent of lawyers, resulting in discipline against 0.4 percent of the country's lawyers.[48]

Deborah Rhode argued convincingly for more effective and accountable disciplinary systems, including making attorney complaint records available to the public and providing more resources, wider jurisdiction, and a greater range of available remedies for disciplinary agencies.[49] Information about attorney disciplinary action is not as available to the public as is information about doctors or other professionals.[50] Rhode's recommendations include "random financial audits, free assistance with complaints, and enforcement of rules requiring lawyers to report serious ethical violations."[51] Each would do more to protect the public than current character and fitness practices. Let's get on with it.

Part Four

THE FUTURE

Competence-Based Alignment of Experience,
Education, and Exams

11

TWELVE GUIDING PRINCIPLES

STATE SUPREME COURTS and bar examiners try to protect the public by ensuring that newly licensed attorneys are at least minimally competent to practice law. The challenges are enormous.

Practicing law is complex and undertaken in a wide array of disparate settings. Minimum competence is hard to define and even harder to assess. Current licensing practices rest on traditions that were created, in the best scenario, instinctively, and at worst, to shut out competition and elevate the status of lawyers by keeping the profession wealthy, male, and white. Oversight of licensing can be a secondary function of overworked and underfunded state supreme courts. Boards of bar examiners are typically strong on commitment to public service but short on resources and expertise about testing. The NCBE is a testing organization that produces highly reliable bar exams but offers almost no leadership about how and why jurisdictions could approach licensing beyond tests. And NCBE test products have suffered from a weak nexus to legal practice, raising serious validity, fairness, and racial equity questions.

I offer twelve foundational principles as a framework for thinking about how attorney licensing can protect the public more effectively moving forward.

1. *Base every licensing requirement on evidence about understanding, ensuring, and assessing minimum competence to practice law, not just hunches, tradition, and good faith.*
Our licensing traditions are well entrenched but built on suppositions and intuition, not evidence. High hopes, good faith, hard work, and "I know it when I see it" are no longer sufficient. Licensing tests and other requirements today are very similar to what I faced in 1980. Some bar exam questions look like questions from the 1800s. Ensuring minimum competence requires careful consideration and alignment of what a candidate should have learned in school, what lawyering experience a candidate should have had, and what kind of licensing tests may be appropriate. Until very recently, courts and bar examiners did not have solid research about minimum competence to practice law. Now we do. Next, we must use it.

2. *Address racial, ethnic, and gender disparities as if required by law.*
Like other aspects of our society, legal education and bar exams carry legacies of purposeful racism and other biases that have morphed into unexamined premises cemented by decades of earnest good faith. We have become complacent about achievement gaps in law school and bar exams. Unlike employers, bar examiners have been successfully immunized from Title VII scrutiny of the undisputed racial, ethnic, and gender disparities in bar exam pass rates. Even if no court compels it, our values and principles require us to commit unrelentingly to understanding disparate results and reducing them.[1] Self-scrutiny should replace defensiveness, complacency, and self-serving good faith. As Sherrilyn Ifill, then president of the NAACP Legal Education Fund, told the ABA upon accepting an award in 2021, "I challenge you to stop talking about diversity and inclusion and make it happen."[2] Our history is humbling.

Public protection requires both an unyielding focus on minimum competence and an uncompromising commitment to a diverse and inclusive profession. Medical outcomes are better studied than legal outcomes, so we should learn from the dismal truth that African American babies with African American doctors have a much higher survival rate than African American babies with white doctors.[3] A diverse legal profession will serve the entire public better.[4] To best protect a diverse public, especially underserved communities, licensing authorities should audit every policy decision—educational and practice requirements, tests, and cut scores—to determine whether they exacerbate or reduce our longstanding racial disparities in licensing. We should recognize enduring problems with high-stakes tests.[5] Our goals of competence and inclusivity require us to seriously consider paths to licensure based on lawyering competence proved in supervised practice—not just predicted by aptitude for time-pressured standardized tests.

3. *License no one who has not successfully practiced law under supervision, preferably in an academic clinical residency.*
   Law is exceptional among the professions in not requiring substantial clinical experience prior to licensure.[6] Jurisdictions should require every candidate to have successfully completed a residency prior to licensure as an attorney, using student practice rules to impose professional standards on both the student lawyer and the supervisor. This is a single, relatively simple step that jurisdictions can take now to dramatically improve public protection.

   Requiring these residencies will expand the lawyering competencies[7] and advance the professional identity[8] that law students bring to licensure, neither of which are easily or effectively assessed in bar exams. The public deserves assurance that a newly licensed lawyer has practiced with a copilot before flying solo.[9]

4. *Align bar exams more closely with minimum competence to practice law.*
   Attorney licensing exams are overdue for a major overhaul. Today's bar exam components have been in place since the introduction of the MBE in 1972 and performance tests in 1980. Changes in the profession demand new tests; innovations in technology, computer-assisted grading, machine learning, and psychometric scoring make better tests possible. If attorney licensing tests

should exist—and I believe most jurisdictions will want at least the option of a test of some kind—the bar exams of the future must be reworked to become more valid assessments of minimum competence to practice law.

Current exams focus too much on memorization of volumes of legal rules at a picky level of detail, rules that may not be the correct law of the jurisdiction administering the exam. Memorization should be reduced or eliminated and replaced by a new emphasis on assessing fundamental methods of lawyering. The ungodly speededness and the required memorization of too many rules, neither of which tracks to law practice, make current tests too hard for competent future lawyers who are not rapid-fire memorization superstars. On the other hand, the questions are also too simple, using cardboard scenarios with falsely stable rules and artificially firm facts. Lawyering is about handling ambiguity—knowing, above all, what is not known and needs to be pursued, whether in factual investigation or legal argumentation. Current technology invites more dynamic question sets that can move beyond doctrine to strategy, organization, case management, and other higher order legal thinking. Luckily, the stage is set for the NCBE to undertake some of this work and for independent jurisdictions to create better tests as well.[10]

5. *Establish competence-based educational or training requirements.*
Jurisdictions typically rely on graduation from an accredited law school as the educational requirement for licensure, without scrutiny of the courses taken. This simplicity is appreciated by candidates, law school administrators, and bar examiners. Rigid yet differing educational licensing requirements would be an administrative nightmare for law schools and would undermine the recent gains in portability of licensure of new lawyers in this mobile age. But with or without a bar exam, in a time of largely elective law school curricula, public protection is not served by mere graduation. Administrative ease and public protection can both be achieved with licensing requirements of coursework *or* training in certain crucial aspects of minimum competence.[11]

6. *Reduce the expense of becoming a lawyer.*
   Protecting the public requires eliminating barriers to the profession based on anything other than potential for and then demonstration of competence as a lawyer. The focus on public protection requires rethinking traditions that were designed to create a path for young men of means. Access to the profession today requires controlling the cost of legal education, the cost and expense of licensing tests, and the costs of bar preparation courses. Three years of post-graduate education should be enough time to produce and assess minimum competence to practice law. If exams are used, a better alignment between those exams and competence to practice law could help close the gaping hole between legal education and bar exams. That chasm is now filled by a billion-dollar bar prep industry funded by candidates. Educators and licensers should consider what law school and licensing tests could and should look like without the voracious commercial behemoth that prepares today's graduates for bar exams, but not for practice.

   Multiple pathways achieve the goal of licensing upon law school graduation, including Arizona's early testing,[12] Wisconsin's diploma privilege,[13] New Hampshire's Daniel Webster Scholars program,[14] or new ideas such as combining a clinical residency with multiple, staged performance tests that could be taken during law school.[15] Law graduates who take care of children or work in non-law jobs have a harder time passing bar exams.[16] The public is hurt when licensing mechanisms exclude competent candidates who do not have the resources to succeed in our expensive gatekeeping system.

7. *Make licenses portable from state to state.*
   Whether or not states use identical licensing tests or requirements, a mobile and dynamic profession requires portability of licensure. Limits on reciprocity are artifacts of protectionism. Jurisdictions should approach reciprocity with the premise that the public benefits from the availability of competent attorneys, not the long-dominant premise that lawyers should protect their business by keeping out interlopers. Attorneys licensed in one state should be presumed competent to practice law in other states. Concern

about state-specific rules and law can be addressed through required state-specific training and tutorials.

8. *Use uniform cut scores to protect the public—including by eliminating unnecessary racial disparities—not to keep out competition.*

Current bar exam cut score practices are indefensible.[17] States have used cut scores to keep out competition, and the NCBE has chosen to look away instead of providing the expertise that jurisdictions should expect and certainly need. Thus, states choose different passing scores on the same test (the multiple-choice Multistate Bar Exam, or MBE) to supposedly establish the same thing: minimum competence to practice law. But minimum competence does not magically appear or disappear when someone crosses the state line, especially because the MBE tests general law, not the law specific to any state. Arguments for higher cut scores generally rest on current practitioners' preferences: to keep out competition, to impose the familiar hazing rituals on future lawyers, or to assert lofty but ungrounded claims about public protection.[18]

Every bar examiner and state supreme court justice should understand that "[a]rtificially high bar passage standards are of special concern because those standards can have a disproportionate impact on minority applicants to the bar."[19] Disparate impact having been established, jurisdictions should show evidence of job relatedness to select any cut score above that of any other state with competent lawyers. A cut score of 130 is currently being used successfully by Alabama, Minnesota, Missouri, New Mexico, and North Dakota.[20] These five states cover different regions of the country and include a variety of practice areas, such as international firms in Minnesota and Missouri; rural practices in several of these states; and private practice, government, and nonprofit practice in all five. No evidence suggests that the public suffers from lawyers in these states being less competent than in the forty-five states that choose higher MBE cut scores. Indeed, recent research suggests that higher cut scores bear no relationship to attorney competence as measured in disciplinary rates.[21]

Bar examiners read terrible essay answers, shudder, and worry that too many passing candidates lack the minimum competence to practice law. But the artificial aspects of bar exams—especially the unrealistic time limits and the inability to research anything—render suspect judgments about minimum competence based on these bar exam essays. No one would give a new associate twenty, thirty, or even sixty minutes to produce a memo identifying and analyzing five to ten legal problems suggested by a relatively complicated factual situation without access to the law or sufficient time to proofread. The methodology of standard setting studies for bar exams is just as bad, relying on lawyers' and judges' judgments about which essay answers look like minimum competence without having taken the test themselves, yet knowing that the conditions under which the essays were written do not mimic law practice.[22] We all know that competent lawyers would fail today's bar exams miserably.[23] The unsurprising certainty of mass failure reveals how far today's testing methodologies have strayed from minimum competence in practice.

9. *Provide multiple forms of law licenses.*
   Low-income and middle-class individuals handle legal problems without lawyers in complicated systems created by lawyers for lawyers. Eighty percent of the legal needs of the poor are unmet, as are roughly half of the legal needs of middle-income people.[24] In many courts, most individuals are not represented by counsel, although litigation—structured within complex procedural rules—is arguably the area of legal practice in which licensed attorneys are most important. The current regime of a single general license for any kind of legal practice—enforced through prohibitions on unauthorized practice of law and requirements of three years of postgraduate legal education, substantial debt, and post-JD bar exam requirements—contributes significantly to this emergency in access to justice. Longstanding economic protectionism and racial or ethnic disparities in bar passage limit the number of attorneys, rendering underserved communities—an enormous category that includes most poor and middle-income individuals—less likely to have access to a lawyer.
   The most important licensing reform to address the crisis in access to justice is creation of new types of licenses to deliver legal services.[25] Some jurisdictions are overcoming protectionist resis-

tance from lawyers and are trying new categories of legal service providers, including limited license legal technicians, court navigators, self-represented litigant coordinators, and certified legal document preparers and other categories.

Law students are another pool of potential providers of legal services in areas of great need. Jurisdictions should consider granting licenses to practice law in specified areas of severe unmet need—for example landlord–tenant, elder law, or debtor–creditor—to law students who have completed two years in an accredited JD program.[26] The jurisdiction could impose special educational requirements to be admitted under this program, and the lawyer could choose to return to school in the future to obtain a JD and seek a general license to practice law. This new category of licensure could engage students' passion for public service and social justice, improve access to justice, reduce the debt incurred by providing a full-time earning opportunity after two years, and potentially lead to a more focused and meaningful third year for students who have already gained unsupervised practice experience. New ways to provide legal services—including new types of licenses—are necessary next steps to begin to address the access to justice crisis that is a seemingly intractable feature of our current licensing structures.

10. *Reassess competency following licensure.*
The absence of any evaluation after initial licensure smacks of a licensing system that protects lawyers more than it protects the public. Oddly, the public may need more protection from experienced lawyers than from new ones.[27] But even the most modest periodic evaluation for licensed lawyers will be a harder sell than the boldest reform of initial attorney licensing.

Practicing attorneys would be horrified to have to periodically retake today's bar exams, and rightly so. If the exams were true tests of minimum competence, experienced attorneys would have little to fear. The utter unsuitability of today's bar exams to be repurposed for subsequent checks of competency is a good sign that they do not measure minimum competence. Two current licensing mechanisms could provide more palatable and meaningful periodic reevaluation of competence: (1) performance tests very much like those currently used in bar exams, or (2) structured self-assessment.

Performance tests. Every competent attorney should be able to pass a performance test that provides adequate time to produce a typical attorney work product based on a self-contained file and access to a library provided to the test-taker.[28] Jurisdictions could design the performance test specifications to include changed aspects of practice, building libraries from new procedural or substantive law, continuously updating the task list that alerts test-takers what they could be asked to do, and providing the standards by which test answers will be evaluated. For example, my legal education and bar preparation included nothing related to alternative dispute resolution. If I had been required to pass a performance test every ten years, one or more of the four such tests I would have taken by now could have required me to prepare for a mediation or settlement conference. My preparation for the test would include reviewing the guidelines for any task on the list for which I was not already adept. Experienced lawyers could be given choices, too, among potential tasks to be performed.

Structured self-assessment. Evaluation need not take the form of a test. A more modest assessment system would require licensed attorneys to engage in self-assessment followed by execution of a learning plan. Such systems are in place in Alberta, Canada, and in England and Wales in lieu of mandatory continuing legal education (MCLE).[29] New Zealand essentially structures continuing legal education within a self-designed assessment and reflection structure, requiring each lawyer to develop and maintain an annual continuing professional development plan that includes that attorney's assessment of his or her learning needs for the coming year, an action plan, activities record, and reflection on how the activities undertaken will improve practice.[30] Any kind of ongoing evaluation, whether a test or self-assessment, would signal the importance of continuous learning for competence as a lawyer.[31]

11. ***Design licensing requirements to change with the changing profession.***
Professional standards for licensing tests require examiners to keep tests current by regularly reviewing changes in the profes-

sion.[32] The legal profession has changed profoundly over the last several decades, but the structure and coverage of bar exams have not kept up with these breathtaking changes. Bar exams consist of multiple-choice questions, essays, and performance tests, the same components of the bar exam I took in California in 1980. The doctrinal subjects tested are the same, too, although usually in more detail today. Stagnant testing for the profession of the past undermines the test's validity. Our professional culture that valorizes stability and tradition has kept us in violation of a fundamental testing standard: the requirement to stay current.

12. ***Responsibility for better attorney licensing rests with the states.*** Licensing authority is firmly situated with the states, usually the state supreme courts. Efficiency, technical and psychometric expertise, and greater social mobility have made the last decade a time of national standardization of attorney licensing led by the NCBE. This standardization has produced important advances in test quality, reliability, and portability for students. It has also centralized the challenging work of exam development that was otherwise a significant burden on the jurisdiction's bar examiners, who are sometimes volunteers.

The NextGen Bar Exam currently being designed by the NCBE will further consolidate NCBE control. NCBE's NextGen Bar Exam is an integrated exam, so a state may be forced to take the entire exam from the NCBE or take nothing.[33] The NextGen exam should be an improvement; for example, the integrated test design and inclusion of short-answer questions facilitate assessment of more sophisticated legal analysis and other lawyering skills, and the knowledge tested could extend beyond doctrine to strategic thinking and case management. The *Testing Task Force* and resulting NextGen Bar Exam may be the NCBE's most innovative and ambitious undertaking in its long history. But the NCBE is building on what it currently offers and starting with the premise that all NCBE exams are reliable, valid, and fair. For example, the silly NCBE insistence that current tests do not test memorization opens the door for the continuing memorization currently planned for the NextGen exam. NextGen continues as a one-time, all-or-nothing exam, instead of a staged licensing scheme. And, of course, although its mission is broader, NCBE's focus remains on only one aspect of the three-headed licensing system: the tests.

Better public protection in attorney licensing requires greater jurisdictional leadership, not less. Jurisdictions cannot relinquish authority and should not cede responsibility to the NCBE. The NCBE's role as the producer and seller of bar exams makes it chief apologist for bar exams, no matter their inherent problems. Perhaps in part because of its geographic isolation (in a state with the diploma privilege), its necessary focus on test security, and the big target worn by anyone producing bar exams, NCBE corporate culture can be defensive and opaque. Most importantly, the NCBE has not addressed structural inequities in bar exams or shown leadership in urging jurisdictions to address them. Instead, as chief defender of current licensing practices, the NCBE explains the racial and ethnic disparities in bar exam pass rates, rather than pressing to change them.[34] For example, as the testing expert for bar examiners, the NCBE should be leading efforts to eliminate cut scores that exacerbate racial disparities, not watching from the sidelines.

The states are our laboratories for licensing for a client-centered, inclusive legal profession. States should seriously consider what minimum competence looks like and use their authority to design licensing systems to align education, experience, and exams toward that competence. Important research on minimum competence has been done by the NCBE, the California Bar, and IAALS. We also have important new research—from the California bar and researchers funded by AccessLex—about bar exam disparate impact and fairness concerns. These studies support a range of approaches—from profound changes to relatively easy tweaks—that every jurisdiction should consider as it aims its licensing system more directly at minimum competence and protection of the public.

The remaining chapters present licensing reforms regarding practice experience, educational requirements, and better bar exams. Each proposal is intended to align preparation for the profession more closely with competence to practice law.

12

CLINICAL RESIDENCIES

NEW LAWYERS SHOULD NOT BE unleashed on the public unless they have successfully practiced law under the watchful eye—and license—of an experienced attorney.[1] Jurisdictions should use student practice rules—a logical step prior to full licensure—to authorize and require every law graduate to complete a clinical residency prior to receiving a full license to practice law.[2] Student practice rules require both the student lawyer and the supervising lawyer to conform to formal rules of professional responsibility for the protection of the clients.

Why call this a clinical residency instead of an apprenticeship? As a path to becoming a lawyer in the United States, apprenticeships have been loose, unstructured, and based largely on personal relationships and connections. By contrast, medical residencies are a formal clinical stage during which new doctors are granted a training certificate to practice medicine under supervision before they are fully licensed.[3] Borrowing "residency" from medicine situates supervised practice as an established, crucial stage in the educational progression of a new lawyer and drives home the need for formal structures, requirements, and assessment.

Structured residencies will expand the lawyering competencies[4] and strengthen the professional identities[5] that law graduates bring to their first work as lawyers. The purpose of the residency is to instill the habits of professionalism and competence that transcend specialization, so the residency can be in any substantive area of legal practice. But to instill those habits effectively, residencies should feature: client representation; with supervision by an excellent attorney; in the context of an academic program that includes (a) key learning goals, (b) habits of reflective practice, and (c) assessment of the competencies expected to be learned.[6] This is more than simply learning from experience; it is learning how best to learn from experience.

Client representation. Ethical and competent client representation is the heart of being a lawyer. Oddly and indefensibly, in most U.S. jurisdictions new attorneys can be licensed without ever having seen a client, let alone represented one. The residency required for licensure should feature supervised first-chair client representation in clinics and externships, whether oriented to public policy, transactions, or litigation.[7] Direct client representation is akin to practice requirements in medicine,[8] veterinary medicine,[9] dentistry,[10] social work,[11] and many other professions. The unpredictability of actual client matters—and the weight of assuming responsibility for clients' interests in the face of those uncertainties—should be experienced to be understood. Optimal public protection requires this learning to begin in the context of professional education, not after licensure.

Attorney supervision. The key distinction between client representation under a student practice rule in a residency compared to client representation as an attorney is that the student lawyer is actively supervised by an attorney, whether a law professor, field supervisor, or both. In essence, the attorney supervisor ensures that the representation provided by the law student meets or exceeds the level of professional competency owed to the client.[12] The student lawyer and the supervising attorney both sign court documents, and both are present when the student attorney appears in court. But under the first-chair model, the oral argument is made by the student. The supervising attorney stands ready to intervene if necessary. Standards and pedagogies for such supervision are well developed.[13]

Learning outcomes, reflective practice, self-regulation, and assessment. Learning from experience is central to the residency. But undertaking initial client representations in the context of a structured, purposeful academic setting expands the professional learning far beyond simply having had the experience. Medical residencies are instructive:

> What a resident learns in the course of her residency education is not the result of random patient experiences. It is purposeful and developmental and reflects—or should reflect—a careful structuring, sequencing, and progression of roles, activities, and responsibilities to support learning.[14]

Three features of the clinical residency's academic context are especially important: (1) identified learning goals; (2) purposeful inculcation of habits of reflective practice and self-regulation; and (3) assessment of competencies learned. Learning goals can be established for clinical residencies based on recent research on minimum competence to practice law[15] and experience with learning goals now required by the ABA accreditation process for clinical[16] and externship[17] courses. Instilling habits of reflection is a longstanding purpose of clinical[18] and externship[19] pedagogy and a hallmark of professional identity formation more generally.[20] Professor Timothy Casey has explained why reflection matters: "Deliberate reflection provides the new professional with a process to develop professional judgment."[21] By itself, gaining professional experience and even learning from one's mistakes is not reflective practice. Reflection without structure may be superficial.[22] The goal, rather, is to instill habits of critical reflection to promote a lifetime of self-knowledge and continuous learning.[23] The residency allows a novice lawyer to form ethical habits by confronting the challenges of client representation for the first time in a setting designed to promote ethical practice[24] with an expert supervising attorney who has the time to mentor and instruct the novice attorney.[25]

Rubrics used to assess the student should be based on learning goals using research about lawyering competence, such as the building blocks identified in *Building a Better Bar*.[26] Assessment should be part of the residency's formal structure and should be continuous throughout the residency, creating context and support for the ultimate judgment of successful (or unsuccessful) completion of the entire residency. Practicing law and dentistry are quite different, thank goodness, but lawyers could learn from the process the Dental Board of California has used since 2011 that provides detailed training and grading rubrics for dental school professors to be able to evaluate minimum competence in six areas of dental practice.[27]

The supervising attorney should not only identify the competencies demonstrated by the candidate but should also assess whether the quality of the work meets a standard of minimum competence. Whether or not the residency is used in lieu of a licensing test, the supervisor should be required to submit an affidavit certifying that the candidate has demonstrated successful completion of specified lawyering tasks that the jurisdiction recognizes as part of minimum competence.[28] Even better, jurisdictions can also use bar examiners to assess students' work product when a residency substitutes for a traditional bar exam, as has been done for many years in New Hampshire and is now proposed in Oregon.[29]

Credits and timing of academic residencies. The residency required for licensure should be the equivalent of fifteen academic credits, of which at least six consist of clinics that include direct client representation. More ambitious experiential credit requirements have been proposed[30] and are well established in some law schools,[31] but a typical semester is fifteen credits. The State Bar of California's Task Force on Admissions Regulation Reform recommended that California require fifteen credits of experiential learning prior to licensure.[32] The Council for the ABA Section on Legal Education sought comment in 2013 on an "alternate proposal" to make fifteen credits of experiential education an accreditation requirement.[33]

Although neither California's proposal nor the ABA's proposal for fifteen experiential credits has been adopted, the New York Court of Appeals established fifteen credits of "practice-based experiential coursework designed to foster the development of professional competencies" as one way a candidate could establish compliance with the skills competencies required for admission to the New York bar.[34] The residency could be concentrated in a single semester or extended over more time. The University of New Hampshire's Daniel Webster Scholars program[35] is essentially a residency spread over four semesters. These students pursue a highly structured and extensive program of experiential courses, primarily simulations but with a requirement of six credits of client representation,[36] with pervasive highly structured assessment. Bar examiners review samples from portfolios of student work, knowing that Daniel Webster Scholars are admitted to the New Hampshire bar upon graduation from law school without taking the traditional bar exam.[37] The clinical pathway being considered by the Oregon Supreme Court as one of two alternative paths to licensure without a bar exam includes fifteen credits of experiential education but does not yet include the six required credits of client representation.[38]

Post-graduation supervised practice. We need look no further than Utah in the 2020 pandemic emergency[39] or to long-established rules in Canada and Delaware to find attorney licensing systems that require a period of supervised practice following law school prior to licensure as an attorney. Requiring a period of practice after law school addresses the historic tension between learning law as an apprentice versus learning law in an academic setting by requiring both. But serious problems of quality, expense, and equity plague requirements for post-graduation supervised practice.

Excellent supervision of student lawyers requires expertise and time, not just good will. A lawyer's first experience representing clients is best undertaken under the careful, experienced eye of a professor whose core job is teaching. Supervision of a first-chair neophyte requires skill and patience, because the work will take time. The inefficiency is not primarily because the experienced lawyer could do the same work in much less time, although that is generally true. The other structural inefficiency comes from the supervisor's role in slowing down the new lawyer. Instilling habits of reflection, self-awareness, and systematic approaches to legal problems takes time. Leaving responsibility on the student while ensuring that the client does not suffer from the student's inexperience is a balancing act that itself slows down everything. Excellent clinical supervision also requires formal and informal assessment, often critical, of the student's performance. Some practitioners are inspired teachers and mentors, but most practicing lawyers are not well positioned to undertake this kind of time-consuming teaching and mentoring as part of their workday. Clinical professors are the experts.

Post-graduation residencies also create serious inequities because access to supervisors is based on preexisting connections and relationships, problems that have infected supervised practice or articling systems around the world.[40] The pattern of people of color and others who are not well connected not being able to obtain articling positions has caused some jurisdictions, including in Canada and South Africa, to create alternative training paths—based largely on simulations—that are open to all candidates.[41] But new lawyers licensed through those paths can face stigma problems in obtaining employment.

Delaware may best represent the problem of post-graduation supervised practice that protects attorneys as much as the public. Delaware is a small state that has established itself as a capital of corporate governance. Many corporate lawyers would like to be licensed in Delaware. The Delaware bar therefore may have unusually strong incentives to approach attorney licensing with a protectionist mindset.[42] Indeed, Delaware not only administers the hardest bar exam in the country by setting the highest cut score in the nation,[43] but also requires five months of full-time supervised practice prior to licensure.[44] This double whammy of high barriers seems to work: Delaware had only 3,058 licensed attorneys in 2020.[45] For comparison, at the same time Vermont had 3,612 licensed attorneys, 18 percent more than Delaware, although Vermont's population was 27 percent smaller,[46] and Vermont's economy was less than half of Delaware's.[47]

The Delaware requirements combine a cut score known to cause the largest racial and ethnic bar pass disparities[48] with a practice and voucher requirement that necessitates access to a well-established Delaware attorney.[49] These requirements are undoubtedly administered with good faith and sincerity. But other jurisdictions have chosen to abandon high cut scores[50] and clerkship or articling requirements[51] because they are barriers to entry that disproportionately harm unrepresented groups. Twentieth-century bar examiners in Pennsylvania proposed a clerkship requirement for the express purpose of excluding Jewish lawyers.[52] Our history of using the same admissions requirements for odious, purposeful exclusion demands humility and constant self-scrutiny to ensure that our current motivation is to protect the public, not the profession.

Delaying the residency until after graduation from law school also unnecessarily increases the cost of becoming a lawyer by delaying licensure. In sum, compared to a residency during law school, post-graduation supervised practice requirements add barriers to entry while reducing public protection.

Academic residencies within legal education are therefore far preferable. But especially in a period of transition before residency requirements are prevalent, jurisdictions adopting a residency requirement should permit the alternative of post-graduation supervised practice. The Oregon Supreme Court recently endorsed the recommendation of the Board of Bar Examiners to develop two pathways to licensure that would not require a bar exam: one based on a structured experiential law school curriculum, and another that would require 1,000–1,500 hours of supervised practice following graduation, including evaluation by bar examiners of a portfolio of work product.[53] Any jurisdiction considering a supervised practice pathway to licensure can elevate the quality of supervision with formal training of supervisors, agreements about the supervision to be undertaken, oversight by bar examiners, and standardized rubrics, certifications, and affidavits for assessment as contemplated in the Oregon Board of Bar Examiners' proposals.[54]

Lawyers Justice Corps. A proposal by Professor Eileen Kaufman for a "Lawyers Justice Corps"[55] is an intriguing model of post-graduation supervised practice as an alternative to a traditional bar exam. According to Professor Kaufman's proposal, a jurisdiction's highest court would designate public service organizations serving underrepresented individuals and communities to qualify for the program. Qualifying organizations would use the ordinary hiring process to employ law graduates for job openings. The Justice Corps lawyers will begin working for their organizations shortly after law school graduation rather than deferring work to prepare for the bar exam. Once a new lawyer completed six months of successful full-time supervised practice, documented through assessment rubrics, the organization would certify that lawyer for admission to the bar.

Supervisors would assess the competence of Justice Corps lawyers with rubrics based on building blocks identified in *Building a Better Bar,* and portfolios of candidates' work could be available for review by bar examiners. A certified lawyer would be required to continue to work for the organization for at least an additional six months.

The Lawyers Justice Corps licensing pathway would increase access to justice for the clients of qualifying organizations because law graduates would be available to start work in late May, rather than August, each devoting 400-plus hours to legal services for underserved clients rather than to bar preparation. Support for the Lawyers Justice Corps from government and private funders could provide additional financial support to legal service organizations.

License no one without supervised practice. Some period of supervised practice, whether in an academically based clinical residency or post-graduation, is necessary to assure the public that new lawyers are at least minimally competent to practice law without supervision. Bar exams are no substitute for supervised practice, but carefully assessed supervised practice can substitute for bar exams. The Oregon Board of Bar Examiners Task Force is recommending a clinical path to licensure in part because the bar exam "does not measure the ability to communicate honestly, candidly, and civilly with clients, attorneys, courts, and others; the ability to interact effectively with clients; the ability to conduct research; and the ability to see the big picture."[56] Every jurisdiction should consider adopting a pathway to practice based on a clinical residency without a traditional bar exam, such as what New Hampshire has done and Oregon is considering, to ensure that qualified, competent attorneys are not excluded from the profession because of bar exams with serious deficiencies. Improved public protection also means beefed up educational requirements, including but beyond the clinical residency.

13

ASKING MORE OF LAW SCHOOLS

LICENSING TODAY ASKS TOO MUCH of bar exams and too little of legal education. Most jurisdictions follow the same, simple approach to educational requirements: Only graduates of ABA-accredited law schools are eligible to sit for bar exams. But the range of approaches is wide, from California's readiness to license successful bar-takers without any law school to Wisconsin's willingness to license JD graduates of its in-state law schools without any bar exam. The major deficit of the majority approach—ABA-accredited law school degree plus bar exam—is the lack of any supervised practice requirement, such as a clinical residency. New educational requirements—the clinical residency and beyond—could improve public protection, with or without a post-graduation bar exam.

Today's highway to licensure: ABA-accredited law school plus bar exam. Most jurisdictions have settled on the same quality control formula: New lawyers must have graduated from an ABA-accredited law school and passed a bar exam. The strange distance between law schools and practice, the equally surprising lack of curricular requirements imposed by ABA accreditation, and the long history of ABA accreditation and law school admissions as mechanisms of exclusion are powerful reasons to reconsider what educational requirements would best serve the goal of public protection. As always, the lodestar is what we know about minimum competence to practice law.

Without a clinical residency, the formula of graduation from an ABA-accredited law school and a bar exam guarantees very little about the minimum competence of new lawyers. The standard requirements not only fail to ensure minimum competence but are expensive for the candidate in both time and dollars. ABA accreditation requires JD students to have earned an undergraduate degree plus a law degree, typically a seven-year undertaking, which is a long investment of years compared to the many countries in which law is an undergraduate degree. ABA accreditation requirements also account for some of the expense of a U.S. legal education, along with reduced state funding for higher education, the prestige arms race fueled by *U.S. News* rankings, and other systemic pressures driving up costs. Jurisdictions concerned about access to the profession should pay attention to the expense of the standard formula of ABA-accredited JD followed by a bar exam.

Jurisdictions that would prefer to offer a less expensive option without sacrificing the oversight of accreditation could make graduates of all accredited law schools, whether accredited by the state or by the ABA, eligible to take bar exams, as California does.[1] The California experience is instructive and positive. State-accredited law schools offer legal education to underserved populations and nontraditional law students at much less cost than ABA-accredited law schools. California-accredited Santa Barbara and Ventura Colleges of Law tied for eighth with Chicago and Virginia, just ahead of Berkeley, in a recent ranking of the law schools with the best debt-to-income ratios of its graduates.[2]

Answering to state education accreditors, but not the ABA, invites pedagogical and curricular innovation, such as the online and intensive on-site hybrid JD program of Santa Barbara and Ventura Colleges of Law or the entirely online JD of Concord Law School.[3] Avoiding ABA accreditation standards can also help to reduce the distance between legal education and the legal profession. ABA accreditation standards require that the curriculum be delivered mainly by full-time professors, and law professors typically sit near the high end of professorial salaries within the university. State-accredited law schools can use practicing lawyers as part-time professors, a less expensive model that offers a legal education infused with practice expertise. Few full-time law professors today express the disdain or even contempt for practice that some of my professors inflicted decades ago. But, aside from clinical professors, few law professors today bring extensive practice expertise, let alone passion for representing clients.

Asking more of law schools. States typically rely on graduation from an ABA-accredited law school as a substitute for any requirements regarding what law school courses candidates actually took. This simplicity is welcome to candidates, law school administrators, and bar examiners. During my deanship at Michigan State University, the entering JD class typically included students from more than twenty-five states; many law schools boast even greater geographic diversity. Rigid, differing educational licensing requirements imposed by jurisdictions would be an administrative nightmare for law schools and would undermine the recent gains in portability of licensure for new lawyers in this very mobile age.

But, using minimum competence as the touchstone, public protection may not be served by merely graduating from law school in our era of highly elective law school curricula. In rethinking educational requirements, jurisdictions should reverse engineer from the problems that generate malpractice awards and attorney discipline. Lawyers' failures often relate to law office management, substance abuse, health crises, and the like. Memorizing the rules of professional responsibility—as required to pass the MPRE—is not the same as competently managing the responsibilities of practice.[4] Jurisdictions should consider pushing law schools to emphasize what the *Carnegie Report* called the apprenticeship of identity and purpose or professional identity.[5]

Some of this—law office and practice management, for example—would lend itself to short courses within the JD program or training programs with certificates. But short courses or training certificates are not enough to prepare new lawyers to handle the responsibilities of the profession when facing the added stress of personal challenges. Therefore, states should require candidates for licensure to have completed an interactive and highly reflective foundational professional formation course, preferably in the first year.[6] This course should highlight the lawyer's role as "a public citizen having special responsibility for the quality of justice," an aspect of competence so important that the

IAALS *Building a Better Bar* study recommends required coursework to ensure it.[7]

Jurisdictions can safely resist the impulse to require that long lists of doctrinal courses be completed.[8] Law school academic programs are remarkably consistent with the basics, and new lawyers are prepared to learn new areas of law much more easily than new skills and methods.[9] But public protection probably justifies educational requirements related to lawyering competencies beyond legal analysis. The *Building a Better Bar* study recommends that licensers require coursework in client relations and negotiation because both are critical to competence and are not easily assessed on exams.[10] Administrative ease and public protection can both be achieved through licensing rules that permit JD coursework *or* training certificates in certain crucial aspects of minimum competence, such as law practice management or negotiation. Jurisdictions can also require state-specific training or tests on the jurisdiction's procedure and unique rules that are not necessarily covered in a national bar exam or in the curriculum of many law schools.

Traditional diploma privilege. A traditional diploma privilege, such as that previously used by as many as fifteen states and currently used in Wisconsin, makes graduation from (certain) law schools a substitute for passing a bar exam. Licensure upon graduation from law school has been a licensing option somewhere in the United States since it was first introduced in Virginia in 1843, when it was designed to reward the privileged, those who were able to attend law school instead of learning law through apprenticeships in law offices. Although wrapped in the rhetoric of public protection, racist and elitist goals tainted the motivation for reducing the number of states using diploma privilege through the middle of the twentieth century, leaving Wisconsin standing alone.[11]

Despite being the comically unlikely home of the NCBE, Wisconsin is satisfied with quality and competence of its bar, licensed primarily without a bar exam, through the traditional diploma privilege.[12] Recent research suggests that malpractice rates are the same for Wisconsin lawyers licensed after taking a bar exam or through the diploma privilege.[13] Jurisdictions considering implementing a diploma privilege more focused on minimum competence could also think about imposing certain curricular requirements, building on what Wisconsin does.[14]

A revival of diploma privilege could serve access goals related to the outsized cost of legal education and the rapacious commercial bar prep industry. A diploma privilege avoids the colossal waste of money and time currently devoted to memorization of books of doctrine and exam-preparation drilling. A diploma privilege also eliminates the disparate racial and ethnic impact that plagues bar exams and other high stakes standardized tests. Those are major benefits.

A diploma privilege can also be justified because bar exams replicate the academic project of law school, hence the strong correlation between bar passage and law school grades. Bar exams test aspects of how good a law student you were, not how competent an attorney you would be. If bar exams do not add much, why not make licensing much less expensive with a diploma privilege?

Unfortunately, on balance, legal education has not earned a diploma privilege for our graduates because law schools—still too much in the grip of Langdellian distrust of practice and practitioners—do not do a good enough job of producing minimally competent new lawyers. Asking more of law schools, though, opens the door to better public protection through competence-based diploma licensure.

Competence-based diploma licensure (without a bar exam). Every jurisdiction should consider expanding its attorney licensing system to include the option of competence-based diploma licensure without a bar exam. Competence-based diploma licensure requires candidates to take a law school academic program that is more closely aligned with minimum competence to practice law than what typical law school programs currently require. Competence-based diploma licensure—based on current research related to minimum competence to practice law, rather than history or tradition or elitism—would protect the public well, certainly better than today's reliance on ABA accreditation and bar exams.

Competence-based diploma licensure would enable jurisdictions to license based on the competence demonstrated by the candidate in his or her academic program. Basing a diploma privilege on fulfillment of certain curricular requirements at any accredited law school avoids the dormant clause concerns that may arise when a jurisdiction limits its diploma privilege to graduates of in-state law schools.[15]

Diploma licensure with clinical residency. The quickest, cheapest, easiest way for a state to add an option for licensure without a bar exam is to condition licensure on passing either a bar exam *or* a clinical residency.[16] Fifteen credits (or the post-graduation equivalent) of a structured, assessed, clinical residency would create a foundation in the range of lawyering abilities critical to competent practice, including handling the weight of client responsibility properly. Most of the building blocks identified in the *Building a Better Bar Exam* study would be well covered by such a pathway.

Diploma licensure with structured curriculum and portfolios. Another version of competence-based diploma licensure would supplement the law school degree with assessment by bar examiners of samples of the candidate's lawyering work as a student in a curriculum structured to prepare graduates to practice law competently. Portfolios can provide evidence of actual performance instead of using an exam as a proxy for such competence. Licensing authorities in dentistry, architecture, engineering, teaching, and other fields have begun to use portfolios of actual work products completed by candidates to assess candidates' minimum competence and eligibility to practice.[17] Advances in technology make licensing portfolios newly feasible and scalable. California already uses to portfolios to license teachers.[18] Bar examiners could assess portfolios of work product, rather than bar exams.

Models for similar licensing in law already exist. New Hampshire has adopted a competence-based pathway, and four Canadian provinces have recently replaced traditional bar exams with stepped up education requirements to make new attorneys more competent, providing models for educational requirements within a JD program or afterwards.

New Hampshire's Daniel Webster Scholar Honors Program. The Daniel Webster program is an innovative law school curriculum started fifteen years ago because the New Hampshire Supreme Court and Committee of Bar Examiners were frustrated by the lack of competence of too many new lawyers.[19] Students in the program undertake a rigorous curriculum of a range of core lawyering skills in their second and third years of law school, assessed by law professors, practitioners, bar examiners, and judges.[20] Students who successfully complete the program may be admitted to practice law in New Hampshire upon graduation from law school without taking the bar exam.[21]

The New Hampshire Supreme Court evaluates minimum competence for licensure of Daniel Webster Scholars by using portfolios of student work product created in a sequenced residency in lieu of a traditional licensing exam.[22] Other jurisdictions could replicate New Hampshire's system of using professors, practitioners, judges, and bar examiners to assess agreed-upon lists of required lawyering work product, or jurisdictions could require candidates to submit portfolios of similar work products that would be subject to selected review—spot checks—by licensing examiners.

Research supports the value of the Daniel Webster program's competence-based licensing curriculum. An IAALS study of focus groups and a simulated client interview established that the program graduates were evaluated more highly than other new lawyers and that Daniel Webster law students out-performed new lawyers on a standardized client interview.[23] Is anyone surprised that a two-year program would result in better lawyering competencies than preparation for a two-day paper-and-pencil test?

The IAALS study also established that participation in the Daniel Webster program was the only significant predictor of successful performance of the standardized client interview, and that neither the LSAT nor law school class rank was a significant predictor.[24] This study of a single, albeit crucial, lawyering skill is suggestive, hinting that a shift from high-stakes tests to heightened educational requirements for licensing could improve the validity (job relatedness) of licensing requirements while reducing persistent racial and ethnic disparities.

The Daniel Webster Scholars program is highly regimented, however, and therefore is not attractive or even available to all law students at the University of New Hampshire. And New Hampshire is a relatively small state with a single law school. A simpler and more scalable alternative available to jurisdictions of any size is to condition diploma privilege on completion of a clinical residency.

Oregon experiential pathways. Based on the IAALS *Building a Better Bar* study and using New Hampshire's Daniel Webster Scholars program as a model, the Oregon Supreme Court is pursuing a new pathway to licensure based on a two-year law school curriculum rather than the bar exam.[25] This competence-based diploma licensing would be open to all students at Oregon's three law schools, who would take all but fourteen credits of their upper-level curriculum in a structured academic program designed to satisfy the building blocks of minimum competence identified in the *Building a Better Bar* study. Oregon is developing this new pathway to licensure to promote goals of consumer protection and equity.

Oregon's experiential learning pathway to licensure will probably include foundational substantive courses, like Evidence and Criminal Procedure, and experiential courses that will require completion of lawyering tasks. Three types of assessment of the students' work would be required: "(1) formative feedback from professors throughout the program, (2) intensive self-reflection by participants, and (3) summative feedback and assessment provided by a dedicated bar examiner at the end of each semester."[26]

The proposal for the "Oregon Experiential Pathway" includes a requirement of fifteen experiential credits, of which nine would be in clinic or simulations and six in externships. Except for the absence of any requirement that six credits of these credits be supervised practice representing clients, this pathway is like a clinical residency.

The Oregon Experiential Pathway would also require a capstone assessment, which might be a performance test.[27] Unlike the Daniel Webster Scholars program, the Oregon Experiential Pathway will be open to all students in Oregon law schools, and potentially those from other states. The Oregon Supreme Court is pursuing the Board of Bar Examiners' recommendation to add this Oregon Experiential Pathway, and a new "Supervised Practice Pathway," consisting primarily of supervised practice hours following graduation, as alternative roads to licensure.

Benefits of competence-based diploma licensure. Compared to current systems, competence-based diploma licensure offers greater assurance of minimum competence to practice law, is easier for jurisdictions to administer, is less expensive for candidates, and avoids the discriminatory impact of bar exams.[28] Under current bar exam systems, white candidates have a strong likelihood of eventually passing, assuming they have the resources to continue cramming for bar exam success.[29] The only losers from widespread adoption of competence-based diploma licensing would be the bar prep industry, which would need to pivot to other, perhaps more useful, training products.

Post-graduation curriculum: Canada's Practice Readiness Education Program (PREP). The articling system in Canada by which law graduates must obtain post-graduation law practice experience creates significant problems of unequal access to the profession,[30] as have similar systems in other countries.[31] But a more recent aspect of licensure in Alberta, Manitoba, Nova Scotia, and Saskatchewan offers a potentially more effective and less discriminatory model for attorney licensing in the United States. Each of those provinces now requires, instead of a traditional bar exam, a nine-month, part-time Practice Readiness Education Program (PREP)[32] undertaken during the law graduates' period of articling and offered by the Canadian Centre for Professional Legal Education (CPRED), a nonprofit consortium led by representatives of the four provincial law societies.[33] PREP is a hybrid of in-person workshops and online modules that focus on "practical legal knowledge" and "competencies in lawyer skills, practice management, professional ethics, as well as the personal attributes needed to successfully practice law in Canada."[34]

A consortium of U.S. jurisdictions or law schools could offer a similar program to law students or recent law graduates. Three years of law school should provide enough time for this practice education, which would be less expensive than tacking on a post-graduation program. But compared to our current system, the public would be protected more effectively if new lawyers could use the months following graduation to prepare for practice instead of cramming for bar exams.

14

ESCAPING THE CONCEPTUAL TRAPS
OF TODAY'S BAR EXAMS

BETTER PUBLIC PROTECTION REQUIRES CLOSE alignment between legal practice and attorney licensing exams. Such exams must look forward to candidates' competence to function as lawyers, not backwards to their abilities as law students in traditional classes, or further back, to the way law used to be practiced. To assess whether new practitioners are at least minimally competent, licensing tests need laser focus on the knowledge, skills, and abilities required for competence in practice. From the beginning, bar exams have correctly concentrated on legal analysis, a core lawyering skill. But we do not yet test enough other lawyering competencies, in part because our tests overemphasize knowledge at the expense of legal methods. Even though the demand for knowledge recall has dominated bar exams, we have not understood why or how to test knowledge, or even what knowledge to test.

Competence misconceived. Bar examiners have provided two main answers to the question of what competent lawyers need to be able to do:

1. New lawyers need the ability to apply facts to rules.
2. New lawyers need to memorize the legal rules they may need in practice.

The first answer is correct. The ability to apply facts to rules, otherwise known as legal analysis, is a foundational skill of every new lawyer. Legal analysis should be at the heart of any bar exam, as it has been. The second answer—new lawyers need to have memorized the doctrinal rules they may use—is as wrong as the first is correct. History explains our error.

How bar exams got off track. Written bar exams began in the late 1800s and flourished at the beginning of the twentieth century with the goal of covering all the law that a lawyer was likely to need. Requiring new lawyers to memorize the doctrinal rules they would likely need made good sense when lawyers were generalists who represented people: People's problems were relatively predictable, little law existed, law books were expensive, and law libraries were remote.

Bar examiners have held tight to that same goal, covering the legal rules a new lawyer is likely to use, for 150 years, while the amount and types of law blew up around us.[1] Courts and legislatures proliferated; corporate practice started small but overtook the profession; the regulatory state was born and never stopped growing; lawyers shifted from representing local people with predictable problems to working for people or entities enmeshed in the complex and unwieldy edifice of court decisions, statutes, and regulations that gush steadily from towns, counties, states, and federal systems.

Bar examiners have tried to handle the overwhelming proliferation of laws in part by generally ignoring statutes and regulations, the bread and butter of much legal practice.[2] Bar examiners have also largely abandoned testing state-specific law, choosing instead a typical version of common law rules used by the NCBE. These two significant compromises—testing on typical law instead of the jurisdiction's actual rules and omitting statutes and regulations—took bar exams further from actual law practice, making them less valid measures of minimum competence and driving down public protection.

Even these two big compromises failed to keep the rules to be learned within reasonable limits. Legal doctrine rarely shrinks or becomes simpler. The doctrinal subjects tested on bar exams today are very similar to what I faced in 1980, but over the decades courts and then bar examiners have added rules, exceptions, sub-rules, and exceptions to the sub-rules within the subjects tested.[3] By now the ever-thriving bar review industry produces even thicker encyclopedic volumes of doctrinal rules for their customers to memorize and sets even more punishing schedules for learning them. Bar review courses today include more rules to be memorized than are typically covered in three years of full-time law school.

The other related formidable problem for bar examiners is that the increased volume and complexity of law forced the profession into specialization. No matter how steadfastly and fervently bar examiners hold onto the goal of testing the rules that new lawyers are likely to use, specialization has made it impossible. Matching the rules to be tested with the rules to be used by a new lawyer is no longer a defensible explanation for bar exam coverage. We are chasing a nostalgic fantasy.

Moving doctrinal subjects in and out of bar exams. In the face of the fire hose onslaught of too much law and the challenge of specialization, bar examiners mainly doubled down instead of adapting, proving again that the bar exam has been the defining ritual of a cautious profession. With focus bordering on obsession, examiners concentrate on identifying the correct doctrinal subjects to test, usually based on commonsense judgments about what is important. This explains why Texas has tested oil and gas law and how Florida tests twenty-five different subjects.[4] In the same way that law school curriculum reform has been said to consist of moving constitutional law in and out of the first year, bar exam reform has largely consisted of moving doctrinal subjects in and out of bar exams.

The recent California and NCBE practice studies confirm what most of us understand: The legal doctrine used by new lawyers depends on their practice areas. Even the most widely used knowledge categories in the studies are not as widely used as many skills. No new lawyer will use all the rules learned for the bar exam, and many will not use any of them.

Consider that the NCBE has removed family law and trusts and estates from the list of doctrinal subjects to be tested on the NextGen Bar Exam.[5] This makes sense for most new lawyers who will not practice in these areas. The assumption that the change also makes sense for the new lawyers who will practice only family or estate law suggests that the purpose of the subject categories on bar exams is no longer to be sure that the new lawyer will "know cold" the legal rules needed for the problems that clients bring in the door.

Bar exams more appropriately assess the methods of a minimally competent lawyer, not any specific doctrinal subject knowledge base. Perhaps the important purpose of testing specific doctrinal rules on bar exams is to provide a platform—and almost any doctrinal platform will do—to test the fundamental skill of legal analysis.

Beyond legal analysis, what do competent lawyers need to be able to do? We know more about what competent lawyers must be able to *do* than what they must *know*. Numerous reports and studies over decades present a consistent message about what skills or abilities are necessary for competence in practicing law,[6] and serious empirical research now elevates our understanding of what new lawyers do and how they learn to do it.[7] The foundational abilities of every competent lawyer include legal reading, legal research, legal analysis, and legal writing. Legal analysis includes the ability to use foundational knowledge about sources of law and legal systems to recognize the category of law presented by a new set of facts and identify the type of rule implicated (identify the issue), know or find the relevant rules, and then apply the applicable legal rules to the facts.

Bar exams should emphasize methods instead of knowledge because legal methods cross specializations more easily than doctrinal knowledge. Also, new lawyers are better equipped to learn new areas of doctrinal knowledge than new skills.[8] Novices with the *skills* of a minimally competent lawyer should be able to determine what new area of legal knowledge they need and how to get it.

The appropriate level of cognitive demand. Very fast but shallow legal reasoning—applying uncontested facts to artificially stable (and memorized) rules—is the hallmark of today's bar examinations. Bar examiners need to consider more fully the cognitive demands of legal analysis, also known as "thinking like a lawyer." Mechanical application of legal rules to new facts is a crucial and foundational aspect of the attorney competence that should be tested by licensing authorities. But this is the skill of a novice law student, not a novice lawyer. Mechanical application by itself reinforces a comforting but false impression that legal doctrine is static.[9] In contrast, legal educators emphasize the ambiguity, malleability, and changing nature of doctrine and facts.[10] In other words, competent entry-level lawyering requires the skills of legal analysis, legal research, legal reading, and legal writing to be undertaken in a dynamic context of uncertainty, testing higher order thinking.

Educational researchers Susan Davis and Chad Buckendahl suggest that licensing tests should consider the depth of intellectual work required in performing relevant tasks,[11] considering not only the difficulty of questions (meaning how many candidates get them right) but also their "cognitive demand." The questions should reflect the level of advanced thinking skills required to meet practice-based requirements. For example, is the relevant competency simply remembering content, or is it understanding and applying doctrine in context, analyzing and evaluating a situation, and making judgments? Or perhaps it requires creating solutions by putting together a new approach? These insights are consistent with the best work on law school pedagogy.[12]

The current licensing exam system—requiring legal analysis at a uniform, basic level— creates differing degrees of difficulty based on the prominence or obscurity of the rules being tested; and it does not recognize the different levels of thinking required to address entry-level lawyers' obligations to meet client needs. Legal practice, whether supervised or not, requires creative judgment to handle uncertain facts and ambiguous law, not the skill of minimizing ambiguity that current tests foster. To assess minimum competence, bar exams should evaluate advanced application and synthesis of legal principles, evaluation of options, and even creative problem solving of the sort that clients need.

Minimally competent new lawyers also need higher order thinking skills to evaluate their own strengths and weaknesses and correct their deficiencies: the skills of metacognition. Metacognition is one of a number of higher order skills (also including reasoning, argumentation, problem solving/critical thinking) that lawyers need in order to understand what they *don't know* and what avenues they need to pursue so that they can meet their obligations to clients without falling prey to blind spots.[13] Metacognition and the ability to reflect are among the most important skills that students can develop to meet their obligations to future clients.[14] Every competent lawyer needs the skills to understanding what he or she needs to learn and how to learn it. Accordingly, a bar exam should incorporate questions designed to evaluate applicants' appreciation of what they do not know and how they might proceed in the face of uncertainty.

Knowledge beyond doctrine. Bar exams rest on the fallacy that the necessary knowledge base consists of legal doctrine or rules. Whatever the knowledge is that every competent lawyer must possess, it is much more than rules.[15] What about knowledge of legal methods, skills, culture, or strategies? What knowledge about skills is required to competently perform them? Bar exams can test these kinds of legal knowledge. Ontario's multiple-choice questions require knowledge of law office management and strategy related to litigation, deal-making, and planning.[16] Bar exams should take account of these broader categories of legal knowledge that are crucial for minimum competence and that are more likely than any single doctrinal subject to be needed by competent lawyers in any practice area. Legal methods, again, transcend practice areas.

Internalized foundational knowledge. In an age of specialization, competent new lawyers need to internalize, or memorize, foundational knowledge. Lawyers will use their understanding of core concepts, what *Building a Better Bar* calls threshold concepts,[17] to determine what else they need to know to solve a legal problem that walks in the door.

New lawyers need to be familiar with the categories of law—private and public, civil and criminal; they need to know the sources of law and the hierarchies of authority, structures of government, and systems of adjudication and dispute resolution. New lawyers need to understand the differences and potential overlap among property, torts, contracts, criminal law, criminal procedure, and constitutional law because new lawyers need to be able to determine what category of legal question they are confronting.

A broad doctrinal knowledge base is highly relevant to attorney competence *if* we understand "knowledge" to mean familiarity. Competent lawyers are adept at the categorical thinking or legal method called "issue spotting." Exposure to multiple doctrinal subjects helps attorneys recognize categories of problems, or spot issues. Familiarity with a broad range of subject areas and facility with core concepts related to methods and doctrine is the knowledge content of minimum competence to practice law.[18]

A lawyer's minimum competence requires understanding the complex conceptual framework into which specific doctrinal rules fit, not necessarily remembering any subset of specific rules. For example, a competent lawyer should understand the mental states associated with intentional torts, negligence, and strict liability; should be familiar with their elements and the common defenses; should understand systems of compensation; and should be able to distinguish between direct and vicarious liability. But remembering a specific rule of parental liability for the careless behavior of a five-year-old is not necessary for competence; the skills of a minimally competent lawyer are knowing that a special rule may exist, how to find it, and how to use it.

Our fierce attachment to licensing tradition has left us requiring memorization of exactly the wrong aspect of legal knowledge. Bar exam questions are two-dimensional "mother goose rhymes" of the law because they strip away the context to test only specific rules. The absence of context is what makes MBE questions and too many essays so artificial, populated by cartoon stick figures who exist in bar exam land, untethered to legal structures or systems. But the missing background—procedural context, source of law, client goals, rule ambiguity, etc.—is precisely the foundation of knowledge that every new lawyer needs to understand and know how to manipulate. The precise rules—that differ from jurisdiction to jurisdiction and from practice area to practice area—are not the common denominator of necessary knowledge. The legal knowledge that every lawyer must "know cold" is just the truly core concepts.

Foundational knowledge should be tested in context. Foundational knowledge is too fundamental to meaningfully test by itself. Competence comes from being able to use this foundational knowledge to solve problems, and legal problems, like negligence, do not exist in the air, separate from facts and rules. The well-aged disdain of law professors for bar exams is partly because law professors—both those with little feel for legal practice and those joyfully immersed in it—are most interested in the contextual ambiguity of the rules.

New lawyers need to find, understand, and use doctrinal rules, not memorize them. Bar examiners resent and resist the characterization of bar exams as tests of memorization, insisting instead that bar exams test legal analysis.[19] But current bar exams do both. Bar examiners test legal analysis by requiring applicants to memorize the online equivalent of thick books of rules. Memorization of these rules is no longer necessary and, worse, is directly contrary to the habits of relentless authority checks required for ethical competence in practice.[20] Confusing memorization with understanding is especially foolish when everyone has law libraries at their fingertips. Memorization is particularly wrongheaded when we consider the rules being memorized may conflict with the rules of the jurisdiction doing the testing.

Fixing the over-testing of memorized rules is easy. Wicked problems exist in attorney licensing, but it would be easy to eliminate excessive memorization. Jurisdictions can use exams that require candidates to use libraries of legal materials, like today's performance tests. Bar examiners wedded to short-answer or multiple-choice questions can move to open book bar exams, as are used in Ontario[21] and by some Uniform Bar Exam jurisdictions to test state-specific doctrine,[22] and as was done in Nevada and Louisiana during the pandemic. Getting rid of memorization is difficult mainly because of the powerful hold of the ritual, which has come to mean that real lawyers memorize books of rules. But the compass pointed at minimum competence for public protection directs us elsewhere.

Cramming for bar exams does not create minimum competence. Experienced lawyers, including bar examiners, cannot really believe that the books of doctrine they currently require to be memorized are necessary knowledge for minimum competence. If that stated premise were true, as competent lawyers, bar examiners and judges and practicing lawyers could pass the test at any point without much effort. But experienced, competent lawyers cannot pass bar exams without extensive study.[23] That explains why, for example, the former dean of the Stanford Law School, an experienced U.S. Supreme Court orator licensed in two states, flunked the California bar exam in 2005.[24]

Perhaps the actual purpose of studying all those rules is not to remember what was studied, but to have some familiarity with a wide range of doctrinal areas. This idea is that two months spent cramming a wide swath of legal doctrine will prepare a competent lawyer to recognize enough of the rules for basic issue spotting through a career, even if a test-taker forgets most of what she memorized shortly after walking out of the test. The serious problem with this rationale is that bar exams unfairly exclude competent candidates who are not good at memorizing vast amounts of rules or who do not have the resources to devote weeks of undivided attention to the task. Educational requirements are a more appropriate method to guarantee that a candidate is familiar with a range of subject areas.[25]

Competence in legal analysis is the heart of lawyering. More than ever before, knowing legal methods—when and how to find and use legal knowledge—is more critical than subject matter knowledge itself. Reconceptualizing knowledge and skills—understanding that bar exams should test methods more than knowledge—is the first step to better bar exams. Validity and fairness require a test's fidelity to actual minimum competence; clarity and honesty about the relationship of doctrinal knowledge to minimum competence is way overdue.

1 5

BAR EXAMS

Better, Best, and Other Fixes

MOVING FORWARD, MOST STATES WILL choose a licensing test as part of at least one path toward licensure. With luck and effort, those tests can be much better assessments of minimum competence to practice law than the bar exams familiar to generations of lawyers. The NCBE has recently announced its commitment to producing what could be a much better test—its NextGen Bar Exam. The NextGen Bar Exam is likely to incorporate some aspects of performance tests such as the Multistate Performance Test (MPT). An alternative testing regime consisting entirely of performance tests could be even better than Next-Gen, offering a nimbler design for modification and permitting testing in stages, which the NextGen will not. Whatever tests are used to license new lawyers, what is needed is better standard setting, less speededness, regular periodic review, and more transparency.

A better test: NCBE's NextGen Bar Exam. The NCBE is currently designing what it calls the next generation bar exam, or *NextGen,* expected to replace the NCBE's current exam products in 2026.[1] The NCBE is attempting to address some of the problems with its current bar exams, including testing too many doctrinal subjects at too much detail and not testing enough critical lawyering competencies. The NextGen exam will be a real improvement if the NCBE succeeds with these goals.

The NextGen Bar Exam will require candidates to learn rules from fewer subjects, a positive change. The NCBE has announced that test-takers will be required to recall what the NCBE calls "foundational concepts and principles" in civil procedure, contracts, evidence, torts, business associations, constitutional law, criminal law, and real property, but no longer family law, trusts and estates, conflict of laws, and secured transactions.[2] The NCBE has suggested that it will try to eliminate non-foundational knowledge (picky rules and exceptions) and shift focus from memorized doctrinal knowledge to use of materials provided in closed libraries, like those currently used in performance tests.[3] We know from Deborah Merritt and Logan Cornett's landmark study of minimum competence, *Building a Better Bar*, that the more NextGen shifts away from memorization of rules to familiarity with and understanding of how to use the rules, the better NextGen will be.[4] NextGen's changes in how knowledge is tested could be notable improvements.

The NCBE's proposed expansion of legal skills to be assessed is also impressive. The NextGen Bar Exam will attempt to assess legal research, legal writing, issue spotting and analysis, investigation and evaluation, client counseling and advising, negotiating and dispute resolution, and client relationship and management.[5] These are consistent with many of the building blocks of minimum competence identified in *Building a Better Bar*.[6]

The weaknesses in the NCBE's NextGen test are also potentially critical. The NCBE presents its design process as empirically based and "unencumbered,"[7] but undertook its analysis and study with a set of premises supporting the validity and fairness of its current tests and methods. To the extent that the NextGen design perpetuates its current focus on memorized doctrinal rules, the NCBE will have missed a big opportunity to align the exam with twenty-first century practice.

As planned, the NextGen exam also fails to incorporate any aspect of staged testing; the NCBE has determined that it will remain an all-or-nothing one-shot exam using the familiar twice-a-year timing. The NextGen Bar Exam may also suffer from an inability to adapt to changing realities of law practice. Having taken eight years to develop this test, the NCBE will need to stick with it. Nimbleness in design change may also be hampered by the fact that NextGen is planned as an integrated test, without separate components that can be scored separately or modified more easily.

Finally, the integrated design may mean that the NCBE will want every jurisdiction to take the entire test—or none of it. This could close the door on meaningful innovations by state bar examiners and make any institutional weaknesses of the NCBE even more problematic. Instead of abdicating the responsibility for better bar exams to the NCBE, states should press the NCBE for choices. One such excellent choice would be modeled on today's performance tests.

The best exams: performance tests. We can expect the NextGen Bar Exam to be a better bar exam, but it will not be the best available. The best way to protect the public with improved bar exams is to use performance tests exclusively. Performance tests like the Multistate Performance Test (MPT) offer a feasible, flexible, relatively inexpensive, even elegant licensing test of minimum competence to practice law. Bar examiners can protect the public by ditching the multiple-choice and essay questions and using performance tests exclusively.

Performance tests provide candidates with a case file and library of legal sources to be used to complete lawyering tasks, such as client letters, memos, or discovery documents.[8] Performance tests are currently used in most U.S. jurisdictions,[9] whether the MPT offered by the NCBE or a similar test designed by a jurisdiction, such as those used in California since 1983 or, more recently, in Nevada.

A performance test assesses legal reading and legal analysis (as do the MBE and essay questions) and legal writing (as do essay questions). Performance tests assess legal methods, including critical reading of cases, statutes, and regulations, and legal analysis, at a more sophisticated level than is required for the MBE or typical essay questions. A performance test can test manipulation of facts, legal strategy, case evaluation and development, and other more sophisticated and realistic lawyering tasks. The performance test is the only bar exam component currently being used that is not designed to primarily test doctrinal rules and the only component that does not emphasize memorization.[10]

Even though performance tests are closest to actual law practice, today's scoring formulas typically put performance tests in a weak third place behind multiple-choice and essay questions in determining whether a candidate passes or fails. The MPT takes 25 percent of the time of the UBE, but accounts for just 20 percent of its score.[11]

A large choir sings the praises of performance tests. Stakeholders surveyed by the NCBE at the first stage of research for the *Next Gen Bar Exam* commended performance tests: "The MPT was widely viewed as the component that is most representative of the skills needed for [newly licensed lawyers] at the point of entry to practice."[12] The new attorneys who participated in focus groups for the IAALS study of minimum competence, *Building a Better Bar*, also praised performance tests as "most closely parallel[ing] the work they do during the first year of practice."[13] A lawyer in a *Building a Better Bar* focus group declared, "The performance test is actually exactly what I did as a first year lawyer, and still do regularly."[14] Another recalled, "My first lawyer job I remember thinking, 'Oh my God it's just like the performance test.'"[15] The performance test has the capacity to move beyond the "mother goose" stories of the law, in Leon Green's biting critique of bar exams.

Give multiple performance tests either upon graduation or at stages throughout law school. One or two performance tests may not be sufficient to examine the range of knowledge domains and lawyering tasks that constitute minimum competence. But a series of performance tests, staged to assess learning appropriate for each year of law school, could convincingly assess minimum competence. An early test to ensure basic legal reasoning ability opens possibilities for later assessment of higher order thinking skills and a broader range of lawyering skills.[16] A later post-graduation bar exam could be comprised entirely of performance tests that align more closely with legal practice, including tasks more challenging than basic memos. A jurisdiction could require successful completion (passage) of five performance tests, one of which could be at the 1L level, at least two at the 2L level, and at least two at the 3L level. Performance tests could be offered three times a year. Even if only offered after graduation, a bar exam made entirely of performance tests could be given immediately, without the need for months wasted memorizing rules.

Test a broad range of doctrinal subject areas and legal methods. Current bar exams at least ensure that candidates are exposed to a wide range of doctrinal subjects as a foundation for future issue spotting. Bar examiners could accomplish this by providing a complete compendium of the broad range of doctrinal areas that are potential subjects of the performance tests. Each performance test would provide specific cases, statutes, regulations, or other authority, but understanding the core concepts (or threshold concepts in the language of *Building a Better Bar*) would be necessary for successful completion of the performance test. This is the same knowledge base necessary for competence as a lawyer.

Test a broad range of lawyering tasks. The jurisdiction should also publish a list of possible tasks that could show up in a performance test, including, for example, predictive memo, discovery plan, client letter or email, closing argument, negotiation preparation memo, lease or contract, sentencing or parole statement, client interview plan, and so on. Notice of the range of tasks would nudge students and law schools to prepare for the lawyering tasks listed, improving candidates' readiness to perform them with competence. The list could be modified routinely to reflect changes in law practice.

Put less focus on memorization. Performance tests deemphasize memorization, appropriately, bringing the test much closer to actual legal practice. Prior understanding of general principles of law and of legal methods is required to succeed on a performance test. But memorization of detailed rules is not required because a library of legal sources is provided, as in law practice.

Test analysis of statutes and regulations. The doctrinal knowledge tested on traditional bar exams is almost exclusively common law doctrine, ignoring the explosion of statutory and regulatory practice of the last hundred years. Common law doctrine is much easier to test on traditional essays and multiple-choice questions, even though it represents a shrinking portion of the work of lawyers. Performance tests invite expansion of assessment to include statutory and regulatory analysis.

Require a more demanding legal analysis. By requiring candidates to perform tasks that more closely simulate practice, performance tests can simulate the ambiguity and uncertainty that lawyers must confront in actual practice, requiring higher order cognitive skills and legal judgment. Providing both relevant and irrelevant materials in the library would test more advanced legal analysis and legal research skills.

Avoid the law of nowhere. The NCBE should provide performance tests to any jurisdiction that wants them. NCBE performance tests of the future, like current MPTs, would test on general principles, the law of nowhere or everywhere, depending on one's perspective. Jurisdictions that prefer to test on their own actual law could develop their state-specific performance tests using state statutes, regulations, or cases.[17] Assuming that passage of multiple performance tests is compulsory, a jurisdiction could require, for example, that two of the five use the law of the jurisdiction. The NCBE should develop expertise regarding format, grading, and timing of performance tests to offer jurisdictions.[18] The NCBE could even offer shells of performance tests for which jurisdictions could add their own specific statutes and cases.

Eliminate the cost of months of bar of review cramming after graduation from law school. Bar exams that consist entirely of performance tests would protect the public better with less cost to the test-takers. Performance tests eliminate doctrinal memorization, so they can be taken immediately upon graduation, or even sequentially during the last half of law school. The only stakeholders who should object to performance test–bar exams would be the bar prep industry. Law schools themselves can teach the competencies necessary to perform well on performance tests without any reduction in academic rigor. Three years of postgraduate law school should be sufficient to prepare for any bar exam based on the actual competencies of entry-level law practice.

Routinely adjust tests to change with the profession. Bar examiners have not been successful in making the routine, periodic changes that every licensing test needs to keep up with a changing profession. State courts do not have the resources or expertise to undertake regular, major overhauls of bar exams. The NCBE is investing in a once in a generation new test, but after spending eight years developing it, the NCBE may be stuck with a test that is not easy to change for another generation. Performance tests, on the other hand, are flexible enough to allow efficient, perpetual adjustment to the changing profession. New subjects and tasks can be easily substituted or added.

Develop reliable scoring protocols. The NCBE and jurisdictions will need to work with psychometricians to develop scoring protocols to ensure reliable grading of performance tests. This is a different approach to reliability than the current MBE-centric systems in place, but initial efforts elsewhere are promising. For example, the Law School Admissions Council (LSAC) has developed a possible post-1L formative assessment based on performance tests, piloted as the 1L Skills Check, that includes research into the reliability of grading of performance tests.[19] Multiple graders, careful rubrics, calibration training for graders, and numerous opportunities to pass the requisite number of performance tests should achieve the reliability and fairness necessary for any high-stakes licensing test. Accepting the challenge to develop reliable scoring of performance tests without scaling to the MBE or other multiple-choice tests is more than justified because performance tests are much better assessments of minimum competence to practice law. In other words, we should invest in achieving reliability for exams that offer much stronger validity.

Performance tests work. As a member of the Nevada Board of Bar Examiners, I have written and graded performance tests for recent bar exam administrations. When I score a candidate's performance test as not minimally competent, I am disappointed but confident in the assessment. A candidate who cannot glean the issues from the file and cannot use the library to answer the problem presented does not have the skills of critical reading, legal writing, and legal analysis required of every minimally competent lawyer. MBE scores, by contrast, are tainted by the irrelevancy of super-fast mechanical application of memorized rules. Essay scores of a single candidate can range from excellent to terrible, depending on the happenstance of the match between the subject of the essay and the candidate's interests or memorized knowledge. Licensing should not depend on that kind of luck. A performance test gives a candidate a clean shot to demonstrate the requisite skills and fundamental knowledge to solve a legal problem with nowhere to hide. If given reasonable time, candidates who cannot accomplish the task are not ready to practice law without supervision.

Every jurisdiction should ask itself, why *not* use performance tests to assess minimum competence? Even as the NCBE develops its integrated *NextGen* test, states should push the NCBE to provide performance test alternatives. The *NextGen* Bar Exam will be better than today's tests, but performance tests could be best.

Fix standard setting and speededness; add periodic review and transparency about sources. Whatever bar exams come next—whether performance tests, the NCBE's *NextGen* exam, or something else—several technical improvements are needed to meet professional standards for high-stakes tests.

Use cut scores to determine minimum competence, not to keep out the competition. Setting an appropriate dividing line between passage and failure of any high-stakes pass-fail test is crucial and tough. Even a bar exam with excellent content and appropriate time limits is neither valid nor fair without a defensible cut score to distinguish between *barely* minimally competent and *not* minimally competent. The hodgepodge of cuts scores in today's bar exams sows doubt about the validity of any of them and about the legal profession's competence regarding standard setting.[20]

To follow psychometric best practices, any standard-setting process should start with having well-regarded (thus competent) lawyers and judges *take the test*, not just deliberate on what scores they want candidates to achieve before they are allowed to join the profession.[21] Testing experts say that the standard setters should take the test so that "any difficulty that the judge has with any of the items will be reflected in the scoring of that item."[22] Testing experts explain that, "Participants who have not attempted to answer the test questions on their own are likely to think the test is easier than it is."[23] In fact, the ability or inability of standard setters to succeed on the test is evidence of the test's validity, or lack of validity.[24] The fact that standard setting for bar exams has been undertaken to date without the standard setters having to face their own performance is a symptom of the vast distance between competent practice of law and bar exam success. Further work is needed to design appropriate standard-setting methods for bar exams.

Stop using speededness as a proxy for competence. Alignment of bar exams with lawyering competence requires that the amount of time allotted for the test reflects the actual challenges of practice, not artificially punishing time pressure. Bar examiners are not the late Alex Trebek, orchestrating a game show that entertains because contestants face severe time pressure. An unusual ability to spit out rapid-fire responses is necessary to win at *Jeopardy*, but not to capably practice law. Competent lawyers need time to think.[25] Artificially short time limits reduce the validity of bar exams because excessive speededness is a distractor from minimum competence, not a proxy for it. Thoughtfulness is more important to competent law practice than speed.

Back in the day of handwritten exam answers, law students and bar candidates would suffer cramped hands from writing their exams. Now speedy and accurate typing is a major asset. Law professors and bar examiners have a long tradition of mistakenly using speed as a proxy for judgment and competence. I fell into that trap until I was introduced to the science of speededness in testing.[26] Rapid responses are required for some attorney positions—law clerk in a court with a busy motion docket comes to mind—but not most. Our focus on speed in licensing exams is especially wrong because novices in any field, including legal practice, take longer to perform any task when it is new. That slowness is one reason that new attorneys bill at a lower rate. Supervisors in the *Building a Better Bar* focus groups wanted new lawyers to slow down.[27] One study participant articulated what most of us understand: "[A] lawyer who is thorough will 'chew up and spit out' one who relies on speed."[28]

We need research to establish the correct amount of time to allow for multiple-choice, essay, or performance test answers.[29] During my time as dean of the Michigan State University College of Law, the five law deans in the state formally requested that the Michigan Board of Law Examiners reduce the length of their essay questions to no more than one single-spaced page. Candidates had to answer those lengthy, dense questions in twenty minutes. We deans were operating on common sense, knowing that a question to be answered in twenty minutes should be shorter than one to be answered in thirty or sixty minutes. But we knew nothing about testing standards related to speed, and neither did the bar examiners—fine lawyers and judges—who wrote the essays. Any bar exam time limits that are more stringent than the time to be allotted for a new attorney in practice move bar exams further away from being valid assessments of minimum competence.[30] Time limits are necessary to control costs, including of test administration. But validity suffers if most applicants are rushing furiously to try to finish or wasting weeks of their lives training to answer hundreds of MBE questions in 1.8 minutes each, a decidedly non-transferable skill.

New technologies enable more sophisticated research about speededness. NCBE test experts justify their time limits with claims that most candidates can finish with little diminution of accuracy at the end. They seem not to understand that law schools and bar prep companies train law graduates to replicate the time pressure through countless practice tests, drilling them to spend no more than 18 minutes on each set of ten multiple-choice questions, undercutting the premise of the methodology on which NCBE experts have relied. Bar examiners need to confront the damage that hunches about speed are doing to the fairness and validity of their bar exam products.

Be transparent about sources of law being tested. Another complication arises from the differences between the general rules tested on the multistate tests versus the state rules tested on state-specific questions. Applicants in many states today must memorize one set of general rules for the MBE and conflicting state rules for state-constructed essays. The Uniform Bar Exam (UBE) and the future *NextGen* exam eliminate this problem by testing only general rules, ignoring the rules of the jurisdiction giving the test.

If bar examiners were correct that competence is established by memorizing and applying rules that will be used in practice, these many layers of differences between what is tested and what is used would be deeply problematic. But reconceptualizing the level of knowledge required for licensing—replacing recall with familiarity and encouraging checking sources—mitigates the trouble from testing different law than what will be used in practice. If the sources of law being tested are transparent, ideally with the rules themselves provided in advance to the candidates, any commonly used rule can be the basis of the test. Performance tests solve this problem by providing the applicable library.

Implement routine periodical review. Professional standards for licensing tests require examiners to keep tests current by regularly reviewing changes in the profession.[31] The legal profession has changed profoundly over the last several decades, but the structure and coverage of bar exams have not. Bar exams today consist of multiple-choice questions, essays, and performance tests—the same components of the bar exam I took in California in 1980. The doctrinal subjects tested are the same, too, although often in more detail today.[32]

Bar exams need to be revised routinely to adapt to the changing profession. Creating the NextGen Bar Exam is an eight-year project for the NCBE, and the profession will have changed by the time it is adopted. Bar exam designs need to be sufficiently flexible to allow for adaptations without waiting another generation. The California Supreme Court's 2019 adoption of a Court Rule requiring a validity study of the bar exam every seven years is impressive because jurisdictions rarely adopt any such schedule.[33] Yet, a seven-year cycle may barely meet the schedule for periodic review required by testing standards. As the California Supreme Court has learned, doing a good job of assessing minimum competence to practice law is difficult work that never ends.

AFTERWORD

AFTER DECADES OF RELATIVE STABILITY, attorney licensing is changing. Those of us who have chosen law understand the power of our profession, and therefore the weight of policies and decisions about who is admitted and who excluded. Our history of purposeful exclusion is humbling. Until recently, those of us with gatekeeper roles— bar examiners, legal educators, supreme court justices, members of the profession—have been more comfortable evaluating the people who want to become lawyers than deeply scrutinizing our own licensing habits. Today, many of us are accepting the challenge to break the grip of tradition and return to the fundamentals of public protection. What does public protection look like? What is minimum competence in a lawyer? How is competence most fairly assessed? What does licensing for a competent, inclusive, equitable, client-centered, justice-seeking profession look like?

Having written and thought about these questions for decades, I understand the challenges better than I used to. But, now more than ever, I also appreciate the drive, values, and vision of those of us standing at the entrance to the profession. My optimism is high, and I'm eager to see what, working together, we accomplish next to shape the profession for the public we serve.

ACKNOWLEDGMENTS

COUNTLESS COLLEAGUES AND FRIENDS IN legal education and in the profession have inspired and elevated my work on attorney licensing over several decades. My first efforts were undertaken in memory of Trina Grillo, the kind of law professor I have tried to be. Most recently, this project has been propelled and lifted by my cherished friends in the *Collaboratory on Legal Education and Licensing for Practice:* Claudia Angelos, Sara Berman, Mary Lu Bilek, Carol Chomsky, Andi Curcio, Marsha Griggs, Eileen Kaufman, Debby Merritt, Patty Salkin, and, especially, Judith Wegner.

Over the years the Society of Law Teachers (SALT) created a home for me and for attorney licensing reform. The thousands of law students I have been privileged to teach have in turn taught me well. The Boyd School of Law, UNLV, provided excellent support for this project, both financially and by being a responsible, generous, and intellectually engaged academic home. Everyone at the Wiener-Rogers Law Library has provided excellent support, particularly Jeanne Price and Jim Rich. Carressa Browder has supplied expert and unflappable manuscript assistance. I am especially grateful for my UNLV research assistants, including Grace Warburton, Crystal Washington, Cristiana Wilcoxon, and Justin Williams. My thinking about attorney licensing benefited from thoughtful comments at faculty workshops at the University of

Minnesota and UNLV. My recent return to the Thomas & Mack Legal Clinic rekindled my focus on experiential education, so I am particularly grateful to my clinical and externship colleagues.

Writing this book has coincided with my work helping to develop the 1L Skills Check, a performance test, formative assessment piloted by the Law School Admissions Council, where Judith Wegner and I have been lucky to work with Wayne Camara, Alexa Chew, Lily Knezevich, Kellye Testy, Danielle Tully, and others. I also thank my colleagues on the Nevada Board of Bar Examiners, especially our chair, Rick Trachok, for the opportunity and many rewards of working together to license the newest attorneys in Nevada. I am grateful for all the efforts of the team at the Stanford University Press, including Marcela Cristina Maxfield, Sunna Juhn, Tiffany Mok, Jennifer Gordon, Kate Mertes, and Michelle Lipinski.

This book, like anything I accomplish, is possible because of my family—my sisters Hilary Howarth and Sandra Howarth, and my partner Carmen Estrada.

NOTES

PREFACE

1. *See* STEPHEN P. KLEIN, RELATIONSHIP OF BAR EXAMINATIONS TO PERFORMANCE TESTS OF LAWYERING SKILLS (July 1983).

CHAPTER 1

1. "Occupational licensing is a technique for creating an occupational monopoly." Lawrence Friedman, *Freedom of Contract and Occupational Licensing 1890–1910: A Legal and Social Study*, 53 CALIF. L. REV. 487, 504 (1965). "The primary challenge for any occupation seeking to become a profession is to control supply." Richard L. Abel, *Essay: Lawyer Self-Regulation and the Public Interest: A Reflection*, 20 LEGAL ETHICS 115, 115 (2017) (citation omitted). "The restrictive consequence of licensure is achieved in large part by making entry into the regulated occupation expensive in time or money or both." Walter Gellhorn, *The Abuse of Occupational Licensing*, 44 U. CHI. L. REV. 6, 12 (1976) (footnote omitted).

2. "Doctors and lawyers, unlike small retailers, had considerable success preserving the essential social and economic configurations of their professions, as they existed in 1900." Friedman, *supra* note 1, at 524. "[L]icensing played and plays an important role in the system of control." *Id.*; *see also* Mario Pagliero, *What Is the Objective of Professional Licensing? Evidence from the US Market for Lawyers*, 29 INTER'L J. OF INDUS. ORG. 473, 481 (2011) ("licensing, as implemented, increases salaries and decreases the availability of lawyers, thus significantly reducing consumer welfare"); Larry E. Ribstein, *Lawyers as Lawmakers: A Theory of Lawyer Licensing*, 69 MO. L. REV. 299, 299 (2004). "Existing explanations of lawyer licens-

ing focusing on the need to ensure lawyer quality are unconvincing. A license to practice is a dubious signal of quality, the licensing requirement restricts the availability of legal services, and state licensing is subject to political capture by lawyers." *Id.*

3. DEBORAH L. RHODE, IN THE INTERESTS OF JUSTICE: REFORMING THE LEGAL PROFESSION 150 (2000).

4. ABA, COMMISSION ON THE FUTURE OF LEGAL EDUCATION, PRINCIPLES FOR LEGAL EDUCATION AND LICENSURE IN THE 21ST CENTURY: PRINCIPLES AND COMMENTARY 7 (2020) [hereinafter ABA FUTURE COMM'N], https://www.americanbar.org/content/dam/aba/administrative/future-of-legal-education/cflle-principles-and-commentary-feb-2020-final.pdf. "Legal educators and the profession must embrace the reality that preparation for law practice does not always require seven years of post-secondary education. Shorter, more focused educational tracks are appropriate for some of the varied roles in the legal service delivery ecosystem." *Id.*

5. *J.D. and LL.M. Tuition and Fees,* COLUMBIA LAW SCHOOL, https://www.law.columbia.edu/about/offices-and-departments/office-financial-aid/costs-and-billing/costs-and-budgeting (last visited March 15, 2022); *J.D. Tuition and Financial Aid,* CORNELL LAW SCHOOL, https://www.lawschool.cornell.edu/admissions/jd-admissions/jd-tuition-and-financial-aid/ (last visited March 15, 2022); *Tuition and Fees,* NEW ENGLAND LAW–BOSTON, https://www.nesl.edu/admissions-aid/tuition-aid/tuition-fees (last visited June 6, 2021); *Tuition and Fees,* SOUTHWEST-ERN LAW SCHOOL–LOS ANGELES, https://www.swlaw.edu/admissions-financial-aid/tuition-fees (last visited Sept. 16, 2021).

6. ABA PROFILE OF THE LEGAL PROFESSION 25–26 (2020) [hereinafter ABA PROFILE], https://www.americanbar.org/content/dam/aba/administrative/news/2020/07/potlp2020.pdf; *see also* Debra Cassens Weiss, *Law Student Debt Averages About $165K at Graduation, Creating Stress and Restricting Choices, Survey Says,* ABA J. (Oct. 27, 2020), https://www.abajournal.com/news/article/law-student-debt-averages-165k-at-graduation-creating-stress-and-restricting-choices-survey-says (reporting on ABA survey).

7. *See, e.g.,* DEBORAH L. RHODE & GEOFFREY C. HAZARD JR., PROFESSIONAL RESPONSIBILITY AND REGULATION 201–03 (2002); Edward Rubin, *What's Wrong with Langdell's Method, and What to Do About It,* 60 VAND. L. REV. 609 (2007).

8. *See* Peter A. Joy, *The Uneasy History of Experiential Education in U.S. Law Schools,* 122 DICK. L. REV. 551 (2018).

9. "[A] correlation between examination scores and law school grades . . . is scarcely surprising, since both measure similar skills. How well either predicts success as a lawyer is something else again and has yet to be demonstrated." RHODE, *supra* note 3, at 151; *see also* Andrea A. Curcio, *A Better Bar: Why and How the Existing Bar Exam Should Change,* 81 NEB. L. REV. 363, 364–65 (2002) (urging reform to test additional skills required for law practice).

10. *See, e.g.*, ABA FUTURE COMM'N, *supra* note 4, at 4. "The bar exam tests both too much and too little. On the subjects it tests, success depends on extensive and granular rule memorization and application. At the same time, it fails to test key skills central to the practice of law." *Id.* (under heading "Outdated Bar Exam").

11. David Epstein, the dean of Emory's law school from 1985–89, once famously said, "Give me a room full of educated adults five nights a week for four weeks and I could probably get them through the bar exam. The bar exam is nothing but regurgitation of some very specific information." *Quotes,* 73 ABA J. 23, 29 (1987).

12. Leon Green, *Why Bar Examinations?*, 33 NW. U. L. REV. 908, 911 (1939).

13. NEW YORK STATE BOARD OF LAW EXAMINERS AND ACCESSLEX INSTI-TUTE, ANALYZING FIRST-TIME BAR EXAM PASSAGE ON THE UBE IN NEW YORK, at 38–40 & Table C1 at 78–81 (App. C) (May 19, 2021) [hereinafter ANALYZING BAR PASSAGE], http://www.accesslex.org/NYBOLE

14. AMERICAN EDUCATIONAL RESEARCH ASSOCIATION, AMERICAN PSYCHO-LOGICAL ASSOCIATION, AND NATIONAL COUNCIL ON MEASUREMENT IN EDUCA-TION, STANDARDS FOR EDUCATIONAL AND PSYCHOLOGICAL TESTING 49 (2014) [hereinafter 2014 STANDARDS].

15. Susan M. Case, *Back to Basic Principles: Validity and Reliability,* 75 BAR EXAM'R 23, 23 (Aug. 2006).

16. "[T]ests used for credentialing are designed to verify that candidates have mastered the knowledge, skills and abilities (KSAs) deemed necessary for work in a profession." Mark B. Raymond, *Job Analysis, Practice Analysis and the Content of Credentialing Examinations,* in HANDBOOK OF TEST DEVELOPMENT 144 (Su-zanne Lane, Mark R. Raymond, & Thomas M. Haladyna, eds., 2d ed. 2016) (citing 2014 STANDARDS, *supra* note 14, at 174–75).

17. *See, e.g.*, Deborah Jones Merritt, *Validity, Competence, and the Bar Exam,* AALS NEWS, no. 2017–2, at 11, https://www.aals.org/wp-content/uploads/2017/05 /AALSnews_spring17-v9.pdf (critiquing validity of bar exams); Joan Howarth, *Teaching in the Shadow of the Bar,* 31 U.S.F. L. REV. 927, 930 (1997) (summarizing earlier criticisms of bar examinations); *Society of American Law Teachers State-ment on the Bar Exam,* 52 J. LEGAL EDUC. 446 (2002) (critiquing bar exams for failure to measure professional competence, negative effects on legal education, and creation of significant barriers to diversity); Andrea Anne Curcio, Carol L. Chomsky, & Eileen R. Kaufman, *Testing, Diversity & Merit: A Reply to Dan Sub-otnik and Others,* 9 U. MASS. L. REV. 206, 225 (2014) (referencing 1992 bar associ-ation criticism of NY bar exam); Carol L. Chomsky, Andrea A. Curcio & Eileen Kaufman, *A Merritt-orious Path for Lawyer Licensing,* 82 OHIO ST. L. J. 883 (2021) (describing Professor Merritt's bar exam reform work starting in 1990s in Fest-schrift in her honor).

18. *See, e.g.*, Marjorie M. Shultz & Sheldon Zedeck, *Predicting Lawyer Effective-ness: Broadening the Basis for Law School Admissions Decisions,* 36 LAW & SOC. INQUIRY 620 (2011).

19. Melissa H. Weresh, *Stargate: Malleability as a Threshold Concept in Legal Education*, 63 J. LEGAL EDUC. 689 (2014).

20. Joan W. Howarth, *What Law Must Lawyers Know?*, 19 CONN. PUB. INT. L.J. 1, 13 (2019); DEBORAH JONES MERRITT & LOGAN CORNETT, BUILDING A BETTER BAR: THE TWELVE BUILDING BLOCKS OF MINIMUM COMPETENCE 48 (Dec. 2020) [hereinafter A BETTER BAR]. https://iaals.du.edu/sites/default/files/documents/publications/building_a_better_bar.pdf

21. Joan W. Howarth, *The Case for a Uniform Cut Score*, 42 J. OF LEGAL PROF. 69, 75 (2017) [hereinafter *Uniform Cut Score*] (citing 2014 STANDARDS, *supra* note 14, at 100); John Mattar et al., *Reviewing or Revalidating Performance Standards on Credentialing Examinations*, in SETTING PERFORMANCE STANDARDS: FOUNDATIONS, METHODS, AND INNOVATIONS 399–400 (Gregory J. Cizek, ed., 2d ed. 2012).

22. For explanations of the process by which written answers are scaled to the multiple-choice tests, see *Uniform Cut Score, supra* note 21, at 72; *Case, supra* note 15, at 23.

23. *Multistate Bar Examination*, NCBE (showing that all U.S. jurisdictions but Louisiana use the MBE), https://www.ncbex.org/exams/mbe (last visited May 27, 2021).

24. *Uniform Cut Score, supra* note 21, at 73–74.

25. *Id.* at 69–71.

26. Fairness "to all individuals in the intended population of test takers is an overriding, foundational concern." 2014 STANDARDS, *supra* note 14, at 49.

27. A BETTER BAR, *supra* note 20, at 70.

28. *See* Haley Moss, *Raising the Bar on Accessibility: How the Bar Admissions Process Limits Disabled Law School Graduates*, 28 AM. U. J. GENDER SOC. POL'Y & L. 537 (2020); Caroline M. Mew & Robert A. Burgoyne, *New Regulations Under Titles II and III of the ADA Address Disability Standards Under the ADA Amendments Act*, 86 BAR EXAM'R 7 (June 2017), https://www.ncbex.org/pdfviewer/?file=%2Fassets%2Fmedia_files%2FBar-Examiner%2Fissues%2F860217-BE-Abridged.pdf

29. *See* John Passmore, *Everything You Need to Know About ADA Accommodations for the MPRE and Bar Exams*, BAR EXAM TOOLBOX (Oct. 25, 2017), https://barexamtoolbox.com/everything-you-need-to-know-about-ada-accommodations-for-the-mpre-and-bar-exams/ For a discussion of differences between jurisdictions, see Amanda M. Foster, *Reasonable Accommodations on the Bar Exam: Leveling the Playing Field or Providing an Unfair Advantage?*, 48 VALPO. U. L. REV. 661, 672–81 (2015).

30. *See* Maria Dinzeo, *Disabled Law Grads Get No Relief from Covid-Era State Bar Exam*, COURTHOUSE NEWS (Sept. 30, 2020), https://www.courthousenews.com/disabled-law-grads-get-no-relief-from-covid-era-state-bar-exam/; *see also* Lilith Siegel (@LilithSiegel), TWITTER (June 27, 2020, 2:28 PM), https://twitter.com/LilithSiegel/status/1276628347506712581

31. *See, e.g.*, RHODE & HAZARD, *supra* note 7, at 223 (critics of bar exams claim that "the skills existing exams measure do not adequately predict performance as a lawyer"; *id.* at 224 (the "inadequate link between exam and job performance is of special concern because minority applicants have disproportionately low passage rates," quoting RHODE, *supra* note 3, at 151); Abel, *supra* note 1, at 115. "As Weber noted, examinations became the dominant entry barrier in the twentieth century. These have an unproven—and arguably dubious—relationship to the knowledge lawyers actually utilise in their daily practice (in the language of psychologists: they have never been validated)." *Id.* (footnote omitted).

32. ABA PROFILE, *supra* note 6, at 33.

33. In 2019, only 56.2% of active physicians identified as white. *Diversity in Medicine: Facts and Figures 2019*, AAMC, https://www.aamc.org/data-reports/workforce/interactive-data/figure-18-percentage-all-active-physicians-race/ethni city-2018 (last visited June 1, 2021).

34. The engineering profession is 73.6% white. *Engineer Demographics in the U.S.*, ZIPPIA, https://www.zippia.com/engineer-jobs/demographics/ (last visited June 1, 2021).

35. In 2020, 70.2% of dentists identified as white. J. Tim Wright, Marko Vujicic & Sylvia Frazier-Bowers, *Elevating Dentistry Through Diversity*, 152 JOURNAL OF AMERICAN DENTAL ASSOCIATION 253, 254 (April 1, 2021), https://jada.ada.org/action/showPdf?pii=S0002-8177%2821%2900095-7

36. In 2020, 64.5% of accountants identified as white. *Accountant Demographics in the U.S.*, ZIPPIA, https://www.zippia.com/accountant-jobs/demographics/ (last visited June 1, 2021).

37. *See, e.g.*, Deborah L. Rhode, *Law Is the Least Diverse Profession in the Nation. And Lawyers Are Not Doing Enough to Change That*, WASH. POST (May 27, 2015), https://www.washingtonpost.com/posteverything/wp/2015/05/27/law-is -the-least-diverse-profession-in-the-nation-and-lawyers-arent-doing-enough-to -change-that/ For further analysis, see Jason P. Nance & Paul E. Madsen, *An Empirical Analysis of Diversity in the Legal Profession*, 47 CONN. L. REV. 271, 305–13 (2014) (providing data comparing the diversity of legal profession with the diversity of other prestigious professions). For updated data, see information collected by the ABA showing that in 2020, the legal profession was composed of 2% Asians, 5% Hispanics, 5% Blacks, 2% multiracial, and 85% whites. ABA PROFILE, *supra* note 6, at 33.

38. *See, e.g.*, RICHARD L. ABEL, AMERICAN LAWYERS 68 (1989) ("Although the bar examination no longer excludes a substantial proportion of non-minority graduates in most jurisdictions, it still represents a substantial barrier for many minority law graduates"); Alex M. Johnson, *Knots in the Pipeline for Prospective Lawyers of Color: The LSAT Is Not the Problem and Affirmative Action Is Not the Answer*, 24 STAN. L. & POL'Y REV. 379, 405 (2013) ("Almost all would agree that the individual state bar examinations act as a severe impediment to certain

members of underrepresented minority groups becoming practicing attorneys"); Kristin Booth Glen, *Thinking Out of the Bar Exam Box: A Proposal to "MacCrate" Entry to the Profession*, 23 PACE L. REV. 343, 381–83 (2004) (discussing studies showing white applicants' bar passage rates were 30% higher than Black applicants' bar passage rates). Because of disparate impact concerns, ABA entities focused on diversity have actively opposed efforts to ratchet up the bar pass rates required for law schools to retain ABA accreditation. *See, e.g., Letter from Chairs of the ABA Goal III Entities in Response to Standard 316* (Jan. 11, 2019), https://www.americanbar.org/content/dam/aba/administrative/legal_education_and_admissions_to_the_bar/council_reports_and_resolutions/feb19/3-aba-diversity-entities-response-to-standard-316.pdf

39. ABA: LEGAL EDUCATION AND ADMISSION TO THE BAR, SUMMARY BAR PASS DATA: RACE, ETHNICITY, AND GENDER, 2020 AND 2021 BAR PASSAGE QUESTIONNAIRE, https://www.americanbar.org/content/dam/aba/administrative/legal_education_and_admissions_to_the_bar/statistics/20210621-bpq-national-summary-data-race-ethnicity-gender.pdf

40. *See* State Bar of California, *California Bar Exam Statistics*, http://www.calbar.ca.gov/Admissions/Law-School-Regulation/Exam-Statistics (last visited May 27, 2021). California's published results for other categories of test-takers and other years, going back to 2006, February and July administrations, are similar. California's recent cut score reduction has reduced but not eliminated racial disparities.

41. *See* Douglas R. Ripkey & Susan M. Case, *A National Look at MBE Performance Differences Among Ethnic Groups*, 76 BAR EXAM'R 21, 24 (Aug. 2007).

42. The most recent New York statistics come from a report that studied the impact of New York's adoption of the Uniform Bar Exam (UBE) in July 2016 by examining test results for the five administrations from July 2015 to July 2017. Disparate results preceded and followed adoption of the UBE. For each of the five bar exam administrations studied, for both all test-takers and domestic, first-time test-takers, the pass rate for Caucasian/white was above the overall average. The pass rate for each of the minority categories was below the average. NCBE, RESEARCH DEPARTMENT, IMPACT OF ADOPTION OF THE UNIFORM BAR EXAMINATION IN NEW YORK 149, 166 (2019), https://www.nybarexam.org/UBEReport/NY%20UBE%20Adoption%20Part%202%20Study.pdf

43. Ripkey & Case, *supra* note 41, at 26–27 ns. 6–7.

44. State Bar of New Mexico, *The Status of Minority Attorneys in New Mexico Report* 60 (2019), https://www.sbnm.org/Portals/NMBAR/AboutUs/committees/Diversity/StatusMinorityAttys2019.pdf?ver=dHrv4Oo2AO4sSUA1VrigWQ%3d%3d

45. *See* State Bar of California, *supra* note 40.

46. Ripkey & Case, *supra* note 41, at 26.

47. *See* Joan W. Howarth, *The Professional Responsibility Case for Valid and Nondiscriminatory Bar Exams*, 33 GEO. J. LEGAL ETHICS 931, 931 (2020).

NOTES TO CHAPTER 1 157

48. *See id.*

49. 2014 STANDARDS, *supra* note 14, at 54.

50. *See, e.g.,* Mark R. Raymond, April Southwick, and Mengyao Zhang, *The Testing Column: Ensuring Fairness in Assessment,* 90 BAR EXAM'R 73 (Spring 2021), https://thebarexaminer.ncbex.org/article/spring-2021/the-testing-column -ensuring-fairness-in-assessment/; Joanne Kane & April Southwick, *The Testing Column: Writing, Selecting, and Placing MBE Items: A Coordinated and Collaborative Effort,* 88 BAR EXAM'R 46 (2019), https://thebarexaminer.org/article /spring-2019/the-testing-column-writing-selecting-and-placing-mbe-items-a -coordinated-and-collaborative-effort/

51. *See* Mitchel Winick, Victor D. Quintanilla, Sam Erman, Christina Chong-Nakatsuchi, & Michael Frisby, *Examining the California Cut Score: An Empirical Analysis of Minimum Competency, Public Protection, Disparate Impact, and National Standards* (Oct. 15, 2020), https://papers.ssrn.com/sol3/papers.cfm?abstract _id=3707812; Johnson, *supra* note 38, at 419 (urging adoption of a uniform cut score, 130, to diversify the profession); Michael B. Frisby, Sam C. Erman, & Victor D. Quintanilla, *Safeguard or Barrier: An Empirical Examination of Bar Exam Cut Scores* 46 (2021) ("no evidence to support the claim that lower cut scores lead to greater lawyer misconduct" so jurisdictions should lower cut scores to protect public with more lawyers and more diverse profession), https://papers.ssrn.com/ sol3/papers.cfm?abstract_id=3793272

52. Winick et al., *supra* note 51, at 17.

53. "[E]nforcement agencies and many courts have taken the position that sufficient proof of job relatedness must support the use of a cutoff score that increases disparate impact." BARBARA T. LINDEMANN, PAUL GROSSMAN, & C. GEOFFREY WEIRICH, I EMPLOYMENT DISCRIMINATION LAW 2.II.A.1 4–55 to 4–56 & n. 273 (5th ed. 2012).

54. *2008 Statistics,* 78 BAR EXAM'R (May 2009), at 9, 15.

55. *2019 Statistics,* BAR EXAM'R, https://thebarexaminer.ncbex.org/2019 -statistics/ (last visited March 2, 2021). In 2020, the chaotic pandemic year, 61% of candidates and 76% of first-time test-takers passed. *2020 Statistics,* BAR EXAM'R, https://thebarexaminer.org/2020-statistics/2020-statistics-snapshot/ (last visited Oct. 21, 2021).

56. *See* Aaron N. Taylor, *The Marginalization of Black Aspiring Lawyers,* 13 FIU L. REV. 489 (2019); ABA, 2020 LAW SCHOOL STUDENT LOAN DEBT: SURVEY REPORT, https://www.americanbar.org/content/dam/aba/administrative/young_ lawyers/2020-student-loan-survey.pdf

57. ANALYZING BAR PASSAGE, *supra* note 13, at 38–40 & App. C, Table C1 at 87–91.

58. *See* Steven Chung, *Farewell Whittier Law School,* ABOVE THE LAW (Aug. 28, 2019), https://abovethelaw.com/2019/08/farewell-whittier-law-school/#:~:text =The%20leaders%20of%20Whittier%20College,eventually%20close%20the

%20law%20school; Paul Bowers, *Fewer Than Half of Charleston School of Law Grads Passed the July Bar Exam*, POST AND COURIER (Sept. 14, 2020), https://www.postandcourier.com/news/fewer-than-half-of-charleston-school-of-law-grads-pass/article_3f20d90e-bfob-11e7-b94a-ff78b9fc72co.html; Press, *Concordia University School of Law Closing*, U.S. NEWS (June 25, 2020), https://www.usnews.com/news/best-states/idaho/articles/2020-06-25/concordia-university-school-of-law-closing#:~:text=In%20February%2C%20Concordia%20University%20in,closing%20due%20to%20financial%20troubles.&text=Hotchalk%2C%20a%20private%20California%20company,Concordia%20St

59. *See* Karen Sloan, *The Big Fail: Why Bar Pass Rates Have Sunk to Record Lows*, LAW.COM (April 14, 2019), https://www.law.com/2019/04/12/the-big-fail-why-bar-pass-rates-have-sunk-to-record-lows/

60. *Id.*

61. *Memorandum from Erica Moeser, President of NCBE, to Law School Deans* (Oct. 23, 2014), https://online.wsj.com/public/resources/documents/2014_1110_moesermemo.pdf

62. ROGER BOLUS, PERFORMANCE CHANGES TO THE CALIFORNIA BAR EXAMINATION: PART 2 (2018), http://www.calbar.ca.gov/Portals/0/documents/admissions/Examinations/Bar-Exam-Report-Final.pdf

63. *See, e.g.*, ABA STANDARDS AND RULES OF PROCEDURE FOR APPROVAL OF LAW SCHOOLS, Standard 316 at 25 (2020–21) (requiring 75% bar passage within two years of graduation), https://www.americanbar.org/content/dam/aba/administrative/legal_education_and_admissions_to_the_bar/standards/2020-2021/2020-21-aba-standards-and-rules-for-approval-of-law-schools.pdf (last visited Oct. 22, 2021).

64. Nancy Rapoport calls these "modal" law schools, as they are the largest group. *See* Nancy B. Rapoport, *Changing the Modal Law School: Rethinking U.S. Legal Education in (Most) Schools*, 122 DICK. L. REV. 189 (2017).

65. *See* David L. Hudson, *Schools Add Bar Exam Class to Curriculum and Find Success*, ABA J. (April 1, 2016), https://www.abajournal.com/magazine/article/schools_add_bar_exam_class_to_curriculum_and_find_success; Stephanie Francis Ward, *More Law Schools Are Covering Bar Review Costs: Is It Improving Pass Rates?*, ABA J. (Oct. 20, 2016), https://www.abajournal.com/news/article/more_law_schools_covering_bar_review_costs_is_it_improving_pass_rates

66. *See, e.g.*, ABA FUTURE COMM'N, *supra* note 4, at 4. "Given its gatekeeper role and influence on legal education, [the bar exam] thus discourages curricular innovation and inhibits the imagination of what a legal professional will be in the 21st century." *Id.*

67. *See JD Admissions: The Juris Doctor Program*, YALE LAW SCHOOL, https://law.yale.edu/study-law-yale/degree-programs/jd-program/jd-degree-requirements (last visited March 5, 2021); *Course List*, MICHIGAN LAW, https://www.law

.umich.edu/CurrentStudents/Registration/ClassSchedule/Pages/CourseList.aspx (last visited March 5, 2021).

68. *See Harvard Law School Handbook of Academic Policies 2020–2021*, HARVARD LAW SCHOOL, https://hls.harvard.edu/dept/academics/handbook/rules -relating-to-law-school-studies/requirements-for-the-j-d-degree/c-first-year-j-d -course-and-credit-requirements/ (last visited March 5, 2021).

69. *See* Erica Moeser, *President's Page*, 83 BAR EXAM'R 6 (Dec. 2014) ("the rise of experiential learning may have crowded out time for students to take additional 'black-letter' courses that would have strengthened their knowledge of the law and their synthesis of what they learned during the first year"); Mark A. Albanese, *Testing Column: The July 2014 MBE: Rogue Wave or Storm Surge*, 84 BAR EXAM'R, 35, 46 (June 2015) ("There has also been a trend toward incorporating non-core courses and clinical experiences into the law school curriculum. These, too, can take students' time away from learning the core concepts that are tested on the bar examination"); *see also* Deborah J. Merritt, *Experiential Education and Bar Passage*, LAW SCHOOL CAFÉ (Jan. 22, 2016) (discussing these statements), https://www.lawschoolcafe.org/2016/01/22/experiential-education-and-bar-passage/; Green, *supra* note 12, at 911 (claiming that licensing "embarrasses every university law school in the country in its attempts to develop broader curricula and better methods of teaching").

70. Lawyers surveyed by the State Bar of California overwhelmingly told the Court to keep the extremely high cut score that was being reconsidered. STATE BAR OF CALIFORNIA, REPORT TO THE ADMISSIONS AND EDUCATION COMMITTEE AND THE COMMITTEE OF BAR EXAMINERS REGARDING PUBLIC COMMENTS ON THE STANDARD SETTING STUDY 4 (2017), http://apps.calbar.ca.gov/cbe/docs/agendaItem/Public/agendaitem1000001998.pdf

71. Gillian K. Hadfield, *The Price of Law: How the Market for Lawyers Distorts the Justice System*, 98 MICH. L. REV. 953, 960–62, 983–84 (2000). "The moral hazard in such control [self-regulation and control over entry] is evident and has been well appreciated throughout the history of the profession." *Id.* at 983 (footnote omitted). For a critique of lack of process and transparency typical of licensing in other professions, see Bobbi Jo Boyd, *Do It in the Sunshine: A Comparative Analysis of Rulemaking Procedures and Transparency Practices of Lawyer-Licensing Entities*, 70 ARK. L. REV. 609, 616 (2017).

72. Barristers (litigators) must have membership in one of the Inns of Court in London and complete a "pupillage" as a means of receiving intensive mentoring and education over the years. *See* BAR COUNCIL, https://www.barcouncil.org.uk / (last visited Sept. 3, 2018). For information on "qualifying as a barrister," see BAR STANDARDS BOARD, https://www.barstandardsboard.org.uk/qualifying-as-a -barrister/ (last visited Sept. 3, 2018). Solicitors (office lawyers) are regulated by the Law Society and must pass a theoretical examination as well as complete a pro-

gram of "articling." *See Becoming a Solicitor*, LAW SOC'Y, https://www.lawsociety .org.uk/law-careers/becoming-a-solicitor/ (last visited Sept. 3, 2018).

73. *See* STANDING COMMITTEE ON PROFESSIONAL REGULATION OF THE ABA, CENTER FOR PROFESSIONAL RESPONSIBILITY, 2018 SURVEY ON LAWYER DISCI-PLINE SYSTEMS (SOLD) (2020), https://www.americanbar.org/content/dam/aba/ administrative/professional_responsibility/2018sold-results.pdf

74. "[I]t is absurd to pretend that any test of competence administered to some-one at the age of twenty-five, no matter how well constructed, can ensure quality throughout a fifty-year career." ABEL, *supra* note 38, at 151–52.

75. NCBE, IRS Form 990 (2020), PROPUBLICA, https://projects.propublica.org/ nonprofits/organizations/362472009

76. *See* NCBE, OVERVIEW OF PRELIMINARY RECOMMENDATIONS FOR THE NEXT GENERATION OF THE BAR EXAMINATION (2020), https://testingtaskforce.org/wp -content/uploads/2021/01/TTF-Preliminary-Bar-Exam-Recommendations2.pdf

77. Hadfield, *supra* note 71, at 995. "Looking at the market imperfections as a whole, it is possible to identify three fundamental features of the market for lawyers as the source of the market power lawyers possess: the complexity of legal reasoning and process, the monopoly the profession holds over coercive dispute resolution, and the unified nature of the profession." *Id.* "We train all our lawyers in essentially the same way, and they receive the same license to practice." *Id.* at 997.

78. ABA FUTURE COMM'N, *supra* note 4, at 4 ("we cannot improve access to jus-tice without significant changes in how we educate and license the next generation of legal professionals").

79. *See* Rebecca Buckwalter-Poza, *Making Justice Equal*, CENTER FOR AMERI-CAN PROGRESS (Dec. 8, 2016), https://www.americanprogress.org/issues/criminal -justice/reports/2016/12/08/294479/making-justice-equal/; *see also* Jessica K. Steinberg, *Demand Side Reform in the Poor People's Court*, 47 CONN. L. REV. 741, 741, https://scholarship.law.gwu.edu/cgi/viewcontent.cgi?referer=&httpsredir= 1&article=2383&context=faculty_publications; Gillian K. Hadfield & Deborah L. Rhode, *How to Regulate Legal Services to Promote Access, Innovation, and the Quality of Lawyering*, 67 HASTINGS L. J. 1191 (2016); Cassandra Burke Robertson, *How Should We License Lawyers*, 89 FORDHAM L. R. 1295 (2021) (urging client-centered system that abandons one-size-fits-all licenses).

80. Lyle Moran, *How the Washington Supreme Court's LLLT Program Met Its Demise*, ABA J. (July 9, 2020), https://www.abajournal.com/web/article/how-wash ingtons-limited-license-legal-technician-program-met-its-demise

81. For a leading analysis and criticism of unauthorized practice limitations, see Deborah L. Rhode, *Policing the Professional Monopoly: A Constitutional and Empirical Analysis of Unauthorized Practice Prohibitions*, 34 STAN. L. REV. 1 (1981); *see also* ABA FUTURE COMM'N, *supra* note 4, at 3. "In almost every legal arena in

the United States, most people and organizations cannot afford competent and cost-effective legal services. Failure to acknowledge and aggressively respond to these challenges threatens America's competitiveness and democratic institutions." *Id.*; *see also* RHODE, *supra* note 3, at 208. "Control over legal processes and legal ethics has often been left to the organized bar, the very group least capable of disinterested decision making. Although lawyers' regulatory codes claim to protect the public, the public has had almost no voice in their content or enforcement. The result is an oversight structure that is unresponsive to consumer concerns." *Id.*

82. THOMAS D. MORGAN, THE VANISHING AMERICAN LAWYER 125 (2010). "Negotiating contracts, troubleshooting discrimination claims, even writing court documents can all be done by non-lawyers within an organization receiving a level of lawyer supervision and training to which unauthorized practice rules cannot effectively speak." *Id.* (citations omitted).

83. *See, e.g.*, Randolph N. Jonakait, *The Two Hemispheres of Legal Education and the Rise and Fall of Local Law Schools*, 51 N.Y.L. SCH. L. REV. 864 (2006–2007).

84. Julie D. Lawton, *Am I My Client? Revisited: The Role of Race in Intra-Race Legal Representation*, 22 MICH. J. RACE & L. 13 (2016).

85. This could change. The State Bar of California is considering a proposal to license paraprofessionals, a role that could be available to law graduates who have not passed a bar exam. *See Frequently Asked Questions: California Paraprofessional Program Working Group*, STATE BAR OF CALIFORNIA, http://www.calbar.ca.gov/paraprofessionals-FAQ (last visited June 24, 2021).

86. Thirty percent of the national workforce is covered by licensing laws, with over 1,100 occupations licensed in at least one state. Deborah L. Rhode, *Virtue and the Law: The Good Moral Character Requirement in Occupational Licensing, Bar Regulation, and Immigration Proceedings*, 43 LAW & SOC. INQUIRY 1027, 1028 (2018).

CHAPTER 2

1. Richard L. Abel, *Lawyer Self-Regulation and the Public Interest: A Reflection*, 20 LEGAL ETHICS 115, 115 (2017) (citation omitted).

2. Roscoe Pound, *Legal Profession in America*, 19 NOTRE DAME L. REV. 334, 334–35 (1944).

3. ALFRED Z. REED, TRAINING FOR THE PUBLIC PROFESSION OF THE LAW: HISTORICAL DEVELOPMENT AND PRINCIPAL CONTEMPORARY PROBLEMS IN THE UNITED STATES WITH SOME ACCOUNT OF CONDITIONS IN ENGLAND AND CANADA (Carnegie Foundation for the Advancement of Teaching, Bulletin #15) 36 (1921); ROBERT STEVENS, LAW SCHOOL: LEGAL EDUCATION IN AMERICA FROM THE 1850S TO THE 1980S 111 n. 40 (1983) (citing to REED, *supra*).

4. STEVENS, *supra* note 3, at 21 (referencing Blackstone's lectures at Oxford in the 1700s).

5. State Bar of California, *California Bar Examination: Information and History* (undated) at 3.

6. Pound, *supra* note 2, at 339.

7. *Id.*

8. REED, *supra* note 3, at 81–83; STEVENS, *supra* note 3, at 111–12 (citing to REED).

9. STEVENS, *supra* note 3, at 7.

10. Walter Gellhorn, *The Abuse of Occupational Licensing*, 44 U. CHI. L. REV. 6, 8 (1976) (citing to LAWRENCE FRIEDMAN, A HISTORY OF AMERICAN LAW 525 (1973)).

11. Robert M. Jarvis, *An Anecdotal History of the Bar Exam*, 9 GEO. J. OF LEG. ETHICS 359, 377 (1996).

12. STEVENS, *supra* note 3, at 18 (citation omitted). Indiana's open admission provision was repealed by popular vote in 1932. Indiana was the only state whose open attorney admissions survived into the twentieth century. *Id.*

13. REED, *supra* note 3, at 90; STEVENS, *supra* note 3, at 9 (citing REED).

14. FREDERICK HOXIE, THIS INDIAN COUNTRY: AMERICAN INDIAN ACTIVISTS AND THE PLACE THEY MADE 50 (2013). Tribal courts maintain their own systems of licensure, which today are more likely than states to permit appearances by lay advocates. Lauren van Schilfgaarde, *Indigenizing Professional Responsibility: The Role of Ethics in Tribal Courts*, JUDGES J. (May 13, 2020) (n. 27 and accompanying text), https://www.americanbar.org/groups/judicial/publications/judges_journal/2020/spring/indigenizing-professional-responsibility-role-ethics-tribal-courts/

15. JEROLD S. AUERBACH, UNEQUAL JUSTICE: LAWYERS AND SOCIAL CHANGE IN MODERN AMERICA 19 (1976). "Ethnic homogeneity had been one of the salient characteristics of the legal profession during most of the nineteenth century." *Id.*

16. STEVENS, *supra* note 3, at 9–10.

17. *Id.* at 19.

18. Kenneth S. Tollett, *Black Lawyers, Their Education, and the Black Community*, 17 HOW. L. J. 326, 330 (1972) (citing to P. Stolz, *Clinical Experience in American Legal Education: Why Has It Failed?* in CLINICAL EDUCATION AND THE LAW SCHOOL OF THE FUTURE at 59, 62 (1970)).

19. *See* Deborah L. Rhode, *Moral Character as a Professional Credential*, 94 YALE L.J. 491, 496 (1985).

20. STEVENS, *supra* note 3, at 25.

21. Bobbi Jo Boyd, *Do It in the Sunshine: A Comparative Analysis of Rulemaking Procedures and Transparency Practices of Lawyer-Licensing Entities*, 70 ARK. L. REV. 609, 616–18 (2017).

22. Jarvis, *supra* note 11, at 374.

23. *Id.*

24. Len Tang Smith, *Abraham Lincoln as a Bar Examiner*, 37 BAR EXAM'R 51 (1982).

25. STEVENS, *supra* note 3, at 32.

26. *Id.* at 32–33.

27. Paul Finkelman, *Not Only the Judges' Robes Were Black: African-American Lawyers as Social Engineers*, 47 STAN. L. REV. 161, 201 (1994) (citing to J. CLAY SMITH JR., EMANCIPATION: THE MAKING OF THE BLACK LAWYER, 1844–1944, at 152 (1993) [hereinafter EMANCIPATION]).

28. J. Clay Smith Jr., *Justice and Jurisprudence and the Black Lawyer*, 69 NOTRE DAME L. REV. 1077, 1077–78 (1993) (citing to EMANCIPATION, *supra* note 27, at 93; Tollett, *supra* note 18, at 329).

29. *See* Finkelman, *supra* note 27, at 175 (citing to JAMES OLIVER HORTON & LOIS E. HORTON, BLACK BOSTONIANS 56 (1979)); Tollett, *supra* note 18, at 329 (describing Morris as having been admitted in either 1843 or 1850 and having participated in first separate but equal litigation in 1850).

30. Finkelman, *supra* note 27, at 173; *but see* Tollett, *supra* note 18, at 328 (describing Draper as leaving for Liberia after being admitted to the Baltimore bar).

31. Finkelman, *supra* note 27, at 201 (citing EMANCIPATION, *supra* note 27, at 279, quoting JAMES WELDON JOHNSON, ALONG THIS WAY 141 (1933)). Johnson passed and joined the Florida bar. *Id.*

32. BARBARA BABCOCK, WOMAN LAWYER: THE TRIALS OF CLARA FOLTZ 31 (2011) (citations omitted).

33. *Id.* (citations omitted).

34. REBELS IN LAW: VOICES IN HISTORY OF BLACK WOMEN LAWYERS 283 (J. Clay Smith Jr., ed. 1998).

35. Hong Yen Chang was posthumously granted admission in 2015. *See* Maura Dolan, *Chinese Immigrant, Denied Law License in 1890, Gets One Posthumously*, L.A. TIMES (March 16, 2015).

36. STEVENS, *supra* note 3, at 8 (quoting *An Address to Law Students*, 1 ALBANY L. J. 165 (March 5, 1870)).

37. STEVENS, *supra* note 3, at 94.

38. *Id.*

39. *Id.* at 173.

40. *Id.* at 25–26.

41. REED, *supra* note 3, at 101 n.3; Jarvis, *supra* note 11, at 374 (citing to REED). The practice was revived in 1876 by the Suffolk County Board in Massachusetts. *Id.*

42. *Id.* at 374 (citations omitted).

43. *Id.* at 101 n.3; Jarvis, *supra* note 11, at 373 (citing to REED).

44. Will Shafroth, *Bar Examiners and Examinees*, Preface to 1 BAR EXAM'R 1, 3–6 (1931) (appearing in the bound edition) (text and chart noting prevalence of written exams with continuing presence of oral exams).

45. STEVENS, *supra* note 3, at 94.

46. *Id.* at 44 (referencing *How Shall Our Bar Exams Be Conducted?*, 3 WESTERN RESERVE L. J. 129, 133 (1897)).

47. Leon Green, *Why Bar Examinations?*, 33 IL. L. REV. 908, 911 (1938–39).

48. STEVENS, *supra* note 3, at 25–26; Jarvis, *supra* note 11, at 374 (quoting STEVENS).

49. REED, *supra* note 3, at 100–03; Jarvis, *supra* note 11, at 375 (quoting REED). The ABA recommended that states create boards of bar examiners in the 1880s, joined by the AALS at the turn of the century. CORINNE LATHROP GILB, HIDDEN HIERARCHIES: THE PROFESSIONS AND GOVERNMENT 63 (1966).

50. GILB, *supra* note 49, at 63; STEVENS, *supra* note 3, at 95 (citing GILB, *supra* note 49).

51. STEVENS, *supra* note 3, at 23 (citing GILB, *supra* note 49).

52. *Id.* at 49.

53. REED, *supra* note 3, at 48–53; STEVENS, *supra* note 3, at 26–27; Jarvis, *supra* note 11 at 369 (citing REED).

54. Olufunmilayo B. Arewa, Andress P. Morriss, & William D. Henderson, *Enduring Hierarchies in American Legal Education*, 89 IND. L. J. 941, 946 (2014) (citing *Report of the Committee on Legal Education*, 14 ANN. REP. ABA 301, 318 (1891)).

55. REED, *supra* note 3, at 265–66. Diploma privilege in this era had many permutations. Starting in 1859, Albany and then Columbia and NYU obtained legislation that made their faculty the bar examiners, who then used their own final exams for licensure. *Id.* at 251. Not having any local law schools to support, before 1870 the Oregon Supreme Court granted diploma privilege to graduates of any law school with the diploma privilege in its home state. *Id.* at 253. Conversely, the Cincinnati YMCA Night Law School conferred its degree only when the graduate had been admitted to practice in his home jurisdiction. *Id.* at 251 n. 3.

56. Arewa et al., *supra* note 54, at 947 (citing ASSOCIATION OF AMERICAN LAW SCHOOLS, A BIT OF HISTORY: REPORT OF AALS LONG RANGE PLANNING COMMITTEE (1989), reprinted in 2 THE HISTORY OF LEGAL EDUCATION IN THE U.S.: COMMENTARIES AND PRIMARY SOURCES 1169, 1170).

57. STEVENS, *supra* note 3, at 34 n.57.

58. *Id.* at 57.

59. *See* Beverly I. Moran, *The Wisconsin Diploma Privilege: Try It, You'll Like It*, 2000 WIS. L. REV. 645 (2000). The ABA's adamant campaign against the diploma privilege showed up again in 2020, when some jurisdictions considered emergency diploma privilege because the COVID-19 pandemic made proceeding in the traditional way impossible. *See* Stephanie Francis Ward, *What Alternatives for the July Bar Exam Are Being Considered in Light of COVID-19?*, ABA J. (March 23, 2020) (the then-managing director of accreditation and legal education noted that "passing a bar examination is an important requirement for becoming a fully licensed lawyer"), https://www.abajournal.com/news/article/in-light-of-the-coronavirus-crisis-working-paper-suggests-alternatives-to-the-july-bar-exam

60. *See* STEVENS, *supra* note 3, at 94–95.

61. *Id.* at 32. "Although not well chronicled, clerkship in law offices was already [by 1897] in decline." *Id.*

62. *Id.* at 22 (quoting Albany critic in late 1800s).

63. *Id.* at 25.

64. *Id.* at 38 (citation omitted).

65. *Id.* at 38.

66. *Id.* at 37 (quoting 4 ABA REPORTS 287 (1881)).

67. *Id.* at 134 (citing AUERBACH, *supra* note 15, at 82–83).

68. *See* Lynn M. LoPucki, *Dawn of the Discipline-Based Law Faculty*, 65 J. LEGAL EDUC. 506, 508 (2016) (finding increased hiring of PhDs who are "decreasingly likely to have legal experience"); Justin McCrary, Joy Milligan, & James Phillips, *The Ph.D. Rises in American Law Schools, 1960–2011: What Does It Mean for Legal Education*, 65 J. LEGAL EDUC. 543, 548–49, 563 (2016) (describing strategy of some law schools to hire PhDs and noting that traditional credentials do not include practice expertise); Sarah Lawsky, *Lawsky Entry Level Hiring Report 2021*, PRAWFSBLAWG (May 18, 2021) (over 40% of new tenure-track law professor hires have had PhDs each of the last five years), https://prawfsblawg.blogs.com/prawfsblawg/2021/05/lawsky-entry-level-hiring-report-2021.html

69. STEVENS, *supra* note 3, at 13 (citing CHARLES WARREN, A HISTORY OF THE AMERICAN BAR 2, 396 (1911)).

70. Robert Stevens, *The Nature of a Learned Profession*, 34 J. LEGAL EDUC. 577, 580 (1984).

CHAPTER 3

1. RICHARD L. ABEL, AMERICAN LAWYERS 71 (1989) ("American Lawyers have been extraordinarily successful in constructing and raising entry barriers during the last century and a half").

2. MAGALI SARFATTI LARSON, THE RISE OF PROFESSIONALISM: A SOCIOLOGICAL ANALYSIS 113 (1977). "The ultimate success of professionalization as a collective assertion of status . . . was itself attendant on the emergence and consolidation of national institutions and national frames of reference." *Id.*

3. JEROLD S. AUERBACH, UNEQUAL JUSTICE: LAWYERS AND SOCIAL CHANGE IN MODERN AMERICA 22 (1976) (quoting Robert Stevens, *Aging Mistress: The Law School in America*, 2 CHANGE IN HIGHER EDUCATION 32, 32 (1970)).

4. Olufunmilayo B. Arewa, Andress P. Morriss, & William D. Henderson, *Enduring Hierarchies in American Legal Education*, 89 IND. L. J. 941, 946 (2014) (citing Barrie Thorne, *Professional Education in Law, in* EDUCATION FOR THE PROFESSIONS OF MEDICINE, LAW, THEOLOGY, AND SOCIAL WELFARE 101, 105 (1973)).

5. AUERBACH, *supra* note 3, at 29.

6. *Id.*

7. Arewa et al., *supra* note 4, at 952.

8. *See, e.g.,* AUERBACH, *supra* note 3, at 24 (describing the Cravath method, including the desire to "make him to order" and the credentialed path (fancy law school and law review), "warmth and force of personality" and "physical stamina").

9. ROBERT STEVENS, LAW SCHOOL: LEGAL EDUCATION IN AMERICA FROM THE 1850S TO THE 1980S 119–20 (1983).

10. DEBORAH L. RHODE, IN THE INTERESTS OF JUSTICE: REFORMING THE LEGAL PROFESSION 150 (2000). "For most of this nation's history, bar admission standards were notably permissive. Until the twentieth century, law school was not required, apprenticeships were often undemanding, and entrance exams were seldom rigorous." *Id.*

11. *The Standard Rules for Admission to the Bar: As Adopted by the Section on Legal Education and Recommended to the American Bar Association,* 4 AMER. L. SCH. REV. 201 (1915–22). Richard Abel found that law joined other professions in using examinations as the "dominant entry barrier in the twentieth century." Richard L. Abel, *Essay: Lawyer self-regulation and the public interest: a reflection,* 20 LEGAL ETHICS 115, 115 (2017) (referencing Weber on professional entry barriers). According to Abel, the "bar examination did not become a significant entry barrier until half a century after it was introduced." ABEL, *supra* note 1, at 72.

12. Dorothy E. Finnegan, *Raising and Leveling the Bar: Standards, Access, and the YMCA Evening Law Schools,* 1890–1940, 55 J. LEGAL EDUC. 208, 209 (2005).

13. STEVENS, *supra* note 9, at 125–26.

14. *Id.* at 176 (describing xenophobia, economic concerns, and genuine concern for the public interest as carrying the day in ABA efforts to keep ratcheting up standards in the 20s).

15. AUERBACH, *supra* note 3, at 108. For example, the Illinois Board of Bar Examiners urged higher standards after reporting in 1922 that "a significantly higher proportion of successful applicants to the bar was foreign born." *Id.*

16. STEVENS, *supra* note 9, at 115.

17. Abel, *supra* note 11, at 116. "Professional associations progressively lengthened educational requirements." *Id.*

18. STEVENS, *supra* note 9, at 157; *accord* Arewa et al., *supra* note 4, at 999 (twelve law schools had adopted the case method in 1902; just over thirty in 1907).

19. *See* Donna Fossum, *Law School Accreditation Standards and the Structure of American Legal Education,* 3 A.B.F. RESEARCH J. 515, 515 n. 3 (1978); Standards Archives—History, ABA, https://www.americanbar.org/groups/legal_education /resources/standards/standards_archives/#:~:text=Standards%22Archives-,His tory,that%20met%20the%20ABA%20Standards

20. ALFRED Z. REED, REVIEW OF LEGAL EDUCATION IN THE UNITED STATES AND CANADA FOR THE YEARS 1926 AND 1927, at 6 (1928).

21. *See* STEVENS, *supra* note 9, at 177; Arthur Karcher, *The Continuing Role of*

the NCBE in the Bar Admissions Process, 65 BAR EXAM'R 14 (1996) (giving date of 1931).

22. STEVENS, *supra* note 9, at 185 (citation omitted).

23. *Id.*

24. *Id.* (footnotes omitted).

25. *Id.* at 191 (quoting HICKS, YALE LAW SCHOOL, 1895–1915 at 45); *see also* AUERBACH, *supra* note 3, at 27. "The Anglo-Saxon Protestant retreat to corporate enclaves was facilitated by changing patterns of legal education, which enabled corporate firms to camouflage their prejudices under the cover of academic achievement." *Id.*

26. *See* Finnegan, *supra* note 12, at 233 (some part-time law schools failed because of the expense of ABA requirements for full-time faculty, libraries, and better facilities). Jerold Auerbach described the higher educational standards as "an instrument of professionalization and, simultaneously, professional purification." AUERBACH, *supra* note 3, at 94.

27. STEVENS, *supra* note 9, at 185.

28. *Id.* "Graduates of AALS schools might still pass, but it was just as likely that those from non-AALS schools could pass too." *Id.*

29. *Id.* at 186 (citing Douglas B. Maggs, *How the Common Objectives of Bar Examiners and Law Schools Can Be Achieved,* 13 OR. L. REV. 147, 147 (1934)).

30. *Id.* at 185 (citation omitted).

31. AUERBACH, *supra* note 3, at 126.

32. STEVENS, *supra* note 9, at 213. For a comprehensive history of how expensive accreditation standards and increasingly difficult bar exams were used to prevent the entry into the profession of Black lawyers, see George B. Shepherd, *No African-American Lawyers Allowed: The Inefficient Racism of the ABA's Accreditation of Law Schools,* 53 J. LEGAL EDUC. 103 (2003). For the efforts by the ABA to keep Black lawyers out of the organized bar, see JAMES WILLARD HURST, GROWTH OF AMERICAN LAW: THE LAW MAKERS 255 (1950).

33. AUERBACH, *supra* note 3, at 65–66 (citations omitted).

34. Paul Finkelman, *Not Only the Judge' Robes Were Black: African-American Lawyers as Social Engineers,* 47 STAN. L. REV. 161, 205 (1994) (citing J. CLAY SMITH JR., EMANCIPATION: THE MAKING OF THE BLACK LAWYER, 1844–1944, at 545).

35. Separate seating and sequential exam numbers for Black candidates was still practiced by bar examiners, at least in Philadelphia, as late as 1970. *See* Donald Janson, *Philadelphia Bar Sees Bias in Exam,* N.Y. TIMES (Dec. 22, 1970), https://www.nytimes.com/1970/12/22/archives/philadelphia-bar-sees-bias-in-exam-panel-says-state-test-only-weeds.html?searchResultPosition=6

36. AUERBACH, *supra* note 3, at 226.

37. For a discussion of NAACP equal protection challenges regarding access to law school, see Kenneth S. Tollett, *Black Lawyers, Their Education, and the Black Community,* 17 HOW. L.J. 326, 334–35 (1972).

38. Finkelman, *supra* note 34, at 200. "The American Bar Association, for example, under the guise of improving the standard of the profession, revamped its accreditation criteria in such a way that black law schools were unable to meet them and were pressured to close." *Id.* (citing SMITH, *supra* note 34, at 42); *see also* LAWRENCE FRIEDMAN, A HISTORY OF AMERICAN LAW 648–54 (2d ed. 1985) (describing the development of the ABA, its exclusionary practices and motivations, and the development of formal bar admission requirements); STEVENS, *supra* note 9, at 92–111 (same). George B. Shepherd wrote that access to the legal profession was in some ways worse in the early twenty-first century than eighty years before. "In contrast, in 1920 a place existed at law school for any black man, and at a much more affordable price." Shepherd, *supra* note 32, at 113.

39. Duke's law school, for example, was desegregated in 1961. https://exhibits .library.duke.edu/exhibits/show/desegregation/progress. For a description of the halting initiatives for racial desegregation by the AALS, see Michael H. Cardozo, *Racial Discrimination in Legal Education, 1950–1963*, 43 J. LEGAL EDUC. 79 (March 1993) (also noting that Richmond was in violation of the AALS nondiscrimination policy in 1962).

40. Tollett, *supra* note 37, at 346. The National Bar Association was founded in 1925 and by 1930 had only 331 members. AUERBACH, *supra* note 3, at 211.

41. STEVENS, *supra* note 9, at 205–06.

42. *Id.*; *see also* LARSON, *supra* note 2, at 210 (the link between licensing and increased educational requirements "connects the sale of professional labor power with the educational system—that is to say, with the principal legitimator of social inequality in advanced industrial capitalism").

43. Finkelman, *supra* note 34, at 200 ("In defending the requirement that all law students first complete a undergraduate degree, one New York lawyer declared it was 'absolutely necessary' that lawyers be 'able to read, write and talk the English language—not Bohemian, not Gaelic, not Yiddish, but English'" (citation omitted)).

44. Robert Stevens, *The Nature of a Learned Profession*, 34 J. LEGAL EDUC. 577, 583 (1984).

45. STEVENS, *supra* note 9, at 210 (quoting John G. Hervey, *The ABA's Survey of the Legal Profession*, as quoted in NICHOLSON, LAW SCHOOLS OF THE UNITED STATES 21).

46. Abel, *supra* note 11, at 116 (2017). "There is strong circumstantial evidence that professional associations in [England and the United States] manipulated the difficulty of exams to regulate supply." *Id.*

47. *Id.*

48. *Id.*

49. *See, e.g.,* Stillwell v. State Bar, 29 Cal.2d 119 (1946) (interpreting Bus. & Prof. Code §6060.5 that enabled law school graduates who served in the Armed Forces in WWII to become licensed without examination).

50. *See, e.g.,* Benjamin Hoorn Barton, *Why Do We Regulate Lawyers: An Economic Analysis of the Justifications for Entry and Conduct Regulation,* 33 ARIZ. ST. L.J. 429 (2001) (finding barriers to entry offer more protection to attorneys than to consumers); J. F. Barron, *Business and Professional Licensing: California, A Representative Example,* 18 STAN. L. REV. 640, 649–50, 653 (1966) (providing examples of industries making self-protective arguments for higher educational credentials, including embalmers who sought a two-year college requirement and a barber's test that was 20% anatomy (e.g., "What is the chemical composition of bones?")); *see also* Lawrence Friedman, *Freedom of Contract and Occupational Licensing 1890–1910: A Legal and Social Study,* 53 CALIF. L. REV. 487, 531 (1965) ("the lawyers could and did react in the usual professional pattern, by forming bar associations and through the licensing movement").

51. *See, e.g.,* Arewa et al, *supra* note 4, at 943 ("For better or worse, the quest for status is endemic to lawyers and law professors").

52. KARL N. LLEWELLYN, THE BRAMBLE BUSH: OUR LAW AND ITS STUDY 144–45 (1951, 1930).

53. *See, e.g.,* ARTHUR M. COHEN, THE SHAPING OF AMERICAN HIGHER EDUCATION: EMERGENCES AND GROWTH OF THE CONTEMPORARY SYSTEM 195 (1998).

54. *See* Arewa et al, *supra* note 4, at 941.

55. *See* NICHOLAS LEMANN, THE BIG TEST: THE SECRET HISTORY OF THE AMERICAN MERITOCRACY 29–34 (2000).

56. *See Mission & History,* LSAC, https://www.lsac.org/about/mission-history#:~:text=February%2028%2C%201948%3A%20Administering%20the,complete%20and%20contained%2010%20sections (last visited Jan. 5, 2021). The College Board became the Educational Testing Service just a few months before it offered the first LSAT. LEMANN, *supra* note 55, at 70.

57. *See* Arewa et al., *supra* note 4, at 941.

58. ABEL, *supra* note 1, at 151 (citing to Alfred B. Carlson & Charles E. Werts, *Relationships Among Law School Predictors, Law School Performance and Bar Examination Results,* 3 REPORTS OF LAW SCHOOL ADMISSIONS COUNCIL SPONSORED RESEARCH 211 (Princeton, LSAC) (1976)).

59. Robert J. Sternberg, *College Admissions: Beyond Conventional Testing,* CHANGE: THE MAGAZINE OF HIGHER LEARNING 6, 12 (Sept.– Oct. 2012).

60. *See* Arewa et al, *supra* note 4, at 941; WENDY ESPELUND & MICHAEL SAUDER, ENGINES OF ANXIETY: ACADEMIC RANKINGS, REPUTATION, AND ACCOUNTABILITY (2016) (describing how U.S. News rankings have shaped legal education).

61. *See, e.g.,* Robert J. Sternberg, *Reform Education: Teach Wisdom and Ethics,* 94 THE PHI DELTA KAPPAN 44 (2013) ("to an unknown extent, our society manufactures these correlations [between high test scores and high achievement] by allowing primarily those who test at high levels to have access to the highest-paying and most prestigious jobs").

62. Richard Delgado, *Rodrigo's Tenth Chronicle: Merit and Affirmative Action*, 83 GEO L.J. 1711, 1721 (1995) (citation omitted). More succinctly, "Merit is what the victors impose." *Id.*

63. R. Scott Baker, *The Paradoxes of Desegregation: Race, Class, and Education, 1935–1975*, 109 AMERICAN JOURNAL OF EDUCATION 320, 340 (2001).

64. *Florida ex Rel. Hawkins v. Board of Control*, 350 U.S. 413 (1956).

65. Baker, *supra* note 63, at 329 (citation omitted). The committee's "sole effort and intention was to devise ways and means of preventing or slowing down the integration of our public schools." *Id.*

66. *Id.*, citing to *New York Times* (March 17, 1956).

67. *See id.*; *Virgil D. Hawkins Story*, UF LAW, https://www.law.ufl.edu/areas-of-study/experiential-learning/clinics/virgil-d-hawkins-story (last visited Jan. 5, 2021).

68. Delgado, *supra* note 62, at 1723–24.

69. Baker, *supra* note 63, at 330.

70. *Id.* (citing to *Richardson v. McFadden* (1976)).

71. *Id.* at 331.

72. *Id.*

CHAPTER 4

1. Ernest Gellhorn, *The Law Schools and the Negro*, 1968 DUKE L. J. 1069, 1092 n. 84 (1968).

2. Donald Janson, *Philadelphia Bar See Bias in Exam*, N.Y. TIMES (Dec. 22, 1970) at 22; Iver Peterson, *Rise in Black Students Brings Disputes on Law School Recruiting*, N.Y. TIMES (April 7, 1974) at 48; JEROLD S. AUERBACH, UNEQUAL JUSTICE: LAWYERS AND SOCIAL CHANGE IN MODERN AMERICA 294 (1976) (citing these *New York Times* stories); Alex Poinsett, *The "Whys" Behind the Black Lawyer Shortage: Disproportionate Bar Exam Failure Rates Raise Suspicion of Racism*, EBONY (Dec. 1, 1974) at 95.

3. Janson, *supra* note 2, at 22. The study found that Pennsylvania had 1 Black lawyer for every 8,000 Black citizens and 1 non-Black lawyer for every 800 non-Black citizens. *Id.*

4. Peterson, *supra* note 2, at 48.

5. *Id.*

6. R. Scott Baker, *The Paradoxes of Desegregation: Race, Class, and Education, 1935–1975*, 109 AMERICAN JOURNAL OF EDUCATION 320, 331 (citing *Richardson v. McFadden* (1976), trial transcript, vol. 1, p. 10).

7. Peterson, *supra* note 2, at 48.

8. AUERBACH, *supra* note 2, at 19.

9. *Id.*

10. *Id.*

11. Peterson, *supra* note 2, at 48.

12. ALFRED ZANTZINGER REED, TRAINING FOR THE PUBLIC PROFESSION OF THE LAW: HISTORICAL DEVELOPMENT AND PRINCIPAL CONTEMPORARY PROBLEMS IN THE UNITED STATES WITH SOME ACCOUNT OF CONDITIONS IN ENGLAND AND CANADA 411 (Carnegie Foundation for the Advancement of Teaching, Bulletin #15) (1921) (noting that one of Langdell's innovations was to teach "national" law instead of "local or severely practical law").

13. *Id.* at 255 (Harvard graduates during Langdell's tenure failed county board's bar exams).

14. Susan M. Case, *Back to Basic Principles: Validity and Reliability,* 75 BAR EXAM'R 23, 23 (Aug. 2006).

15. For a detailed description of the MBE scaling and equating processes, see Deborah J. Merritt, Lowell L. Hargens, & Barbara F. Reskin, *Raising the Bar: A Social Science Critique of Recent Increase to Passing Scores on the Bar Exam,* 69 U. CIN. L. REV. 929, 932–35 (2001).

16. For explanations of bar exam scaling written for bar examiners, see Susan M. Case, *Frequently Asked Questions About Scaling Written Scores to the MBE,* 75 BAR EXAM'R 41 (Nov. 2006); and Susan M. Case, *Demystifying Scaling to the MBE: How'd You Do That?,* 74 BAR EXAM'R 45–46 (May 2005).

17. COMPREHENSIVE GUIDE TO BAR ADMISSIONS, NCBE AND ABA SECTION OF LEGAL EDUCATION AND ADMISSIONS TO THE BAR 30–31 (2021).

18. Richard L. Abel, *Essay: Lawyer Self-Regulation and the Public Interest: A Reflection,* 20 LEGAL ETHICS 115, 115 (2017) ("Bar exams "have an unproven—and arguably dubious—relationship to the knowledge lawyers actually utilize in their daily practice (in the language of psychologists: they have never been validated)").

19. *See* GILLIAN K. HADFIELD, RULES FOR A FLAT WORLD: WHY HUMANS INVENTED LAW AND HOW TO REINVENT IT FOR A COMPLEX GLOBAL ECONOMY 114–21 (2017).

20. *See, e.g.,* DEBORAH L. RHODE & GEOFFREY C. HAZARD JR., PROFESSIONAL RESPONSIBILITY AND REGULATION (2002) (noting claims that "the skills existing exams measure do not adequately predict performance as a lawyer" (at 223) and that the "inadequate link between exam and job performance is of special concern because minority applicants have disproportionately low passage rates" (at 224, quoting DEBORAH L. RHODE, IN THE INTERESTS OF JUSTICE: REFORMING THE LEGAL PROFESSION 151 (2000)).

21. For further depth, see Joan W. Howarth, *The Professional Responsibility Case for Valid and Nondiscriminatory Bar Exams,* 33 GEO. J. LEG. ETHICS 931 (2020); Cecil J. Hunt II, *Guests in Another's House: An Analysis of Racially Disparate Bar Performance,* 23 FLA. ST. U. L. REV. 721, 733–50 (1996); Maurice Emsellem & Richard S. Barrett, *The Bar Examination Debate (Continued),* 16 T. MARSHALL L. REV. 531 (1991).

22. 517 F.2d 1089 (5th Cir. 1975).

23. *Id.* at 1092.

24. *Id.*

25. *Id.* at 1096.

26. *Id.*

27. *Id.* The dissenting judge found that the dismissal on summary judgment was inappropriate because the question of racial motivation was inherently fact-bound and that "reference to the good faith judgment of the bar examiners" should not be sufficient when "the selection of cut-off scores" may be arbitrary and is not subject to review." 517 F.2d 1089, 1105–06 (Adam, J., dissenting). The good faith of bar examiners is precisely what supports bar exam cut scores in many jurisdictions today. *See, e.g.,* STATE BAR OF CALIFORNIA, FINAL REPORT ON THE 2017 CALIFORNIA BAR EXAM STUDIES (2017), at 45–46, http://www.calbar.ca.gov/Portals/0/documents/reports/2017-Final-Bar-Exam-Report.pdf

28. 533 F.2d 942 (5th Cir. 1976). In an earlier stage of the case, the Fifth Circuit had upheld denial of the plaintiffs' motion to recuse the trial judge. *See Parrish v. Bd. of Com'rs of St. B. of Alabama,* 524 F.2d 98 (1975). The motion to recuse rested on the facts that two years previously the trial judge had served as the president of the Montgomery Bar Association when its bylaws explicitly excluded African Americans from membership. The Fifth Circuit rejected the bar association allegation as "essentially an allegation based on the judge's background [that] states no specific facts that would suggest he would be anything but impartial" and that the "claim of bias is general or impersonal at best." 524 F.2d at 101.

29. 533 F.2d at 944.

30. *Id.* at 947.

31. *Id.* at 949.

32. *Id.* at 946–47.

33. The bar examiners asserted the circular argument that the documentation was irrelevant because no evidence had contradicted their own "positive affirmation . . . that they were not guilty of any improper conduct." *Id.* at 947.

34. *Richardson v. McFadden,* 540 F.2d 744 (4th Cir. 1976), *on reh'g,* 563 F.2d 1130 (4th Cir. 1977).

35. *Richardson,* 540 F.2d at 746–48 (citation omitted).

36. *See id.* at 747.

37. *Id.* (parenthetical in original).

38. *Id.* at 746. For a history of the law school at South Carolina State College, see Alfred D. Moore III, *Turning the Tide of Segregation: The Legacy of the Law School at the South Carolina State College,* JOURNAL OF BLACKS IN HIGHER EDUCATION (Sept. 7, 2017), https://perma.cc/7QXZ-MAFV

39. *Richardson,* 540 F.2d at 747.

40. *Id.* at 747–48.

41. *Id.* at 749.

42. *Id.*

43. *Id.*

44. *Id.*

45. *Id.*

46. *Id.* at 751.

47. *Id.*

48. *Id.* at 751–52.

49. *Id.* at 751.

50. *Id.* at 751–52.

51. Instead, the court affirmed the district court that had denied relief, differing on whether the federal court lacked subject-matter jurisdiction (deferring to the Supreme Court of South Carolina's authority over bar admission) or whether the claim had not been established. *Richardson v. McFadden*, 563 F.2d 1130, 1130–32 (4th Cir. 1977).

52. *Id.* at 1132 (emphasis added).

53. *See also Woodard v. Virginia Bd. of B. Exam'rs*, 598 F.2d 1345 (4th Cir. 1979) (per curiam opinion holding that Title VII does not apply to bar exams); *Pettit v. Ginerich*, 582 F.2d 869 (4th Cir. 1978) (per curiam decision rejecting claims of seven African American applicants to the bar in Maryland based on *Richardson*; *Delgado v. McTighe*, 522 F. Supp. 886 (E.D. Pa. 1981) (upholding Pennsylvania bar exams as "neutral on their face and rationally serv[ing] the purpose for which they have been designed" (*id.* at 894–95) and noting that *Richardson* upheld bar exam essay questions with no model answer and multiple grading methods (*id.* at 897).

54. *See* Howarth, *supra* note 21.

CHAPTER 5

1. *See* CLIFFORD WINSTON, DAVID BURK, & JIA YAN, TROUBLE AT THE BAR: AN ECONOMICS PERSPECTIVE OF THE LEGAL PROFESSION AND THE CASE FOR FUNDAMENTAL REFORM 30 (2021) (pointing out that admission to and graduation from law school is a higher barrier than bar passage because ultimate bar passage after multiple tries is high); *but see* Mitchel L. Winick, Victor D. Quintanilla, Sam Erman, Christina Chong-Nakatsuchi, & Michael Frisby, *Examining the California Cut Score: An Empirical Analysis of Minimum Competency, Public Protection, Disparate Impact, and National Standards* (Oct. 15, 2020) (between 2008 and 2019, 24.2% of bar-takers never passed (at 13); of these never-passers, "49 percent were minorities (10% Black, 25.5% Asian, and 13.5% Hispanic/Latinx) while only 46 percent were Whites" (at 14)), https://papers.ssrn.com/sol3/papers.cfm?abstract_id=3707812

2. *See* Phoebe A. Haddon & Deborah W. Post, *The Misuse and Abuse of the LSAT: Making the Case for Alternative Evaluative Methods and a Redefinition of*

Merit, 80 ST. JOHNS L. REV. 41, 45–48 (2006).

3. *See, e.g.,* Aaron N. Taylor, *Robin Hood, in Reverse: How Law School Scholarships Compound Inequality,* 47 J. L. & EDUC. 41 (2018); AARON N. TAYLOR & CHAD CHRISTENSEN, LAW SCHOOL SCHOLARSHIP POLICIES: ENGINES OF INEQUITY (Feb. 2017) (Law School Survey of Student Engagement Annual Results 2016), http://lssse.indiana.edu/annual-results/

4. Aaron N. Taylor, *The Marginalization of Black Aspiring Lawyers,* 13 FIU L. REV. 489, 496 (2019) ("In 2016–17, 49 percent of Black law school applicants received no offers of admission").

5. *Id.*; MEERA E. DEO, CHAD CHRISTENSEN, & JACQUELINE PETZOLD, THE CHANGING LANDSCAPE OF LEGAL EDUCATION: A 15-YEAR LSSSE RETROSPECTIVE 10–11 (Dec. 2020) (LSSSE Spl. Rep.).

6. *Cf.* WINSTON ET AL., *supra* note 1, at 182 ("Many capable individuals are either unwilling or unable to spend three years in law school and graduate with debts that can easily exceed $150,000, not to mention the opportunity cost of not earning income during that period").

7. ABA SECTION OF LEGAL EDUCATION AND ADMISSIONS TO THE BAR, STANDARDS OF THE ABA FOR LEGAL EDUCATION: FACTORS BEARING ON THE APPROVAL OF LAW SCHOOLS 14 (1969).

8. ABA SECTION OF LEGAL EDUCATION AND ADMISSIONS TO THE BAR, ABA STANDARDS AND RULES OF PROCEDURE, Standard 302(b) (1973) [hereinafter ABA STANDARDS].

9. From 1973 through 2003–2004, this prohibition remained in ABA Standard 302, at some point becoming 302(f). ABA STANDARDS (2003–2004).

10. In 2005, ABA Standard 302 was modified to remove 302(f), but Interpretation 302–7 was adopted: "If a law school grants academic credit for a bar examination preparation course, such credit may not be counted toward the minimum requirements for graduation established in Standard 304. A law school may not require successful completion of a bar examination preparation course as a condition of graduation." ABA STANDARDS, Standard 302 (2005–2006).

11. ABA STANDARDS, Standard 302 (2008–2009).

12. Standard 301 has required that law schools "maintain an educational program that prepares its students for admission to the bar, and effective and responsible participation in the legal profession." Interpretation 301–6 was added in 2008, providing a complicated formula to measure bar passage that added teeth to the bar admission aspect of Standard 301 for the first time. Interpretation 301–6 was converted to a new Standard 316 in 2014. For a discussion of the purpose and earlier versions of Standard 316, see Gregory G. Murphy, *Revised Bar Passage Standard 316: Evolution and Key Points,* 88 BAR EXAM'R 21 (Summer 2019).

13. For information on law school academic support professors, see ASSOCIATION OF ACADEMIC SUPPORT EDUCATORS, https://associationofacademicsuppor

teducators.org/

14. Stephanie Francis Ward, *ABA House of Delegates Rejects Changes to the Bar Passage Standard for Law Schools,* ABA J. (Jan. 28, 2019), https://www.abajournal .com/news/article/resolution-105-fails

15. Stephanie Francis Ward, *10 Law Schools Are Out of Compliance with Bar Passage Standard, ABA Legal Ed Section Says,* ABA J. (May 28, 2020), https://www .abajournal.com/news/article/legal-ed-posts-public-notice-for-schools-out-of -compliance-with-bar-passage-standard

16. ABA STANDARDS, Standard 205 (2021–22).

17. By 1996 bar review was a $50 million industry annually, dominated by BARBRI. Robert M. Jarvis, *An Anecdotal History of the Bar Exam,* 9 GEO. J. OF LEGAL ETHICS 359, 370 (1996).

18. *BARBRI, a Portfolio Company of Leeds Equity Partners, Completes Acquisition of the Center for Legal Studies,* PR NEWSWIRE (June 13, 2019), https://www .prnewswire.com/news-releases/barbri-a-portfolio-company-of-leeds-equity -partners-completes-acquisition-of-the-center-for-legal-studies-300867410.html

19. *See About BARBRI Legal Ed,* BARBRI, https://legaled.barbri.com/about-us/ (last visited March 31, 2022).

20. *See BARBRI Global Acquires West Academic,* MARKETS INSIDER (Jan. 4, 2022), https://markets.businessinsider.com/news/stocks/barbri-global-acquires -west-academic-1031076476?op=1

21. James E. Brenner, *A Standard Bar Examination,* 9 AM. L. SCH. REV. 1205 (1938–1942) (speech of NCBE secretary from 1941 urging a uniform bar exam as better quality and more efficient).

22. *Jurisdictions That Have Adopted the UBE,* NCBE, https://www.ncbex.org/ exams/ube/ (last visited Jan. 11, 2022).

23. For arguments that bar exams should emphasize methods, not knowledge, see Joan W. Howarth, *What Law Must Lawyers Know?,* 19 CONN. PUB. INT. L.J. 1 (2019).

24. *See, e.g., Admission Eligibility Requirements for Exam Applicants,* MISSOURI BOARD OF BAR EXAMINERS (requiring passage of Missouri Educational Component Test on Missouri law), https://www.mble.org/admission-eligibility -requirements

25. *See Snapshot of NextGen Bar Exam,* NCBE: NEXTGEN BAR EXAM OF THE FUTURE, https://nextgenbarexam.ncbex.org/ (last visited Jan. 1, 2022).

26. *See* Claudia Angelos, Sara J. Berman, Mary Lu Bilek, Carol L. Chomsky, Andrea A. Curcio, Marsha Griggs, Joan W. Howarth, Eileen Kaufman, Deborah J. Merritt, Patricia E. Salkin, & Judith W. Wegner, *The Bar Exam and the COVID-19 Pandemic: The Need for Immediate Action* (March 22, 2020), https://ssrn.com/ abstract=3559060

27. For comprehensive analyses of the bar exam problems of 2020, see Marsha

Griggs, *An Epic Fail*, 64 HOWARD L. REV. 1 (2020); Leslie C. Levin, *The Politics of Bar Admission: Lessons from the Pandemic* 50 HOFSTRA L. REV. 81 (2021).

28. *July 2020 MBE Mean Score Increases*, NCBE (Sept. 1, 2020), https://www.ncbex.org/news/july-2020-mbe-mean-score-increases/

29. Karen Sloan, *Diploma Privilege Leader: "This is a Good Moment to Try Something New*," LAW.COM (Aug. 19, 2020), https://www.law.com/2020/08/19/diploma-privilege-leader-this-is-a-good-moment-to-try-something-new/?slreturn=20210006141153

30. *July 2020 Bar Exam Status by Jurisdiction*, NCBE, https://www.ncbex.org/ncbe-covid-19-updates/july-2020-bar-exam-jurisdiction-information/ (last visited Oct. 11, 2020).

31. *Order Approving Modified July 2020 Bar Examination*, Exhibit A at 2, In re Matter of the July 2020 Nevada State Bar Examination, No. ADKT 0558 (May 20, 2020), https://www.ncbex.org/pdfviewer/?file=%2Fdmsdocument%2F252

32. *2020 Bar Exam Process Comes to an End: Approximately 38,000 Applicants Took Bar Exam in July, September, or October*, NCBE (Oct. 7, 2020), https://www.ncbex.org/news/2020-bar-exam-process-comes-to-an-end-approximately-38000-applicants-took-bar-exam-in-july-september-or-october/

33. Twitter hashtag led by Vanderbilt law professor Caitlin Moon, @inspiredcat, and others.

34. For an explanation of the benefits of proving competence through supervised practice instead of predicting it with a standardized test, see Claudia Angelos, Mary Lu Bilek, Carol L. Chomsky, Andrea A. Curcio, Marsha Griggs, Joan W. Howarth, Eileen Kaufman, Deborah Jones Merritt, Patricia E. Salkin, & Judith Welch Wegner, *Licensing Lawyers in a Pandemic: Proving Competence*, HARV. L. REV. BLOG (April 7, 2020), https://blog.harvardlawreview.org/licensing-lawyers-in-a-pandemic-proving-competence/

35. Donna Saadati-Soto, Pilar Margarita Hernández Escontrías, Alyssa Leader, & Emily Croucher, *Why This Pandemic Is a Good Time to Stop Forcing Prospective Lawyers to Take Bar Exams*, WASH. POST (July 13, 2020), https://www.washingtonpost.com/education/2020/07/13/why-this-pandemic-is-good-time-stop-forcing-prospective-lawyers-take-bar-exams/

36. Leaders of DiplomaPrivilege4All (@DiplomaPriv4All) have established the National Association for Equity in the Legal Profession, a "nonprofit organization to advocate for racial, gender, economic, and disability justice in the legal profession." @NAE4ELP, https://twitter.com/na4elp

37. For a compilation of commentaries and state-by-state advocacy and responses, see *Coming Together to Fight a Pandemic*, THE COLLABORATORY, https://barcovid19.org/ (last visited Oct. 11, 2020).

38. See Karen Sloan, *Diploma Privilege Leader: "This Is a Good Moment to Try Something New*," LAW.COM (Aug. 19, 2020), https://www.law.com/2020/08/19/

diploma-privilege-leader-this-is-a-good-moment-to-try-something-new/

39. *See, e.g.,* Brian L. Frye, *NCBE Is a Joke, Give "Judge Judy" the Boot,* THE JURIST (Aug. 5, 2020), https://www.jurist.org/commentary/2020/08/brian-frye -ncbe-judith-gundersen/; Joe Patrice, *Like COVID-19, Online Bar Exam Is a Disaster and Was Entirely Preventable,* ABOVE THE LAW (Oct. 6, 2020), https:// abovethelaw.com/2020/10/like-covid-19-online-bar-exam-is-a-disaster-and-was -entirely-preventable/; Sam Skolnik, *Examsoft "Deeply Sorry" for Glitches That Crashed Bar Exams,* BLOOMBERG LAW (Aug. 17, 2021), https://news.bloomberglaw .com/business-and-practice/examsoft-deeply-sorry-for-malfunctions-that -crashed-bar-exams

40. *See, e.g.,* Joe Patrice, *It's Time for a Serious Inquiry into State Bar Examiner Behavior,* ABOVE THE LAW (Oct. 21, 2020), https://abovethelaw.com/2020/10 /its-time-for-a-serious-inquiry-into-state-bar-examiner-behavior/; Joe Patrice, *NCBE Prez Issues Threat to Tie Up Licenses of Bar Exam Critics,* ABOVE THE LAW (Aug. 6, 2020), https://abovethelaw.com/2020/08/ncbe-prez-issues-threat-to-tie -up-licenses-of-bar-exam-critics/

41. *Order for Temporary Amendments to Bar Admission Procedures During Covid-19 Outbreak,* SUPREME COURT OF UTAH, https://www.ncbex.org/pdfviewer /?file=%2Fdmsdocument%2F240

42. *See* Zane Sparling, *Oregon Supreme Court Supports Alternative to Bar Exam Requirement, Adding Options for New Lawyer,* THE OREGONIAN/OREGON-LIVE (Jan. 12, 2022), https://www.oregonlive.com/news/2022/01/oregon-supreme -court-approves-dropping-bar-exam-requirement-adding-options-for-new -lawyers.html; *OSB Task Force,* OREGON STATE BAR, https://taskforces.osbar.org/ (last visited Jan. 12, 2022).

43. *See Blue Ribbon Commission on the Future of the Bar Exam,* STATE BAR OF CALIFORNIA, http://www.calbar.ca.gov/About-Us/Who-We-Are/Committees/ Blue-Ribbon-Commission (last visited Oct. 16, 2021).

CHAPTER 6

1. *See, e.g.,* Brian E. Clauser, Melissa J. Margolis, & Susan M. Case, *Testing for Licensure and Certification in the Professions, in* EDUCATIONAL MEASUREMENT 720 (Robert L. Brennan ed., 4th ed. 2006).

2. WILLIAM SULLIVAN, ANNE COLBY, JUDITH WELCH WEGNER, LLOYD BOND, & LEE S. SHULMAN, EDUCATING LAWYERS: PREPARATION FOR THE PROFESSION OF LAW 47–74 (2007) (also known as the *Carnegie Report).*

3. *See* Mark B. Raymond, *Job Analysis, Practice Analysis, and the Content of Credentialing Examinations, in* HANDBOOK OF TEST DEVELOPMENT 144 (Suzanne Lane, Mark R. Raymond, & Thomas M. Haladyna eds., 2d ed. 2016) (citing AMERICAN EDUCATIONAL RESEARCH ASSOCIATION, AMERICAN PSYCHOLOGI-CAL ASSOCIATION, & NATIONAL COUNCIL ON MEASUREMENT IN EDUCATION,

STANDARDS FOR EDUCATIONAL AND PSYCHOLOGICAL TESTING 49 (2014) [hereinafter 2014 STANDARDS], https://www.testingstandards.net/uploads/7/6/6/4/76643089/standards_2014edition.pdf

4. *See, e.g.*, Michael T. Kane, *The Role of Licensure Tests*, 74 BAR EXAM'R 27 (Feb. 2005).

5. *See* 2014 STANDARDS, *supra* note 3, at 11, 174–78, 181–83.

6. *See, e.g.*, Deborah Jones Merritt, *Validity, Competence, and the Bar Exam*, AALS NEWS, no. 2017–2, at 11[hereinafter *Validity*] (critiquing validity of bar exams), https://www.aals.org/wp-content/uploads/2017/05/AALSnews_spring17 -v9.pdf; Joan Howarth, *Teaching in the Shadow of the Bar*, 31 U.S.F. L. REV. 927, 930 (1997) (summarizing earlier criticisms of bar examinations); *Society of American Law Teachers Statement on the Bar Exam*, 52 J. LEGAL EDUC. 446 (2002) (critiquing bar exams for failing to adequately measure professional competence).

7. "A lawyer shall provide competent representation to a client. Competent representation requires the legal knowledge, skill, thoroughness and preparation reasonably necessary for the representation." *Model Rules of Professional Conduct*, Rule 1.1 (ABA 2019) [hereinafter *Model Rules*].

8. *Model Rules, supra* note 7, Rule 1.1 comment 1.

9. *Model Rules, supra* note 7, Rule 1.1 comment 2.

10. *Model Rules, supra* note 7, Rule 1.1 comment 2. The comment also reminds us that "[a] lawyer can provide adequate representation in a wholly novel field through necessary study." *Id.*

11. ABA SECTION OF LEGAL EDUCATION AND ADMISSIONS TO THE BAR, ABA STANDARDS AND RULES OF PROCEDURE, Standard 302 (2021–22), https:/ /qa.americanbar.org/content/dam/aba/administrative/legal_education_and _admissions_to_the_bar/standards/2021-2022/2021-2022-aba-standards-and -rules-of-procedure-chapter-3.pdf

12. *See* ABA COMMISSION ON THE FUTURE OF LEGAL EDUCATION, PRINCIPLES FOR LEGAL EDUCATION AND LICENSURE IN THE 21ST CENTURY: PRINCIPLES AND COMMENTARY 3 (2020) ("Our established system of legal education and licensure is preparing the next generation of legal professionals for yesterday rather than for tomorrow"); STATE BAR OF CALIFORNIA, THE PRACTICE OF LAW IN CALIFORNIA: FINDINGS FROM THE CALIFORNIA ATTORNEY PRACTICE ANALYSIS AND IMPLI-CATIONS FOR THE CALIFORNIA BAR EXAM 4 (May 11, 2020) [hereinafter CAPA REPORT] ("Moreover, these studies need to be updated periodically as changes over time in the practice of a given profession could easily drift away from the content of the licensing exam"), https://www.calbar.ca.gov/Portals/0/documents/ reports/2020/California-Attorney-Practice-Analysis-Working-Group-Report.pdf

13. The CAPA REPORT identified the challenge of the vastness of "domains of law, practice setting, and tasks." *Id.*

14. "[T]he systematic collection of data describing the responsibilities required

of a professional and the skills and knowledge needed to perform these responsibilities is the foundation upon which to build a viable and legally defensible licensing examination." Joan E. Knapp & Lenora G. Knapp, *Practice Analysis: Building the Foundation for Validity, in* LICENSURE TESTING: PURPOSES, PROCEDURES, AND PRACTICES 93–94 (James C. Impara ed., 1995).

15. *See, e.g.,* Chad W. Buckendahl & Susan L. Davis-Becker, *Setting Passing Standards for Credentialing Programs, in* GREGORY J. CIZEK, SETTING PERFORMANCE STANDARDS: FOUNDATIONS, METHODS, AND INNOVATIONS 487 (2012) (providing graphical representation of stages in developing and checking possible high-stakes tests).

16. THOMAS M. HALADYNA & MICHAEL C. RODRIGUEZ, DEVELOPING AND VALIDATING TEST ITEMS 283 (2013) (emphasis in original). "In the case of the bar exam, practice analysis is needed to assess how accurately the questions on the exam, or the measures, capture the KSAs necessary to practice law in California at an entry-level of proficiency." CAPA REPORT, *supra* note 3, at 4 n. 3.

17. The suit was filed directly in the California Supreme Court on June 20, 1972, as a petition for writ of review and/or writ of mandate and/or application to exercise rule-making power. It was denied November 9, 1972. Justice Peters would have granted the petition. *See* Supreme Court Minutes, case no. S.F. 22928, Nov. 9, 1972.

18. Morris Ballerd, *The Minority Candidate and the Bar Examination Symposium, Panel No. 3: "Search for Solutions,"* 5 BLACK L. J. 165, 194 (1977) [hereinafter *Minority Candidate Symposium, Panel No. 3*].

19. David K. Robinson, *Minority Candidate Symposium, Panel 3, supra* note 18, at 169 (former member of the commission).

20. Richard S. Barrett, *Minority Candidate Symposium, Panel No. 3, supra* note 18, at 169 (*quoting* CALIFORNIA COMMISSION TO STUDY THE BAR EXAM. PROCESS, FINAL REPORT TO THE BOARD OF GOVERNORS OF THE STATE BAR OF CALIFORNIA (Aug. 1975)).

21. David K. Robinson, *Minority Candidate Symposium, Panel No. 3, supra* note 18, at 169.

22. Clyde O. Bowles Ill, *The Minority Candidate and the Bar Examination Symposium, Panel No. 1,* 5 BLACK L. J. 130, 134 (1977) [hereinafter *Minority Candidate Symposium, Panel No. 1*].

23. Kenneth D. McCloskey, *Minority Candidate Symposium, Panel No. 1, supra* note 22, at 147.

24. Richard S. Barrett, *Minority Candidate Symposium, Panel No. 3, supra* note 18, at 176 (explaining that it is "essential" that "the evidence of validity should include a complete description of job duties, including relative frequency, importance, and skill level of such duties").

25. *Id.* at 174.

26. *Id.*

27. Peter J. Liacouras, *The Minority Candidate and the Bar Examination Symposium, Panel No. 2, Factors Contributing to Bar Examination Failure*, 5 BLACK L. J. 149, 149 (1977).

28. *Id.* at 155–56.

29. Susan E. Brown and Claire Levay, *Melendez v. Burciaga: Revealing the State of the Art in Bar Examinations*, 51 BAR EXAM'R 4, 4 (May 1982).

30. *Id.* at 6 ("The obvious question is how one can adequately measure a criterion that eludes definition").

31. *Id.* (Armando M. Menocal III, a former chair of the California Board of Bar Examiners who later served as NCBE chair).

32. *Id.* at 7.

33. David K. Robinson, *Minority Candidate Symposium, Panel No. 3, supra* note 18, at 169.

34. *See* STEVEN S. NETTLES & JAMES HELLRUNG, A STUDY OF THE NEWLY LICENSED LAWYER: CONDUCTED FOR THE NATIONAL CONFERENCE OF BAR EXAMINERS (2012); *id.* at 9 (surveys sent to more than 20,000 new admittees, but only 1,669 responses (8.4%) were returned and usable). For discussion of this job analysis, see Susan Case, *The NCBE Job Analysis: A Study of the Newly Licensed Lawyer*, 82 BAR EXAM'R 52 (March 2013).

35. *See id.* at 53 (addition of civil procedure was planned prior to the study); NCBE, TESTING TASK FORCE, FIRST YEAR REPORT 1 (April 2019) (describing addition of civil procedure following evaluation of 2012 study results), https:// thebarexaminer.ncbex.org/latest-news/testing-task-force-shares-overview-of-its -first-year-activities/

36. *See* Case, *supra* note 34, at 54–55.

37. TRACY A. MONTEZ, OBSERVATION OF THE STANDARD SETTING STUDY FOR THE CALIFORNIA BAR EXAMINATION: PERFORMED FOR THE STATE BAR OF CALIFORNIA 10 (July 2017), http://www.calbar.ca.gov/Portals/0/documents/admissions /Examinations/Tracy-Montez-ReviewBarExamstudy.pdf. Dr. Montez explained that such a study was needed for, among other purposes, "determining content to be measured on the [California Bar Exam]; creating a common frame of reference . . . when establishing passing scores; providing preparation and training information to candidates and schools." *Id.*

38. Letter from Professor Deborah Merritt to California Supreme Court, In re Calif. Bar Exam, Docket No. S244281 (Oct. 1, 2017) (on file with author).

39. In this study, ten lawyers—representing diverse backgrounds and with varying seniority—used the NCBE's 2012 practice analysis to evaluate components of the California bar exam. *See* CHAD W. BUCKENDAHL, CONDUCTING A CONTENT VALIDATION STUDY FOR THE CALIFORNIA BAR EXAM: FINAL REPORT (Oct. 4, 2017) (finding exam components aligned with knowledge and skills identified in the 2012 study and also identifying the need for a design process using a

new job analysis to become the blueprint for the exam), https://www.calbar.ca.gov
/Portals/0/documents/admissions/Examinations/CBEStudy_Attachment_A.pdf

CHAPTER 7

1. *See, e.g.*, Richard S. Barrett, *The Minority Candidate and the Bar Examination Symposium, Panel No. 3: "Search for Solutions,"* 5 BLACK L. J. 165, 176 (1977) ("Validity applies to the bar examination with reference to the potential performance of the examinees as lawyers, not their past performance as students"). Dr. Barrett was Director, Laboratory of Psychological Studies, Stevens Institute of Technology.

2. "[W]e should expect a high degree of overlap between the content of professional school curricula and the content of licensure and certification examinations, since both presumably emphasize knowledge and skills that are viewed as needed for effective practice." Michael T. Kane, *The Future of Testing for Licensure and Certification Examinations*, in THE FUTURE OF TESTING 145 (Barbara S. Plake & Joseph C. Witt, eds. 1986).

3. *See* Joan W. Howarth & Judith Welch Wegner, *Ringing Changes: Systems Thinking About Legal Licensing*, 13 FIU L. REV. 383, 430–31, 447–56 (2019); Peter A. Joy, *The Uneasy History of Experiential Education in U.S. Law Schools*, 122 DICK. L. REV. 551 (2018); Rebecca L. Sandefur and Jeffrey Selbin, *The Clinic Effect*, 16 CLINICAL L. REV. 57, 57 (2009). "Whether viewed as a "curious error in orientation," a "remarkable educational anomaly," or a "complete failure," for more than a century legal education has been out of step with sister professional schools in preparing its graduates for practice." *Id.* (citations omitted).

4. *See, e.g.*, DEBORAH L. RHODE & GEOFFREY C. HAZARD JR., PROFESSIONAL RESPONSIBILITY AND REGULATION 201–03 (2d ed. 2007); Edward Rubin, *What's Wrong with Langdell's Method, and What to Do About It*, 60 VAND. L. REV. 609 (2007).

5. *See* LINDA H. EDWARDS, THE DOCTRINE/SKILLS DIVIDE: LEGAL EDUCATION'S SELF-INFLICTED WOUND (2017) (compelling treatment of the fallacy of differentiating doctrinal courses and faculty from skills courses and faculty); Kate Kruse, *Legal Education and Professional Skills: Myths and Misconceptions About Theory and Practice*, 45 MCGEORGE L. REV. 7 (2013) (proposals to address doctrine/ skills divide).

6. See *UCI School of Law, First-Year Curriculum*, UCI GENERAL CATALOGUE, https://catalogue.uci.edu/schooloflaw/#FirstYearCurriculum (last visited Dec. 27, 2021).

7. "Tort cases declined from 16% of civil filings in state courts in 1993 to about 4% in 2015, a difference of more than 1.7 million cases nationwide, according to an analysis of annual reports from the National Center for State Courts." Joe Palazzolo, *We Won't See You in Court: The Era of Torts Lawsuits Is Waning*, WALL ST.

J. (July 24, 2017), https://www.wsj.com/articles/we-wont-see-you-in-court-the-era -of-tort-lawsuits-is-waning-1500930572

8. *See generally,* WILLIAM SULLIVAN, ANNE COLBY, JUDITH WELCH WEGNER, LLOYD BOND, & LEE S. SHULMAN, EDUCATING LAWYERS: PREPARATION FOR THE PROFESSION OF LAW 47–74 (2007) (describing first-year case dialogue as potentially transformative signature pedagogy).

9. *State Bar Examination Questions,* 2 AM. L. SCH. REV. 524 (1906–1911) (Ohio bar exam, Dec. 7–8, 1909).

10. *See* ABA SECTION OF LEGAL EDUCATION AND ADMISSIONS TO THE BAR, LEGAL EDUCATION AND PROFESSIONAL DEVELOPMENT—AN EDUCATIONAL CONTINUUM: REPORT OF THE TASK FORCE ON LAW SCHOOLS AND THE PROFESSION: NARROWING THE GAP (1992) [hereinafter *MacCrate Report*] (report issued by a task force of practitioners and academics led by former ABA President Bob MacCrate), https://www.corteidh.or.cr/tablas/28961.pdf; *see also* Bryant G. Garth & Joanne Martin, *Law Schools and the Construction of Competence,* 43 J. LEGAL EDUC. 469, 475, 477 (1993).

11. *MacCrate Report, supra* note 10, at 135–221.

12. *See* MARJORIE M. SHULTZ & SHELDON ZEDECK, IDENTIFICATION, DEVELOPMENT, AND VALIDATION OF PREDICTORS FOR SUCCESSFUL LAWYERING (2008) [hereinafter PREDICTORS], http://www.law.berkeley.edu/files/LSACREPORTfinal -12.pdf; Marjorie M. Shultz & Sheldon Zedeck, *Predicting Lawyer Effectiveness: Broadening the Basis for Law School Admissions Decisions,* 36 LAW & SOC. IN-QUIRY 620 (2011).

13. PREDICTORS, *supra* note 12, at 26–27.

14. *See* Neil Hamilton, *Empirical Research on the Core Competencies Needed to Practice Law: What Do Clients, New Lawyers, and Legal Employers Tell Us?,* 83 BAR EXAM'R 6, 10 (Sept. 2014) (evaluating survey data from junior and senior lawyers in Minnesota, interviews, job analysis by the NCBE, and other studies).

15. *See* ALLI GERKMAN & LOGAN CORNETT, FOUNDATIONS FOR PRACTICE: THE WHOLE LAWYER AND THE CHARACTER QUOTIENT 30–34 (2016), http://iaals .du.edu/sites/default/files/documents/publications/foundations_for_practice_ whole_lawyer_character_quotient.pdf

16. *See* ABA SECTION OF LEGAL EDUCATION AND ADMISSIONS TO THE BAR, ABA STANDARDS AND RULES OF PROCEDURE (2021–22), Standard 301(a)(3), Standard 304(a)(1).

17. *Id.,* Standard 302(d).

CHAPTER 8

1. *See* KELLIE R. EARLY, JOANNE KANE, MARK RAYMOND, & DANIELLE M. MOREAU, NCBE TESTING TASK FORCE PHASE 2 REPORT: 2019 PRACTICE ANALYSIS (March 2020) [hereinafter NCBE PRACTICE ANALYSIS], https://nextgenbarexam

.ncbex.org/wp-content/uploads/TestingTaskForce_Phase_2_Report_031020.pdf

2. STATE BAR OF CALIFORNIA, THE PRACTICE OF LAW IN CALIFORNIA: FINDINGS FROM THE CALIFORNIA ATTORNEY PRACTICE ANALYSIS AND IMPLICATIONS FOR THE CALIFORNIA BAR EXAM (May 11, 2020) [hereinafter CAPA REPORT], https://www.calbar.ca.gov/Portals/0/documents/reports/2020/California-Attorney-Practice-Analysis-Working-Group-Report.pdf

3. DEBORAH JONES MERRITT & LOGAN CORNETT, BUILDING A BETTER BAR: THE TWELVE BUILDING BLOCKS OF MINIMUM COMPETENCE (2020), https://iaals .du.edu/sites/default/files/documents/publications/building_a_better_bar.pdf. I was pleased to participate in this project. After training, and along with Boyd School of Law colleague Dean Frank Durand, we convened and led three focus groups in Nevada.

4. NCBE TESTING TASK FORCE, FINAL REPORT OF THE TESTING TASK FORCE (2021) [hereinafter TESTING TASK FORCE FINAL REPORT], https://nextgenbarexam .ncbex.org/reports/final-report-of-the-ttf/

5. NCBE PRACTICE ANALYSIS, *supra* note 1, at 1 (studies undertaken "to ensure that the bar examination *continues* to test the knowledge, skills, and abilities needed for competent entry-level legal practice in a changing profession" (emphasis added)).

6. *Id.* at 1, 13.

7. *Id.* at 4–6.

8. *Id.* at 4.

9. *Id.* at 50. "[F]or a task to be considered eligible for consideration in the test blueprint development process, it must be performed by at least 50% of entry-level practitioners." *Id.* at 5.

10. Marjorie M. Shultz & Sheldon Zedeck, *Predicting Lawyer Effectiveness: Broadening the Basis for Law School Admissions Decisions*, 36 LAW & SOC. INQUIRY 620 (2011).

11. "The list of SAOs included nearly all of the 26 lawyering skills identified through the work of Shultz and Zedeck (2011). The fact that nearly all SAOs were judged to be either moderately or highly critical can be regarded as confirmation of that earlier work." NCBE PRACTICE ANALYSIS, *supra* note 1, at 6.

12. NCBE PRACTICE ANALYSIS, *supra* note 1, at 5–6 (describing "SAOs with the highest mean criticality rating" and contrasting those with "SAOs with the lowest mean criticality ratings," specifically, "Strategic Planning, Leadership, Social Consciousness/Community Involvement, Networking and Business Development, and Instructing/Mentoring").

13. *Id.* at 5.

14. *See* NCBE TESTING TASK FORCE, OVERVIEW OF RECOMMENDATIONS FOR THE NEXT GENERATION OF THE BAR EXAMINATION 2, 4 (2021), https://nextgenbarexam.ncbex.org/wp-content/uploads/TTF-Next-Gen-Bar-Exam

-Recommendations.pdf

15. NCBE PRACTICE ANALYSIS, *supra* note 1, at 57.

16. *Id.* at 57, 62.

17. NCBE TESTING TASK FORCE, YOUR VOICE: STAKEHOLDER THOUGHTS ABOUT THE BAR EXAM: PHASE 1 REPORT OF THE TESTING TASK FORCE (Aug. 2019), https://nextgenbarexam.ncbex.org/wp-content/uploads/FINAL-Listening -Session-Executive-Summary-with-Appendices-2.pdf

18. *See Snapshot of NextGen Bar Exam,* NCBE: NEXTGEN BAR EXAM OF THE FUTURE, https://nextgenbarexam.ncbex.org/ (last visited Jan. 10, 2022).

19. CAPA REPORT, *supra* note 2, at 1.

20. *See id.* at 4. "The response rate for the traditional survey was 8 percent, with 5,100 respondents, while the ESM survey's response rate was higher at 18 percent (11,090 respondents")." *Id.* at 9.

21. *Id.* at 10.

22. *Id.* at 7–8; SCANTRON, STATE BAR OF CALIFORNIA PRACTICE ANALYSIS REPORT 30–31 (March 2020) [hereinafter CAPA TECHNICAL REPORT], https:// board.calbar.ca.gov/docs/agendaItem/Public/agendaitem1000025775.pdf. This scale is based on Bloom's taxonomy. *See* Deborah J. Merritt, *Bloom's Taxonomy and the Bar Exam,* RAISING THE BAR (July 2019), at 3 (describing Bloom's taxonomy, in which application requires more cognitive skill than recall), https://www .accesslex.org/raising-the-bar-july-2019

23. *See* CAPA TECHNICAL REPORT, *supra* note 22, at 31, table 37 (*Criticality and Depth of Knowledge for Legal Topics, ESM Survey*).

24. *Id.* at App. K (*Legal Subtopics Based on Respondents in the First Three Years of Practice, Both Surveys, Tasks and Average Ratings from Traditional Survey for Newly Licensed Attorneys*).

25. *Id.* "Insider Trading" seemed like an odd topic for low cognitive demand, but 2.7 was the result from the single lawyer working on it. The two lawyers interrupted while considering "Securities-Definition" gave an average score of 2.7, as did the two lawyers working on "Secured Transactions—Enforcement & Foreclosure." "Eighth Amendment" got a 2.6 from the twenty-one lawyers working on it and "Mergers & Acquisitions, Disbanding, Winding Up" got a 2.6 from forty-three lawyers.

26. *Id.* By contrast, the highest "depth of knowledge" averages were 4.6 from the seven lawyers working on "Strict Liability" and 4.5 from the five lawyers immersed in "Federalism." "Negligence" landed the most lawyers; the 380 working on it averaged 3.3.

27. CAPA REPORT, *supra* note 2, at 2.

28. *Id.* at 18–19. "[I]t is also recognized that some competencies are more amenable to traditional forms of testing than others. The Working Group exhaustively discussed the challenges of testing these competencies using the tra-

ditional bar exam format and testing methods. Drafting and Writing, Research and Investigation, Issue Spotting and Fact Gathering have been tested using the current Performance Test. However, the Working Group agreed that new testing formats would be necessary to effectively test these recommended competencies, especially Communication and Client Relationships." *Id.* at 18.

29. *Id.* at 2.

30. *Id.* at 2.

31. *Id.* at 18.

32. STATE BAR OF CALIFORNIA, JOINT SUPREME COURT/STATE BAR BLUE RIBBON COMMISSION ON THE FUTURE OF THE CALIFORNIA BAR EXAMINA-TION, https://www.calbar.ca.gov/Portals/0/documents/factSheets/Blue-Ribbon -Commission-Future-of-California-Bar-Exam-Fact-Sheet.pdf (last visited Jan. 10, 2022).

33. *See* MERRITT & CORNETT, *supra* note 3; *see also Exploring Ways to License Lawyers Now and in the Future*, LAWYER LICENSING RESOURCES (licensing materials based on this research), https://lawyerlicensingresources.org/ (last visited April 21, 2022).

34. *Id.* at 9–10.

35. *Id.* at 10 ("our research underscores the difficulty of separating knowledge from skills").

36. *Id.* at 30.

37. *Id.*; *see also* Jennifer A. Gundlach & Jessica R. Santangelo, *Teaching and Assessing Metacognition in Law School*, 69 J. LEGAL EDUC. 156 (2019) (emphasizing importance of awareness about one's learning for academic and professional success).

38. MERRITT & CORNETT, *supra* note 3, at 31.

39. Ronald M. Epstein & Edward M. Hundert, *Defining and Assessing Professional Competence*, 287 JAMA 226, 226 (2002).

40. *Id.*

41. *Id.* (citing JAN H. F. MEYER & RAY LAND, THRESHOLD CONCEPTS AND TROUBLESOME KNOWLEDGE: LINKAGES TO WAYS OF THINKING AND PRACTISING WITHIN THE DISCIPLINES (2003) (report first proposing recognition of threshold concepts); Jan H. F. Meyer, *Threshold Concepts and Pedagogic Representations*, 58 EDUC. + TRAINING 463 (2016) (recent overview).

42. MERRITT & CORNETT, *supra* note 3, at 31.

43. *Id.*

44. *See* BENJAMIN BLOOM ET AL., TAXONOMY OF EDUCATIONAL OBJECTIVES: THE CLASSIFICATION OF EDUCATIONAL GOALS, HANDBOOK I: COGNITIVE DOMAIN (1956). For a discussion in the legal context, see Ruth Jones, *Assessment and Legal Education: What Is Assessment and What the *# Does It Have to Do with the Challenges Facing Legal Education?*, 45 MCGEORGE L. REV. 85, 98 (2013).

45. "[M]etacognition is the concept that individuals can monitor and regulate their own cognitive processes and thereby improve the quality and effectiveness of their thinking." Cheryl B. Preston, Penée Wood Stewart, & Louise R. Moulding, *Teaching "Thinking Like a Lawyer": Metacognition and Law Students*, 2014 BYU L. REV. 1053, 1057 (2014); *see* David R. Krathwohl, *A Revision of Bloom's Taxonomy: An Overview*, 41 THEORY INTO PRAC. 212, 214 (2002).

46. *See* Gregory Schraw, Matthew T. McCrudden, Stephen Lehman, & Bobby Hoffman, *An Overview of Thinking Skills*, *in* ASSESSMENT OF HIGHER ORDER THINKING SKILLS 22, 26–27 (Gregory Schraw & Daniel H. Robinson, eds. 2011) (defining metacognition as "thinking about and regulating one's thinking" and characterizing its attributes as those of "skilled learners").

47. *See* Preston et al., *Metacognition*, *supra* note 45, at 1056, 1059 (suggesting a relationship between the Socratic method and teaching metacognition).

48. *E.g.*, Elizabeth M. Bloom, *A Law School Game Changer: (Trans)formative Feedback*, 41 OHIO N.U. L. REV. 227 (2015) (discussing metacognition and self-regulated learning); Louis N. Schulze Jr., *Using Science to Build Better Learners: One School's Successful Efforts to Raise Its Bar Passage Rates in an Era of Decline*, 68 J. LEGAL EDUC. 230 (2019).

49. *E.g.*, Anthony Niedwiecki, *Teaching for Lifelong Learning: Improving the Metacognitive Skills of Law Students Through More Effective Formative Assessment Techniques*, 40 CAP. U. L. REV. 149 (2012).

50. *E.g.*, John M. A. DiPippa & Martha S. Peters, *The Lawyering Process: An Example of Metacognition at Its Best*, 10 CLINICAL L. REV. 311 (2003).

51. Jerome Frank, *Why Not a Clinical Lawyer-School?*, 81 U. PENN. L. REV. 907, 912–13 (1933) (arguing that doctrine rarely controls).

52. MERRITT & CORNETT, *supra* note 3, at 27, 61–62.

CHAPTER 9

1. *See* Leslie C. Levin, *The Folly of Expecting Evil: Reconsidering the Bar's Character and Fitness Requirement*, 2014 BYU L. REV. 775, 782 (2014) ("By 1928, virtually all of the states had a character and fitness requirement for bar admission" (citation omitted)); *Code of Recommended Standards for Bar Examiners*, *in* COMPREHENSIVE GUIDE TO BAR ADMISSIONS, NCBE AND ABA SECTION OF LEGAL EDUCATION AND ADMISSIONS TO THE BAR viii (2021) [hereinafter *NCBE Code*] ("A record manifesting a significant deficiency in the honesty, trustworthiness, diligence, or reliability of an applicant may constitute a basis for denial of admission"), https://reports.ncbex.org/comp-guide/; *see also NCBE Character and Fitness Sample Application*, NCBE (providing a 36-page sample character and fitness application), https://www.ncbex.org/dmsdocument/134 (last visited Dec. 17, 2021).

2. *See NCBE Code*, *supra* note 1, at viii. States set their own character and fitness rules and processes. *Id.*

3. "Most of the problems that clients have with attorneys do not arise from deficiencies that [bar] exams assess. Rarely do these problems involve a lawyer's inadequate knowledge of the law or of the relevant ethical rules." DEBORAH L. RHODE, IN THE INTERESTS OF JUSTICE: REFORMING THE LEGAL PROFESSION 150 (2000). Instead, the problems come from "poor office management, neglect, overcharging, unrealistic caseloads, or related problems, which are often rooted in personal difficulties such as financial pressures and substance abuse." *Id.* at 150–51.

4. "The primary purpose of character and fitness screening before admission to the bar is the protection of the public and the system of justice. The lawyer licensing process is incomplete if only testing for minimal competence is undertaken. The public is inadequately protected by a system that fails to evaluate character and fitness as those elements relate to the practice of law." *NCBE Code*, *supra* note 1, at vii.

5. RHODE, *supra* note 3, at 150. "[M]ost states now require graduation from an accredited law school, passage of a demanding bar exam, and proof of good moral character. In theory, these requirements serve to protect the public from incompetent or unethical attorneys. In practice, they are highly imperfect means of accomplishing either." *Id.*

6. *See, e.g.*, Levin, *supra* note 1 at 779 ("it may be impossible to predict at the time of bar admission which applicants will become problematic lawyers"); Leslie C. Levin, Christine Zozula, & Peter Siegelman, *The Questionable Character of the Bar's Character and Fitness*, 40 LAW & SOC. INQUIRY 51 (2015) (study of Connecticut lawyers showing that the information gathered in the character and fitness inquiry is of little value in predicting who will subsequently be disciplined).

7. *See* Jason O. Billy, *Confronting Racists at the Bar: Matthew Hale, Moral Character, and Regulating the Marketplace of Ideas*, 22 HARV. BLACKLETTER L. J. 25, 52 (2006) (First Amendment values suggest that candidates for the bar should not be excluded on the basis of racist ideologies); Carla D. Pratt, *Should Klansmen Be Lawyers—Racism as an Ethical Barrier to the Legal Profession*, 30 FLA. ST. U. L. REV. 857 (2003) (white supremacists do not have the necessary character to be admitted to the bar).

8. *See, e.g.*, Tim Gallagher, *Innocent Until Proven Guilty? Not for Bar Applicants*, 31 J. LEGAL PROF. 297, 305 (2007) (describing dilemma of candidates who have been told that expunged conviction no longer exists).

9. Levin, *supra* note 1, at 784 ("Lack of candor during the character inquiry—rather than the past misconduct itself—is a common reason for denial of admission"); Deborah Rhode, *Moral Character as a Professional Credential*, 94 YALE L. J. 491, 544 (1985) [hereinafter *Moral Character*] ("Nondisclosure, even about relatively trivial matters, may evidence the wrong 'mental attitude,' and 'glib, equivocal responses,' even if technically accurate, may prove more damning than the conduct at issue").

10. Deborah L. Rhode, *Virtue and the Law: The Good Moral Character Requirement in Occupational Licensing, Bar Regulation, and Immigration Proceedings*, 43 LAW & SOC. INQUIRY 1027, 1036 (2018) [hereinafter *Virtue*] (citing to *Moral Character, supra* note 9, at 568). Jerold Auerbach summarized: "Good character re-emerged as a flexible test to exclude aspirants whose political activism displeased admissions committees." JEROLD S. AUERBACH, UNEQUAL JUSTICE: LAWYERS AND SOCIAL CHANGE IN MODERN AMERICA 291 (1976).

11. The Briggs Initiative was defeated by a vote of 2,823,293 to 3,396,120. *See* https://ballotpedia.org/California_Proposition_6,_Ban_on_Lesbian_and_Gay_Teachers_Initiative_(1978)

12. "Although the number of applicants formally denied admission has always been quite small, the number deterred, delayed, or harassed has been more substantial." *Moral Character, supra* note 9, at 493–94. For research on psychological distress caused by anticipated stigma, see Diane M. Quinn & Valerie A. Earnshaw, *Concealable Stigmatized Identities and Psychological Well-Being*, 7 SOCIAL AND PERSONALITY PSYCHOLOGY COMPASS 40 (2013) and Diane M. Quinn & Stephenie R. Chaudoir, *Living with a Concealable Stigmatized Identity: The Impact of Anticipated Stigma, Centrality, Salience, and Cultural Stigma on Psychological Distress and Health*, 97 JOURNAL OF PERSONALITY AND SOCIAL PSYCHOLOGY 634 (2009).

13. Karen Sloan, *"I Understand the Anxiety and the Anger," Says Top Bar Exam Official*, LAW.COM (July 13, 2020) (reporting that some diploma privilege advocates felt threatened by bar examiners' criticism tied to character and fitness), https://www.law.com/2020/08/13/i-understand-the-anxiety-and-the-anger-says-top-bar-exam-official/

14. Jennifer Aronson, *Rules Versus Standards: A Moral Inquiry into Washington's Character & Fitness Hearing Process*, 95 WASH. L. REV. 997 (2020).

15. A character and fitness issue can result in four possible outcomes: licensure, no licensure, deferred licensure, or conditional licensure. Six jurisdictions currently have some sort of program for deferred admission, and twenty-five jurisdictions currently have a conditional licensure program through which they attach strings to the license. *NCBE Code, supra* note 1, at 5–6. For criticism of conditional admission programs, see Stephanie Denzel, *Second-Class Licensure: The Use of Conditional Admission Programs for Bar Applicants with Substance Abuse and Mental Health Histories*, 43 CONN. L. REV. 889 (2011).

16. *NCBE Code, supra* note 1, at 5–6.

17. *See Virtue, supra* note 10, at 1039 ("The bar refuses to certify fewer than 1 percent of applicants") (citation omitted); Levin, *supra* note 1, at 779 ("The process can also become embarrassing, stressful, and career-damaging for applicants who must explain to employers why their bar admission is delayed") (citation omitted).

18. "For a time, the American Bar Association even considered an examination for all law students that would 'identify those significant elements of char-

acter that may predictably give rise to misconduct in violation of professional responsibilities.'" AUERBACH, *supra* note 10, at 292 (citation omitted).

19. *Virtue, supra* note 10, at 1031.

20. Levin, *supra* note 1, at 785 (quoting *Moral Character, supra* note 9, at 556).

21. Levin, *supra* note 1, at 792.

22. "Efforts to predict violence by psychologists and psychiatrists based on clinical judgment are not especially accurate." *Id.* at 790 (citation omitted).

23. *See Virtue, supra* note 10, at 1029–30 (describing and citing to the famous Milgram studies at Stanford).

24. *See id.* at 1030 (describing and citing to 1973 study at Princeton Theological Seminary).

25. *Moral Character, supra* note 9, at 493–94 (1985). "In the absence of meaningful standards or professional consensus, the filtering process has proved inconsistent, idiosyncratic, and needlessly intrusive. We have developed neither a coherent concept of professional character nor effective procedures to predict it. Rather, we have maintained a licensing ritual that too often has debased the ideals it seeks to sustain." *Id.*

26. Rhode identified the purposes of character inquiry as predictive and symbolic, neither of which, according to Rhode, justified current practices. *Virtue, supra* note 10, at 1031. Other determinations are hard to explain in terms other than cronyism and favoritism. One Michigan committee excluded a candidate based on a fishing license violation ten years prior, while, also in Michigan at around the same time, other examiners admitted candidates convicted of child molestation and conspiracy to bomb a public building. *Id.* at 1037 (citing to *Moral Character, supra* note 9, at 538).

27. AUERBACH, *supra* note 10, at 12 (citing to JAMES WILLARD HURST, THE GROWTH OF AMERICAN LAW: THE LAW MAKERS, 251, 254–55 (1950)).

28. ALFRED ZANTZINGER REED, TRAINING FOR THE PUBLIC PROFESSION OF THE LAW: HISTORICAL DEVELOPMENT AND PRINCIPAL CONTEMPORARY PROBLEMS IN THE UNITED STATES WITH SOME ACCOUNT OF CONDITIONS IN ENGLAND AND CANADA 36 (1921).

29. Levin, *supra* note 1, at 781 (quoting RICHARD L. ABEL, AMERICAN LAWYERS 25 (1989)).

30. *Virtue, supra* note 10, at 1035 (describing Pennsylvania).

31. *Id.* (citation omitted).

32. *Id.* (citation omitted).

33. AUERBACH, *supra* note 10, at 123. "In 1922 the [Illinois] state board of bar examiners, reporting that a significantly higher proportion of successful applicants to the bar was foreign born, urged higher standards as a restrictive weapon against members of ethnic minority groups. References to the 'morally unfit' began to punctuate debates." *Id.*

34. MAGALI SARFATTI LARSON, THE RISE OF PROFESSIONALISM: A SOCIO-LOGICAL ANALYSIS 125 (1977).

35. Ernest Gellhorn, *The Law Schools and the Negro*, 1968 DUKE L.J. 1069, 1092 n. 84 (1968).

36. *Virtue, supra* note 10, at 1036 (citations omitted).

37. AUERBACH, *supra* note 10, at 7.

38. During the 1950s, character and fitness rules were used to exclude those "whose political and professional commitments deviated from Cold War ortho-doxy." AUERBACH, *supra* note 10, at 233.

39. Konigsberg v. State Bar of California, 353 U.S. 252, 262 (1957); *see also* Schware v. Bd. of Bar Examiners, 353 U.S. 232 (1957) (state may not deny bar ad-missions based on Communist Party membership); ABEL, *supra* note 29, at 38. "Although professions portray self-regulations as a means of reducing client un-certainty, they deliberately draft ethical rules in vague and ambiguous language to preserve the indeterminacy that is a foundation of professional power." *Id.*

40. AUERBACH, *supra* note 10, at 250.

41. Hallinan v. Committee of Bar Examiners, 65 Cal. 2d. 447 (1966).

42. AUERBACH, *supra* note 10, at 291 n. 58.

43. For examples of law student activism raising character and fitness con-cerns, see Theresa Keeley, *Good Moral Character: Already an Unconstitutionally Vague Concept and Now Putting Bar Applicants in a Post 9/11 World on an Ele-vated Threat Level*, 6 U. OF PA. J. CONST. L. 844, 844–45 (2004) and Steven Lubet, *The Contretemps at Yale*, REAL CLEAR EDUCATION (Oct. 27, 2021) (character and fitness implications of law school condemnation of email about "Trap House" party), https://www.realcleareducation.com/articles/2021/10/27/the_contretemps _at_yale_110658.html

44. *Brief Against Homophobia at the Bar: To Law School Dean: Mid 1960s*, 10 COLUM. J. GENDER & L. 63, 71 (2000) ("Conversations with the Associate Dean (who spoke discreetly with a high official of the Bar) and others, leave virtually no doubt that disclosure of Mr. Lawson's 'problem' would result in automatic denial of a license to practice law").

45. In re Kimball, 40 A.D.2d 252, 339 N.Y.S.2d 302 (1973).

46. *See Guide to the Harris L. Kimball papers*, circa 1973–2003, Division of Rare and Manuscript Collections, CORNELL UNIVERSITY LIBRARY, https://rmc.library .cornell.edu/EAD/htmldocs/RMM07823.html

47. 40 A.D.2d 252, 257; 339 N.Y.S.2d 302, 308–09 (Martuscello and Shapiro, JJ., dissenting).

48. 33 N.Y.S.2d 686 (1973).

49. In re Petition of Kimball, 425 So. 2d 531 (Fla. 1982).

50. In re Fla. Bd. of Bar Examiners, 358 So. 2d 7, 7–8 (Fla. 1978).

51. 358 So. 2d 7, at 9. One justice dissented. "There should not be admitted to

The Florida Bar anyone whose sexual life style contemplates routine violation of a criminal statute." In re Fla. Bd. of Bar Examiners, 358 So. 2d 7, 10 (J. Boyd, dissenting) (Fla. 1978).

52. 358 So. 2d 7, at 8.

53. Florida Board of Bar Examiners Re N.R.S., 403 So.2d 1315 (Fla. 1981). As in Kimball, *supra* note 49, this case concerned a gay candidate who had passed all parts of the Florida bar exam and was licensed elsewhere.

54. *Id.* at 1317.

55. *Id.* at 1318 (Boyd, J., dissenting).

56. *Id.* (Alderman, J., dissenting).

57. 403 So.2d 1315, 1318 (Alderman, J., dissenting).

58. Florida Board of Bar Examiners Re N.R.S., 403 So.2d 1315, 1317 (Fla. 1981).

59. *Id.*

60. Elizabeth B. Cooper, *The Power of Dignity*, 84 FORDHAM L. REV. 3, 3 (2014); *see also* Joel Jay Finer, *Gay and Lesbian Applicants to the Bar: Even Lord Devlin Could Not Defend Exclusion, Circa 2000*, 10 COLUM. J. GENDER & L. 231 (2001) (noting that gay and lesbian applicants to the bar may have difficulties satisfying the "good moral character" standard).

61. *Moral Character, supra* note 9, at 539. Applicants occasionally had to answer questions about the intimate details of their sex lives and living arrangements. *Id.* at 579. One official expressed relief that issues such as cohabitation rarely arose: "Thank God we don't have much of that [in Missouri]." *Id.* at 539.

62. Finer, *supra* note 60, at 260.

63. E. R. Shipp, *Homosexual Lawyers Keep Fighting Barriers*, N.Y. TIMES, Sec. B, p. 11 (Feb. 3, 1989).

64. Carol M. Langford, *Barbarians at the Bar: Regulation of the Legal Profession Through the Admissions Process*, 36 HOFSTRA L. REV. 1193, 1221 (2008).

65. Frances McMorris, *Nathan Bruemmer, a Transgender Man, Graduated from Law School and Now Faces Complications in His Quest to Become a Lawyer*, TAMPA BAY BUS. J. (Sept. 1, 2017), https://www.bizjournals.com/tampabay/news/2017/09/01/nathan-bruemmer-switched-genders-graduated-from.html

66. Telephone conversation of Cristiana Wilcoxon with Kylar Broadus (July 2, 2020).

67. *See, e.g.*, CAROLINE COHN, DEBBIE A. MUKAMAL, & ROBERT WEISBERG, UNLOCKING THE BAR: EXPANDING ACCESS TO THE LEGAL PROFESSION FOR PEOPLE WITH CRIMINAL RECORDS IN CALIFORNIA 4 (2019), https://www-cdn.law.stanford.edu/wp-content/uploads/2019/07/Unlocking-the-Bar-July-2019.pdf; *see also* Reginald Dwayne Betts, *Getting Out*, N.Y. TIMES MAGAZINE (Oct. 16, 2018) (titled *Could an Ex-Convict Become an Attorney? I Intended to Find Out*), https://www.nytimes.com/2018/10/16/magazine/felon-attorney-crime-yale-law.html; *see generally* Devah Pager, *The Mark of a Criminal Record*, 108 AM. J. OF SOCIOLOGY

937 (2003) (research on employment consequences of incarceration for Black and white men).

68. Levin, *supra* note 1, at 784. "In a few states, felony convictions are automatically disqualifying, at least for a period of time." *Id.* (citation omitted).

69. Susan Saab Fortney, *Law School Admissions and Ethics—Rethinking Character and Fitness Inquiries*, 45 S. TEX. L. REV. 983, 985 (2004) (describing controversy regarding James Hamm's application); *id.* at n. 7 (citing to Paul Davenport, *Paroled Murderer Passes Bar Exam*, THE LEGAL INTELLIGENCER 4 (Oct. 15, 1999).

70. *See, e.g.*, In re Manville, 538 A.2d 1128 (D.C. Crt. App. 1988) (deciding in favor of bar admission of candidate previously convicted of voluntary manslaughter for killing in drug deal); *see also* Sheila Pursglove, *A Changed Man: Law Professor Spearheads MSU Civil Rights Clinic*, DETROIT LEGAL NEWS (April 13, 2012), http://www.legalnews.com/detroit/1283324

71. *See* Levin, *supra* note 1, at 778 (citing to Fortney, *supra* note 69, at 991–92).

72. "Seventy million Americans have criminal records, and character-based licensing requirements are a substantial barrier to their economic livelihood and rehabilitation. Because racial and ethnic minorities are disproportionately likely to have run ins with the criminal law, they pay a special price for these requirements." *Virtue, supra* note 10, at 1027; *see also* COHN ET AL., *supra* note 67, at 4 (finding that character and fitness inquiry into prior criminal activity creates barrier to diversity of the profession with little public protection).

73. *See, e.g.*, Maureen M. Carr, *The Effect of Prior Criminal Conduct on the Admission to Practice Law: The Move to More Flexible Admission Standards*, 8 GEO. J. LEGAL ETHICS 367, 369 (1995).

74. *See* Kurt L. Schmoke, *Gone but Not Forgotten: Bar Examiners Cheat Would Be Lawyers of a Second Chance by Asking Them to Disclose Expunged Convictions*, 2006 LEGAL AFF. 27 (Jan.–Feb.).

75. N.Y. State Supreme Court App. Div., *Application for Admission to Practice as an Attorney and Counselor-at-Law in the State of New York*, https://www.nybarexam.org/Admission/B-Bar_Admissions-Questionaire.pdf (last visited Dec. 7, 2021).

76. New York State Bar Association, *Report and Recommendations of the Working Group on Question 26 of the N.Y. Bar Application* (Jan. 2022), https://nysba.org/app/uploads/2021/11/H6.-Working-Group-on-Question-26-NYS-Bar-Exam-Admission-App-APPROVED-HOD-1.22.2022.pdf; New York City Bar Association, *Letter to Members of the New York Court of Appeals Re: Amending Question 26 of the New York Bar Application* (June 21, 2021), https://s3.amazonaws.com/documents.nycbar.org/files/2020889_AmendingQuestion26oftheNewYorkBar Application.pdf

77. *See* COHN ET AL, *supra* note 67, at 4.

78. For a comprehensive discussion of the issues and argument for inclusion of undocumented lawyers, see Raquel Aldana, Beth Lyon, & Karla Mari McKanders, *Raising the Bar: Law Schools and Legal Institutions Leading to Educate Undocumented Students*, 44 ARIZ. ST. L. J. 5 (2012).

79. *Virtue, supra* note 10, at 1037.

80. "In recent years . . . at least six states—California, Florida, Illinois, Nebraska, New York, and Wyoming—have changed their rules to allow some immigrants who are not fully documented to be admitted to the bar." LISA LERNER & PHILIP SHRAG, ETHICAL PROBLEMS IN THE PRACTICE OF LAW 20 (4th ed., 2018), citing National Conference of State Legislatures, Professional and Occupational Licenses for Immigrants (Jan. 17, 2017) (displaying chart that details the changes in each state), https://www.ncsl.org/research/immigration/professional -and-occupational-licenses-for-immigrants.aspx

81. *Virtue, supra* note 10, at 1039 (citation omitted).

82. *See* In re Garcia, 58 Cal. 4th 440 (2014).

83. Karen Sloan, *California's "Undocumented Lawyer" Obtains U.S. Citizenship After 25-Year Effort*, LAW.COM (July 29, 2019), https://www.law.com/therecorder/ 2019/07/09/californias-undocumented lawyer-obtains-u-s-citizenship/

84. Levin, *supra* note 1, at 783. "In the 1970s, bar examiners began to regularly inquire into mental health history and soon thereafter, bar applicants were sometimes denied admission on that basis." *Id.* (citations omitted).

85. *Id.* at 778.

86. *See, e.g.*, Phyllis Coleman & Ronald A. Shellow, *Ask About Conduct, Not Mental Illness: A Proposal for Bar Examiners and Medical Boards to Comply with the ADA and the Constitution*, 20 J. LEGIS. 147 (1994).

87. David Jaffe & Janet E. Stearns, *Conduct Yourselves Accordingly: Amending Bar Character and Fitness Questions to Promote Lawyer Well-Being*, 26 PROF. LAWYER 1 (Jan. 2020), https://ssrn.com/abstract=3504290

88. *See, e.g.*, Alyssa Dragnich, *Have You Ever: How State Bar Association Inquiries into Mental Health Violate the Americans with Disabilities Act*, 80 BROOK. L. REV. 677 (2015).

89. Jaffe & Stearns, *supra* note 87, at 3–4.

90. *Id.* at 4.

91. *Id.* at 5–8; Lindsey Ruta Lusk, *The Poison of Propensity: How Character and Fitness Sacrifices the "Others" in the Name of "Protection,"* 2018 ILL. L. REV. 345 (2018) (includes powerful personal narrative of then-law student, now attorney with bipolar diagnosis); Andrea Stempien, *Answering the Call of the Question: Reforming Mental Health Disclosure During Character and Fitness to Combat Mental Illness in the Legal Profession*, 93 U. DET. MERCY L. REV. 185 (2016).

92. *Virtue, supra* note 10, at 1040; *Moral Character, supra* note 9, at 549.

93. Levin et al., *supra* note 6, at 51 (study of Connecticut lawyers showing

information gathered in the character and fitness inquiry to be of little value in predicting who will subsequently be disciplined).

94. *Id.* at 79.

95. *Id.*

96. Levin, *supra* note 1, at 796 (footnote omitted). "Lawyers who were disciplined were more than twice as likely to report having had a pre-application psychological diagnosis/treatment as those who did not (4.1% vs. 1.9%). They were also substantially more likely to report having had a pre-application criminal conviction (5.6% vs. 2.1%), having had their driver's license suspended (13.1% vs. 5.4%), having had delinquent credit accounts (23.8% vs. 7.2%), and having attended a law school ranked in the bottom half (59% vs. 36.8%)." *Id.* at 794 (citing to Levin et al., *supra* note 6, at 63).

97. Levin, *supra* note 1, at 794.

98. *Id.* (citing to Levin et al., *supra* note 6, at 71).

99. *Id.* at 795.

100. *Id.* at 800.

CHAPTER 10

1. Ronald M. Epstein & Edward M. Hundert, *Defining and Assessing Professional Competence*, 287 JAMA 226, 226 (2002). They "propose that professional competence is the habitual and judicious use of communication, knowledge, technical skills, clinical reasoning, emotions, values, and reflection in daily practice for the benefit of the individual and community being served." *Id.*

2. *See* DEBORAH JONES MERRITT & LOGAN CORNETT, BUILDING A BETTER BAR: THE TWELVE BUILDING BLOCKS OF MINIMUM COMPETENCE 32–34 (Dec. 2020), https://iaals.du.edu/sites/default/files/documents/publications/building_a_better_bar.pdf; MARJORIE M. SHULTZ & SHELDON ZEDECK, FINAL REPORT: IDENTIFICATION, DEVELOPMENT, AND VALIDATION OF PREDICTORS FOR SUCCESSFUL LAWYERING 25 (2008); ALLI GERKMAN & LOGAN CORNETT, FOUNDATIONS FOR PRACTICE: THE WHOLE LAWYER AND THE CHARACTER QUOTIENT (2016) [hereinafter FOUNDATIONS FOR PRACTICE].

3. WILLIAM SULLIVAN, ANNE COLBY, JUDITH WELCH WEGNER, LLOYD BOND, & LEE S. SHULMAN, EDUCATING LAWYERS: PREPARATION FOR THE PROFESSION OF LAW 28–33 (2007); *see* Jerome M. Organ, *Is There Sufficient Human Resource Capacity to Support Robust Professional Identity Formation Learning Outcomes?*, 14 U. ST. THOMAS L. J. 458, 462 (2018) ("the authors of *Educating Lawyers* told us legal education has made the least progress with respect to the third apprenticeship of professional identity"); Russell Pearce, *MacCrate's Missed Opportunity: The MacCrate Report's Failure to Advance Professional Values*, 23 PACE L. REV. 575, 585 (2003) (pointing out marginalization of legal ethics in law school).

4. Louis D. Bilionis, *Bringing Purposefulness to the American Law School's*

Support of Professional Identity Formation, 14 U. ST. THOMAS L. J. 480, 480 (2018) (citation omitted).

5. Neil W. Hamilton, *Professional-Identity/Professional-Formation/Professionalism Learning Outcomes: What Can We Learn About Assessment from Medical Education?*, 14 U. ST. THOMAS L. J. 357 (2018) (listing the number of law schools with various professional identity formation learning outcomes). For a database of law schools that have adopted learning outcomes related to professional formation, see *Learning Outcomes 302(c) and (d)*, HOLLORAN CENTER, https://www.stthomas.edu/hollorancenter/learningoutcomesandprofessionaldevelopment/learningoutcomesdatabase/learningoutcomes302c/ (last visited Aug. 24, 2020).

6. See, e.g., NEIL W. HAMILTON & LOUIS D. BILIONIS, LAW STUDENT PROFESSIONAL DEVELOPMENT AND FORMATION: BRIDGING LAW SCHOOL, STUDENT, AND EMPLOYER GOALS (2022).

7. Bilionis, *supra* note 4, at 483. Professor Bilionis's definition also includes "the student's acceptance and internalization of a personal responsibility for her or his continuing development toward excellence in all of the competencies of the profession" (*id.*), helpful recognition that professional identity and competence are not separate.

8. See, e.g., HAMILTON & BILIONIS, *supra* note 6; Louis D. Bilionis, *Professional Formation and the Political Economy of the American Law School*, 83 TENN. L. REV. 895, 901–902 (2016) (discussing various programs); Neil Hamilton & Verna Monson, *Legal Education's Ethical Challenge: Empirical Research on How Most Effectively to Foster Each Student's Professional Formation (Professionalism)*, 9 U. ST. THOMAS L. J. 325, 374 (2009) (meet students where they are).

9. See, e.g., Neil Hamilton & Verna Monson, *Answering the Skeptics on Fostering Ethical Professional Formation (Professionalism)*, 20 PROF. LAW. 3, 3–5 (2011) (describing psychology research of Robert Kegan and Lisa Lahey demonstrating ongoing moral/ethical development across a lifetime).

10. See Danny DeWalt, *Practical Lessons Learned While Building a Required Course for Professional Identity Formation*, 14 U. ST. THOMAS L.J. 433, 434 (2018).

11. See, e.g., PATRICK EMERY LONGAN, DAISY HURST FLOYD, & TIMOTHY W. FLOYD, THE FORMATION OF PROFESSIONAL IDENTITY: THE PATH FROM STUDENT TO LAWYER (2020).

12. The ABA Section on Legal Education has recently added a requirement in Standard 303(b) that law schools provide students with "substantial opportunities" for "the development of a professional identity." *See ABA Standards—Matters for Notice and Comment—Standards 205, 206, 303, 507, and 508*, https://www.americanbar.org/content/dam/aba/administrative/legal_education_and_admissions_to_the_bar/council_reports_and_resolutions/comments/2021/21-may-notice-and-comment-standards-205-206-303-507-508.pdf; *Holloran Center's Comments on Proposed Revisions to Standard 303* (March 25, 2021), https://

www.americanbar.org/content/dam/aba/administrative/legal_education_and_
admissions_to_the_bar/council_reports_and_resolutions/comments/2021/3-21
-comment-std303-holloran-center.pdf

13. *See* DeWalt, *supra* note 10, at 434 (at the beginning of law school, students "seem more inclined to listen to anything that will help them succeed in law school and the profession").

14. *See* Organ, *supra* note 3, at 465–60.

15. HAMILTON & BILIONIS, *supra* note 6, at 191–92.

16. Kennon M. Sheldon & Lawrence S. Krieger, *Does Legal Education Have Undermining Effects on Law Students? Evaluating Changes in Motivation, Values, and Well-Being*, 22 BEHAV. SCI. & L. 261 (2004) (finding significant reductions in well-being during law school).

17. *See, e.g.*, Ian Ayres, Joseph Bankman, Barbara Fried, and Kristine Luce, *Anxiety Psychoeducation for Law Students: A Pilot Program*, 67 J. LEGAL EDUC. 118 (2017) (describing curricular efforts at Stanford and Yale using cognitive behavioral techniques).

18. MERRITT & CORNETT, *supra* note 2, at 60–61.

19. Leslie C. Levin, *The Folly of Expecting Evil: Reconsidering the Bar's Character and Fitness Requirement*, 2014 BYU L. REV. 775, 785 (2014) ("disciplined lawyers often report depression related to work or life circumstances, alcohol abuse, or family or financial crises") (citations omitted).

20. For a critique of legal education's failure to grapple with concepts of justice, see ROBIN WEST, TEACHING LAW: JUSTICE, POLITICS, AND THE DEMANDS OF PROFESSIONALISM (2014).

21. MERRITT & CORNETT, *supra* note 2, at 75.

22. *See, e.g.*, Howard Gardiner & Lee S. Shulman, *The Professions in America Today: Crucial but Fragile*, 134 DAEDALUS 13, 14 (2005) (identifying creation of and participating in responsible professional communities and performing public service as central for all professionals).

23. *See* Organ, *supra* note 3, at 473 (professors who are reluctant to embrace the professional formation project may have concerns about knowledge transfer and preparing graduates to pass the bar exam).

24. MERRITT & CORNETT, *supra* note 2, at 32 (Carson).

25. *See* Robert L. Jones Jr., Gerard F. Glynn, & John J. Francis, *When Things Go Wrong in the Clinic: How to Prevent and Respond to Serious Student Misconduct*, 41 U. BALT. L. REV. 441 (2012).

26. Levin, *supra* note 19, at 787 ("Lawyers often learn their responses to ethical challenges early in practice from other lawyers around them").

27. David Luban, *Integrity: Its Causes and Cures*, 72 FORDHAM L. REV. 279, 284 (2003) ("we respond to situations by checking to see how other people respond, and their response in large measure determines how we perceive the situation and therefore how we ourselves will respond").

28. MERRITT & CORNETT, *supra* note 2, at 58.

29. *Id.* at 68–69, 75–76 (discussing importance of clinical education and recommending that licensers require clinical coursework).

30. *See* Jones et al., *supra* note 25.

31. Levin, *supra* note 19, at 786 ("Lawyers in solo and small firm practice receive over 90% of all discipline, even though they make up less than 50% of all practicing lawyers") (citations omitted).

32. KELLIE R. EARLY, JOANNE KANE, MARK RAYMOND, & DANIELLE M. MOREAU, NCBE TESTING TASK FORCE PHASE 2 REPORT: 2019 PRACTICE ANALYSIS 42 (March 2020) [hereinafter NCBE PRACTICE ANALYSIS], https://nextgenbarexam .ncbex.org/wp-content/uploads/TestingTaskForce_Phase_2_Report_031020.pdf

33. STATE BAR OF CALIFORNIA CAPA WORKING GROUP, THE PRACTICE OF LAW IN CALIFORNIA: FINDINGS FROM THE CALIFORNIA ATTORNEY PRACTICE ANALYSIS AND IMPLICATIONS FOR THE CALIFORNIA BAR EXAM 18 (2020).

34. MERRITT & CORNETT, *supra* note 2, at 58–60.

35. *Id.* at 58.

36. *Id.*

37. Resources exist. *See, e.g.,* KATRINA LEE, THE LEGAL CAREER: KNOWING THE BUSINESS, THRIVING IN PRACTICE (2d ed. 2020).

38. "Focus group members suggested that professional conduct was a 'learned skill' rather than a set of black-letter rules." MERRITT & CORNETT, *supra* note 2, at 32. Deborah Rhode described the standard advice for passing the MPRE as, "If in doubt, pick the second most ethical course of action." DEBORAH L. RHODE, IN THE INTERESTS OF JUSTICE: REFORMING THE LEGAL PROFESSION 150 (2000) (citation omitted).

39. NCBE PRACTICE ANALYSIS, *supra* note 32, at 5 (knowledge area with the highest mean importance rating was "rules of professional responsibility and ethical obligations").

40. *Cf.* Deborah L. Rhode, *Virtue and the Law: The Good Moral Character Requirement in Occupational Licensing, Bar Regulation, and Immigration Proceedings,* 43 LAW & SOC. INQUIRY 1027, 1049 (2018) (advocating for "direct and substantial relationship between legal practice and any potentially disqualifying conduct").

41. *See id.* at 1049. "In all cases, the preeminent concern should be public protection, not professional reputation. Resources now squandered in a vain attempt to predict lawyer misconduct would be better spent on detecting, deterring, and remedying it." *Id.*

42. *Cf.* Linda McGuire, *Lawyering or Lying? When Law School Applicants Hide Their Criminal Histories and Other Misconduct,* 45 S. TEX. L. REV. 709 (2004) (advocating for educating law students about importance of disclosure on law school applications at law school orientation).

43. *See, e.g.,* Florida Board of Bar Examiners, Rules of the Supreme Court Re-

lated to Admission to the Bar, Rule 21–2.2 (2020).

44. "Their problems with their marriages, their mortgages, and other life circumstances often arise years after the character and fitness inquiry occurs." Levin, *supra* note 19, at 785–86 (citation omitted).

45. *Id.* at 785 (citations omitted).

46. Daniel B. Hogan, *The Effectiveness of Licensing: History, Evidence, and Recommendations*, 7 LAW AND HUMAN BEHAVIOR 117, 124 (1983).

47. *Id.* (citation omitted).

48. STANDING COMMITTEE ON PROFESSIONAL REGULATION OF THE ABA, CENTER FOR PROFESSIONAL RESPONSIBILITY, 2018 SURVEY ON LAWYER DISCI-PLINE SYSTEMS (SOLD) (2020), https://www.americanbar.org/content/dam/aba/ administrative/professional_responsibility/2018sold-results.pdf. In 2018, 83,073 complaints were filed against the 1,257,772 active licensed attorneys in the nation. That year 1,921 attorneys were privately disciplined, 2,872 attorneys were publicly disciplined, and 631 disbarred, of which 253 were voluntary. *Id.* at 5, 24.

49. RHODE, *supra* note 38, at 211–12.

50. Debra Moss Curtis, *Attorney Discipline Nationwide: A Comparative Analysis of Process and Statistics*, 35 J. LEGAL PROF. 209, 212 (2011).

51. RHODE, *supra* note 38, at 211–12; *see also* Benjamin Hoorn Barton, *Why Do We Regulate Lawyers: An Economic Analysis of the Justifications for Entry and Conduct Regulation*, 33 ARIZ. ST. L. J. 429, 484–88 (2001) (supporting shift from entry barriers to conduct regulation including transparency of records, height-ened reporting, and deeper investigations).

CHAPTER 11

1. For an argument that principles of professional responsibility require such scrutiny, see Joan W. Howarth, *The Professional Responsibility Case for Valid and Nondiscriminatory Bar Exams*, 33 GEO. J. LEGAL ETHICS 931 (2020).

2. I fill accepted a Spirit of Excellence Award at the midyear meeting of the ABA in February 2021. *See Five Trailblazers Move Needle on Diversity, Inclusion*, ABA (Feb. 19, 2021), https://www.americanbar.org/news/abanews/aba-news-archives/ 2021/02/five-trailblazers-move-needle-on-diversity--inclusion/

3. Brad N. Greenwood, Rachel R. Hardeman, Laura Huang, & Aaron So-journer, *Physician–Patient Racial Concordance and Disparities in Birthing Mortality for Newborns*, 35 PNAS 21194 (2020), https://www.pnas.org/content/117/35/ 21194

4. *See* Milan Markovic & Gabrielle Plickert, *The Paradox of Minority Attorney Satisfaction*, 60 INT'L REV. L. & ECON. 2 (2019); Carla D. Pratt, *Way to Represent: The Role of Black Lawyers in Contemporary American Democracy*, 77 FORDHAM L. REV. 1409, 1424–34 (2008).

5. *See, e.g.*, Deborah Jones Merritt, Carol L. Chomsky, Claudia Angelos, &

Joan W. Howarth, *Racial Disparities in Bar Exam Results—Causes and Remedies*, BLOOMBERG LAW (July 20, 2021), https://news.bloomberglaw.com/us-law-week/ racial-disparities-in-bar-exam-results-causes-and-remedies

6. *See, e.g.*, WILLIAM SULLIVAN, ANNE COLBY, JUDITH WELCH WEGNER, LLOYD BOND, & LEE S. SHULMAN, EDUCATING LAWYERS: PREPARATION FOR THE PROFESSION OF LAW 91–125 (2007); Peter A. Joy, *The Uneasy History of Experiential Education in U.S. Law Schools*, 122 DICK. L. REV. 551 (2018).

7. "Law schools . . . need to give the teaching of practice a valued place in the legal curriculum so that formation of the students' professional judgment is not abandoned to chance." SULLIVAN ET AL., *supra* note 6, at 115.

8. Professional formation "introduces students to the purposes and attitudes that are guided by the values for which the professional community is responsible." *Id.* at 28. Its primary goal "is to teach the skills and inclinations, along with the ethical standards, social roles, and responsibilities that mark the professional." *Id.*

9. Clinical residencies are described more fully in Chapter 12.

10. Bar exams are the focus of Chapters 14 and 15.

11. Chapter 13 explores advisable educational requirements more fully.

12. *See* Ariz. Sup. Ct. R. 34(2) (permitting law students to take the bar exam in their last semester).

13. *See* Wisc. Sup. Ct. R. 40.03 (providing rules for diploma privilege for Marquette and Wisconsin graduates).

14. *See Daniel Webster Scholar Honors Program*, UNH FRANKLIN PIERCE SCHOOL OF LAW, https://law.unh.edu/academics/daniel-webster-scholar-honors -program (last visited March 25, 2022).

15. *See* Chapter 15 (describing better bar exams).

16. AARON N. TAYLOR, JASON M. SCOTT, & JOSH JACKSON, IT'S NOT WHERE YOU START, IT'S HOW YOU FINISH: PREDICTING LAW SCHOOL AND BAR SUCCESS 29 (March 24, 2021) (National Report of Findings for the AccessLex/LSSSE Bar Exam Success Initiative), https://www.accesslex.org/sites/default/files/2021-04/ LSSSE%20National_Report.pdf

17. *See* Joan W. Howarth, *The Case for a Uniform Cut Score*, 42 J. LEGAL PROF. 69 (2017).

18. For these reasons, California lawyers overwhelmingly opposed lowering the cut score when surveyed. *See* STATE BAR OF CALIFORNIA, REPORT TO THE ADMISSIONS AND EDUCATION COMMITTEE AND THE COMMITTEE OF BAR EXAMINERS REGARDING PUBLIC COMMENTS ON THE STANDARD SETTING STUDY (Aug. 31. 2017), http://apps.calbar.ca.gov/cbe/docs/agendaItem/Public/agendaitem 1000001998.pdf

19. Deborah J. Merritt, Lowell L. Hargens, & Barbara F. Reskin, *Raising the Bar: A Social Science Critique of Recent Increase to Passing Scores on the Bar Exam*,

69 U. CIN. L. REV. 929, 965 (2001); *see* Stephen P. Klein & Roger Bolus, *The Size and Source of Differences in Bar Exam Passing Rates Among Racial and Ethnic Groups*, 6 BAR EXAM'R 8, 8 (Nov. 1997) (discussed in Merritt et al., *supra*, at 966–67).

20. A cut score of 130 is the lowest currently used by a cohort of states. *See* NCBE, *Chart 10: Non-Uniform Bar Examination Jurisdictions—MPRE Requirements, MBE Score Transfers, and Attorneys' Exams:, Comprehensive Guide to Bar Admission Requirements 2021,* https://reports.ncbex.org/comp-guide/charts/chart -10/; *see also* Alex M. Johnson Jr., *Knots in the Pipeline for Prospective Lawyers of Color: The LSAT Is Not the Problem and Affirmative Action Is Not the Answer,* 24 STAN. L. & POL'Y REV. 379, 405–19 (2013) (recommending 130 as uniform cut score to diversify the profession).

21. *See* Mitchel L. Winick, Victor D. Quintanilla, Sam Erman, Christina Chong-Nakatsuchi, & Michael Frisby, *Examining the California Cut Score: An Empirical Analysis of Minimum Competency, Public Protection, Disparate Impact, and National Standards* (Oct. 15, 2020), https://papers.ssrn.com/sol3/papers .cfm?abstract_id=3707812. For a study suggesting that lowering the California cut score could increase disciplinary rates, *see* Robert Anderson IV & Derek T. Muller, *The High Cost of Lowering the Bar,* 32. GEO. J. LEGAL ETHICS 307 (2019); *but see* Deborah J. Merritt, *Bar Exam Scores and Lawyer Discipline,* LAW SCHOOL CAFÉ (June 3, 2017) (challenging some Anderson & Muller conclusions), https:// perma.cc/6RMSF62L

22. For information on California bar passage studies generally, see STATE BAR OF CALIFORNIA, FINAL REPORT ON THE 2017 CALIFORNIA BAR EXAM STUDIES (Dec. 1, 2017), https://www.calbar.ca.gov/Portals/0/documents/reports/2017-Final -Bar-Exam-Report.pdf

23. *See* Steven Foster, *Does the Multistate Bar Exam Validly Measure Attorney Competence?,* 82 OHIO ST. L. J. ONLINE 31 (Jan. 4, 2021) (lawyers flunked test of MBE questions administered by researcher).

24. DEBORAH L. RHODE, ACCESS TO JUSTICE 3 (2004).

25. *See, e.g., id.* at 89 (discussing the need to expand provision of legal services by non-lawyer specialists); Rebecca Sandefur, *Break Up Lawyers' Monopoly on the Law,* POLITICO (2019), https://www.politico.com/interactives/2019/how-to-fix -politics-in-america/participation/break-up-lawyers-monopoly-on-law/; Rebecca L. Sandefur & Thomas M. Clarke, *Designing the Competition: A Future of Roles Beyond Lawyers: The Case of the USA,* 67 HASTINGS L.J. 1467 (2016). Academics have advanced serious arguments that attorney licensure itself may not protect the public. *See, e.g.,* CLIFFORD WINSTON, DAVID BURK, & JIA YAN, TROUBLE AT THE BAR: AN ECONOMICS PERSPECTIVE OF THE LEGAL PROFESSION AND THE CASE FOR FUNDAMENTAL REFORM 6 (2021) (clients should have choice between licensed or unlicensed lawyers); Deborah J. Cantrell, *The Obligation of Legal Aid Lawyers to Champion Practice by Nonlawyers,* 73 FORDHAM L. REV. 883, 894 (2004) (unauthorized practice of law rules driven by profession's self-interest); Russell G.

Pearce, *The Professionalism Paradigm Shift: Why Discarding Professional Ideology Will Improve the Conduct and Reputation of the Bar*, 70 N.Y.U. L. REV. 1229, 1269–70 (1995) (proposing that a license not be required to provide legal services but that only licensed practitioners be permitted to call themselves lawyers). But the profession has not engaged meaningfully with this idea since it defeated the open admissions movement of the 1800s.

26. *See* Joan W. Howarth & Judith Welch Wegner, *Ringing Changes: Systems Thinking About Legal Licensing*, 13 FIU L. REV. 383, 446–49 (2019); Renee Newman Knake, *Democratizing Legal Education*, 45 CONN. L. REV. 1281, 1310–12 (2013).

27. Most problems come from middle-aged men with extensive practice experience. *See* Leslie C. Levin, *The Folly of Expecting Evil: Reconsidering the Bar's Character and Fitness Requirement*, 2014 BYU L. REV. 775, 785 (2014), citing to RICHARD L. ABEL, LAWYERS IN THE DOCK: LEARNING FROM ATTORNEY DISCIPLINARY PROCEEDINGS 496 (2008). "Law society statistics indicate that lawyers in their first three years of practice generate fewer competence problems than other cohorts." JORDAN FURLONG, LAWYER LICENSING AND COMPETENCE IN ALBERTA: ANALYSIS AND RECOMMENDATIONS 6 (Nov. 2020) (report prepared for Law Society of Alberta), https://documents.lawsociety.ab.ca/wp-content/uploads/2020/12/08212906/LawyerLicensingandCompetenceinAlbertaReport_Designed.pdf. For an argument that patterns of problems later in practice cast doubt on the current practice of requiring a one-time entry-level exam without further examination, see David Adam Friedman, *Do We Need a Bar Exam . . . For Experienced Lawyers*, 12 U.C. IRVINE L. REV. __ (forthcoming 2022). For criticism that barriers to entry instead of regulation of lawyers protects lawyers more than consumers, see Benjamin Hoorn Barton, *Why Do We Regulate Lawyers: An Economic Analysis of the Justifications for Entry and Conduct Regulation*, 33 ARIZ. ST. L. J. 429, 433 (2001).

28. Performance tests are described more fully in Chapter 15.

29. *See* FURLONG, *supra* note 27, at 50 (noting that Alberta and other Canadian jurisdictions do not require continuing legal education but instead, along with England and Wales, use a "self-assessment and learning plan" system that requires lawyers to annually assess their learning needs, develop a learning plan, and execute that learning plan).

30. The New Zealand requirements are available at *CPD Requirements*, NEW ZEALAND LAW SOC., https://www.lawsociety.org.nz/professional-practice/legal-practice/continuing-professional-development/cpd-requirements/ (last visited April 28, 2021).

31. DEBORAH JONES MERRITT & LOGAN CORNETT, BUILDING A BETTER BAR: THE TWELVE BUILDING BLOCKS OF MINIMUM COMPETENCE 61–62 (Dec. 2020) (describing "the ability to pursue self-directed learning" as a building block of competence), https://iaals.du.edu/sites/default/files/documents/publications/building_a_better_bar.pdf

32. "Practice in professions and occupations often changes over time. . . . Each profession or occupation should periodically reevaluate the knowledge and skills measured in its examination used to meet the requirements of the credential." AMERICAN EDUCATIONAL RESEARCH ASSOCIATION, AMERICAN PSYCHOLOGICAL ASSOCIATION, & NATIONAL COUNCIL ON MEASUREMENT IN EDUCATION, STANDARDS FOR EDUCATIONAL AND PSYCHOLOGICAL TESTING 176–77 (2014).

33. *See Home Page*, NCBE: NEXTGEN BAR EXAM OF THE FUTURE, https://nextgenbarexam.ncbex.org/ (last visited April 28, 2021).

34. *See* Mark R. Raymond, April Southwick, and Mengyao Zhang, *The Testing Column: Ensuring Fairness in Assessment*, 90 BAR EXAM'R 73 (Spring 2021), https://thebarexaminer.ncbex.org/article/spring-2021/the-testing-column-ensuring-fairness-in-assessment/

CHAPTER 12

1. For earlier discussion of many of the ideas in this chapter, see Joan W. Howarth & Judith Welch Wegner, *Ringing Changes: Systems Thinking About Legal Licensing*, 13 FIU L. REV. 383, 428–37 (2019).

2. Most jurisdictions have student practice rules that permit law students to practice law—including as first chair—under the supervision of an experienced lawyer, typically a clinical law professor. *See* Wallace J. Mlyniec & Haley D. Etchison, *Conceptualizing Student Practice for the 21st Century: Educational and Ethical Considerations in Modernizing the District of Columbia Student Practice Rules*, 28 GEO. J. LEGAL ETHICS 207 (2015). For important suggested improvements to student practice rules, see Gillian R. Chadwick, *(Un)supervised Student Practice*, 58 SAN DIEGO L. REV. 497 (2021).

3. For a detailed description and evaluation of residency training for physicians in the United States, see MOLLY COOKE, DAVID M. IRBY, & BRIDGET C. O'BRIEN, EDUCATING PHYSICIANS: A CALL FOR REFORM OF MEDICAL SCHOOL AND RESIDENCY 113–60 (2010).

4. "Law schools . . . need to give the teaching of practice a valued place in the legal curriculum so that formation of the students' professional judgment is not abandoned to chance." WILLIAM SULLIVAN, ANNE COLBY, JUDITH WELCH WEGNER, LLOYD BOND, & LEE S. SHULMAN, EDUCATING LAWYERS: PREPARATION FOR THE PROFESSION OF LAW 115 (2007).

5. Professional formation "introduces students to the purposes and attitudes that are guided by the values for which the professional community is responsible." *Id.* at 28. Its primary goal "is to teach the skills and inclinations, along with the ethical standards, social roles, and responsibilities that mark the professional." *Id.*

6. Insistence on client representation, reflective practice, supervision, and assessment of goals is not new. *See, e.g.,* Gary S. Laser, *Educating for Professional*

Competence in the Twenty-First Century: Educational Reform at Chicago-Kent College of Law, 68 CHI.-KENT L. REV. 243, 244 (1992).

7. *See* Susan L. Brooks, *Meeting the Professional Identity Challenge in Legal Education Through a Relationship-Centered Experiential Curriculum,* 41 U. BALT. L. REV. 395, 395–96 (2012) (advocating that each student progress through simulated practice, mentee, and first-chair roles).

8. Medical students spend two of the four years of medical school in clinical settings. COOKE ET AL., *supra* note 3, at 21.

9. Veterinary students must spend at least one of the four academic years of veterinary college in "hands-on clinical education." *COE Accreditation Policies and Procedures: Requirements,* AMERICAN VETERINARY MEDICAL ASSOCIATION (Sept. 2017), https://www.avma.org/ProfessionalDevelopment/Education /Accreditation/Colleges/Pages/coe-pprequirements-of-accredited-college.aspx.

10. "The comprehensive care experiences provided for patients by students should be adequate to ensure competency in all components of general dentistry practice." *Current Accreditation Standards,* COMMISSION ON DENTAL ACCREDITATION (CODA) 25 (2021), https://coda.ada.org/en/current-accreditation-standards

11. "It is a basic precept of social work education that the two interrelated components of curriculum—classroom and field—are of equal importance within the curriculum." COUNCIL ON SOCIAL WORK EDUCATION, EDUCATIONAL POLICY AND ACCREDITATION STANDARDS (EPAS) FOR BACCALAUREATE AND MASTER'S SOCIAL WORK PROGRAMS 12 (2015), https://www.cswe.org/getattachment/ Accreditation/Standards-and-Policies/2015-EPAS/2015EPASandGlossary.pdf

12. *See* Peter A. Joy, *The Ethics of Law School Clinic Students as Student-Lawyers,* 45 S. TEX. L. REV. 815, 815–16 (2003–2004).

13. *See, e.g.,* Ann Shalleck & Jane H. Aiken, *Supervision: A Conceptual Framework,* in SUSAN BRYANT, ELLIOTT S. MILSTEIN, & ANN C. SHALLECK, TRANSFORMING THE EDUCATION OF LAWYERS: THEORY AND PRACTICE OF CLINICAL PEDAGOGY 169 (2014); Jane H. Aiken & Ann Shalleck, *The Practice of Supervision,* *id.* at 205.

14. COOKE ET AL, *supra* note 3, at 126.

15. *See* DEBORAH JONES MERRITT & LOGAN CORNETT, BUILDING A BETTER BAR: THE TWELVE BUILDING BLOCKS OF MINIMUM COMPETENCE (2020), https: //iaals.du.edu/sites/default/files/documents/publications/building_a_better_bar .pdf; *see also* other research discussed in Chapter 7.

16. For a thoughtful delineation of multiple aspects of fundamental goals for learning in clinics (including, for example, improving capacities to manage uncertainty), see Susan Bryant, Elliott S. Milstein, & Ann Shalleck, *Learning Goals for Clinical Programs,* in BRYANT ET AL., *supra* note 13, at 13; *see also* Lisa Radtke Bliss & Donald C. Peters, *Delivering Effective Education in In-House Clinics,* in BUILDING ON BEST PRACTICES: TRANSFORMING LEGAL EDUCATION IN A CHANGING

WORLD 188–215 (Deborah Maranville, Lisa Radtke Bliss, Carolyn Wilkes Kaas, & Antoinette Sedillo Lopez, eds., 2015) at 188–215 [hereinafter BUILDING ON BEST PRACTICES].

17. Effective externship programs articulate and assess learning goals. *See generally* Kelly S. Terry, *Embedding Assessment Principles in Externships*, 20 CLINICAL L. REV. 467 (2014); Carolyn Wilkes Kaas, Cynthia Batt, Dena Bauman, & Daniel Schaffzin, *Delivering Effective Education in Externship Programs*, *in* BUILDING ON BEST PRACTICES, *supra* note 16, at 224–30.

18. *See, e.g.*, Bryant, Milstein, & Shalleck, *Learning Goals for Clinical Programs*, *supra* note 16, at 34–35.

19. *See* Kaas et al., *supra* note 17, at 219.

20. *See, e.g.*, NEIL W. HAMILTON & LOUIS D. BILIONIS, LAW STUDENT PROFESSIONAL DEVELOPMENT AND FORMATION: BRIDGING LAW SCHOOL, STUDENT, AND EMPLOYER GOALS 71–72 (2022); ROY STUCKEY AND OTHERS, BEST PRACTICES FOR LEGAL EDUCATION: A VISION AND A ROAD MAP 48–49 (2007); Larry O. Natt Gantt II & Benjamin V. Madison III, *Teaching Knowledge, Skills, and Values of Professional Identity Formation*, *in* BUILDING ON BEST PRACTICES, *supra* note 16, at 260–68; Donald A. Schön, *Educating the Reflective Legal Practitioner*, 2 CLINICAL L. REV. 231 (1995) (discussing uncertainty and need for reflection on reflection); Michael Hunter Schwartz, *Teaching Law Students to Be Self-Regulated Learners*, 2003 MICH. ST. D. C. L. L. REV. 447 (2003); Timothy Casey, *Reflective Practice in Legal Education: The Stages of Reflection*, 20 CLINICAL L. REV. 317, 326–27 (2014). Much of the work on reflective practice in legal education builds on DONALD A. SCHÖN, EDUCATING THE REFLECTIVE PRACTITIONER: TOWARD A NEW DESIGN FOR TEACHING AND LEARNING IN THE PROFESSIONS (1987) and DONALD A. SCHÖN, THE REFLECTIVE PRACTITIONER: HOW PROFESSIONALS THINK IN PRACTICE (1983).

21. Casey, *supra* note 20, at 319. "Professionals who engage in reflective practice make a conscious decision to integrate reflection into their practice. For them, the process of engaging in conscious and deliberate reflection becomes integrated into the practice." *Id.* at 319 n.10.

22. *See id.* at 320 n.13.

23. *See* SULLIVAN ET AL., *supra* note 4, at 145.

24. *See* Chapter 9 (proposing clinical residency requirement to help shift character and fitness efforts from prediction to prevention of problems).

25. The 2020 NCBE practice survey found "instructing/mentoring" to be lowest of the twenty-six surveyed skills, abilities, and other characteristics. KELLIE R. EARLY, JOANNE KANE, MARK RAYMOND, & DANIELLE M. MOREAU, NCBE TESTING TASK FORCE PHASE 2 REPORT: 2019 PRACTICE ANALYSIS 13 (March 2020) 26, 63, https://nextgenbarexam.ncbex.org/wp-content/uploads/TestingTaskForce_Phase_2_Report_031020.pdf

26. *See* MERRITT & CORNETT, *supra* note 15.

27. *See Introduction to the Portfolio Examination*, DENTAL BOARD OF CALI-FORNIA, https://www.dbc.ca.gov/applicants/portfolio_binder.shtml (last visited Nov. 10, 2020).

28. Certification of successful completion of identified tasks is different from the checklist of twenty-six experiences currently required for candidates for admission in Delaware, all of which entail watching or reading about, not doing. *See Clerkship Checklist*, DELAWARE COURTS, https://courts.delaware.gov/bbe/ (last visited April 16, 2021).

29. The New Hampshire's Daniel Webster Scholar Honors Program and the Oregon Task Force proposals are discussed more extensively in Chapter 13 about improved educational requirements.

30. *E.g.*, Karen Tokarz et al., *Legal Education at a Crossroads: Innovation, Integration, and Pluralism Required!*, 43 WASH. U. J. L. & POL'Y 11, 15 (2013) (proposing a requirement of twenty-one credits of experiential learning including at least five in a clinic or externship).

31. The Washington and Lee University School of Law requires eighteen upper-level experiential credits, some of which must include client representation. *See Experiential Education at W&L Law*, WASHINGTON & LEE UNIVERSITY SCHOOL OF LAW, https://law.wlu.edu/academics/experiential-education (last visited Jan. 8, 2022). The University of the District of Columbia School of Law requires fourteen credits of clinics alone. *See Curriculum: Full-Time J.D. Program*, UNIVERSITY OF THE DISTRICT OF COLUMBIA SCHOOL OF LAW, https://www.law.udc.edu/page/fulltimecurriculum (last visited Jan. 8, 2022). CUNY Law School has required all students to take sixteen to twenty experiential credits, with a minimum of twelve credits in clinics. *See Academic Planning*, CUNY SCHOOL OF LAW, https://www.law.cuny.edu/academics/planning/ (last visited Jan. 8, 2022).

32. *See* STATE BAR OF CALIFORNIA, TASK FORCE ON ADMISSIONS, REGULA-TION REFORM: PHASE II FINAL REPORT (Sept. 25, 2014), https://www.calbar.ca.gov/Portals/0/documents/bog/bot_ExecDir/2014_TFARRPhaseIIFinalReport_092514.pdf. The Clinical Legal Education Association (CLEA) endorsed this licensing proposal. *See* CLINICAL LEGAL EDUCATION ASSOCIATION, COMMENT OF THE CLINICAL LEGAL EDUCATION ASSOCIATION ON THE PHASE II IMPLEMENT-ING RECOMMENDATIONS OF THE CALIFORNIA TASK FORCE ON ADMISSIONS REGULATION 1 (2014), http://www.cleaweb.org/Resources/Documents/9-1014%20CLEA%20comment%20to%20CA%20Task%20Force%20FINAL.pdf

33. CLEA endorsed this fifteen-credit accreditation proposal. *See* CLINICAL LEGAL EDUCATION ASSOCIATION, COMMENT ON DRAFT STANDARD 303(A)(3) & PROPOSAL FOR AMENDMENT TO EXISTING STANDARD 302(A)(4) TO REQUIRE 15 CREDITS OF EXPERIENTIAL COURSES 1 (2013), http://www.cleaweb.org/Resources/Documents/20140114%20CLEA%20Chapter%203%20comment.pdf. A more lim-

ited six-credit requirement was ultimately adopted. *See* ABA SECTION OF LEGAL EDUCATION AND ADMISSION TO THE BAR, ABA STANDARDS AND RULES OF PROCEDURE FOR APPROVAL OF LAW SCHOOLS 2018–2019, at 16.

34. *New York Rules of the Court of Appeals for the Admission of Attorneys and Counselors at Law §520.18(A)(2),* N.Y. COURT APPEALS, https://www.nycourts.gov/ctapps/520rules10.htm (last visited Feb. 28, 2019).

35. *See Daniel Webster Scholar Honors Program,* UNH FRANKLIN PIERCE SCHOOL OF LAW, https://law.unh.edu/academics/daniel-webster-scholar-honors-program (last visited March 25, 2022).

36. Daniel Webster Scholars must complete six credits of "clinic/residency" (the non-simulation component of the program) before graduation. *See id.* A variety of clinical opportunities are available. *Experiential Education,* UNH FRANKLIN PIERCE SCHOOL OF LAW, https://law.unh.edu/academics/experiential-education (last visited April 15, 2021).

37. The Oregon proposal replicates this aspect of the New Hampshire program. *See Supplemental Report of Alternative to the Exam Taskforce,* OREGON STATE BAR TASK FORCE 16, 20–21, 23 (Nov. 29, 2021) [hereinafter *Or. Supp. Report*], https://taskforces.osbar.org/files/2021-11-29SupplementalReporttoJune182021ATEReport.pdf

38. *See id.*

39. *See Information and Resources Related to the Utah Supreme Court's Temporary Order Waiving the Bar Exam Requirement in Response to the COVID-19 Pandemic,* https://utahdiplomaprivilegeorg.wordpress.com/ (last visited July 7, 2021).

40. *See* Peggy Maisel, *An Alternative Model to United States Bar Examinations: The South African Community Service Experience in Licensing Attorneys,* 20 GA. ST. U. L. REV. 977 (2009); *see also* Lorne Foster, *Lawyers of Colour and Racialized Immigrants with Foreign Legal Degrees: An Examination of the Institutionalized Processes of Social Nullification,* 2 INTERNATIONAL JOURNAL OF CRIMINOLOGY AND SOCIOLOGICAL THEORY 189 (2009).

41. *Id.; see also Articling Reductions and Exemptions from PLTC,* LAW. SOC. https://www.lawsociety.bc.ca/becoming-a-lawyer-in-bc/admission-program/articling-centre/articling-reductions-and-exemptions-from-pltc/ (last visited April 21, 2021).

42. *See* Leslie C. Levin, *The Politics of Bar Admission: Lessons from the Pandemic,* 50 HOFSTRA L. REV. 81, 115 (2021) (bar leader described Delaware as "purposefully exclusive and selective"); at 133 (explaining that Delaware desire to "preserve [it's] reputation for having an elite bar with notoriously difficult admission requirements"); *but see Improving Diversity in the Delaware Bench and Bar Strategic Plan, Report and Recommendations to the Delaware Supreme Court,* NATIONAL CENTER FOR STATE COURTS (Jan. 31, 2022) (recommending numerous proposals to Delaware Supreme Court including a path to licensure without a

bar exam similar to the Daniel Webster Scholars program, reconsideration of the high cut score, reduction in the number of subjects tested, offering the bar exam twice a year, and rethinking of the court observation requirements), https://courts .delaware.gov/forms/download.aspx?id=135148

43. NCBE, COMPREHENSIVE GUIDE TO BAR ADMISSION REQUIREMENTS (2021), https://reports.ncbex.org/comp-guide/

44. *See* Del. Ct. R. 52(A)(8).

45. ABA NATIONAL LAWYER POPULATION SURVEY 2 (2021) ("10-Year Trend in Lawyer Population by State"), https://www.americanbar.org/content/dam/aba/ administrative/market_research/2021-national-lawyer-population-survey.pdf

46. Vermont's population is 628,061 compared to Delaware's 982,895, according to *The 50 US States Ranked by Population,* WORLD ATLAS, https://www .worldatlas.com/articles/us-states-by-population.html#table (last visited April 21, 2021).

47. Vermont's gross domestic product is $32,796.7 million compared to Delaware's $75,512.5 million, according to the Bureau of Economic Analysis of the U.S. Department of Commerce. *See State BEARFACTS,* BUREAU OF ECONOMIC ANALYSIS, https://apps.bea.gov/regional/bearfacts/statebf.cfm (last visited April 21, 2021).

48. Mitchel L. Winick, Victor D. Quintanilla, Sam Erman, Christina Chong-Nakatsuchi, & Michael Frisby, *Examining the California Cut Score: An Empirical Analysis of Minimum Competency, Public Protection, Disparate Impact, and National Standards* (Oct. 15, 2020), https://papers.ssrn.com/sol3/papers.cfm?abstract _id=3707812

49. Candidates (called clerks in Delaware) are required to complete twenty-six activities, including, for example, attending civil and criminal trials and at least two bankruptcy hearings, each of which requires the signature of the clerk and a supervising attorney. *See Clerkship Checklist,* DELAWARE COURTS, https://courts .delaware.gov/bbe/ (last visited April 16, 2021).

50. California and Rhode Island both have lowered cut scores. *See* Debra Cassens Weiss, *Several States Consider Lowering Cut Scores on Bar Exam, Making It Easier to Pass,* ABA J. (March 29, 2021), https://www.abajournal.com/news/article /several-states-consider-lowering-cut-scores-on-bar-exam-making-it-easier-to -pass

51. *See* Avner Levin & Asher Alkoby, *Barriers to the Profession: Inaction in Ontario, Canada, and Its Consequences,* 3 OÑATI SOCIO-LEGAL SERIES 580 (2013), https://autopapers.ssrn.com/sol3/papers.cfm?abstract_id=2283823#

52. JEROLD S. AUERBACH, UNEQUAL JUSTICE: LAWYERS AND SOCIAL CHANGE IN MODERN AMERICA 126–27 (1976).

53. *See* Zane Sparling, *Oregon Supreme Court Supports Alternative to Bar Exam Requirement, Adding Options for New Lawyers,* OREGONIAN/OREGONLIVE (Jan.

12, 2022), https://www.oregonlive.com/news/2022/01/oregon-supreme-court-approves-dropping-bar-exam-requirement-adding-options-for-new-lawyers.html; *Recommendations of Alternatives to the Bar Exam Task Force,* OREGON STATE BOARD OF BAR EXAMINERS 14–24 (June 18, 2021), https://taskforces.osbar.org/files/Bar-Exam-Alternatives-TFReport.pdf

54. *See id.* and *Or. Supp. Report, supra* note 37.

55. *See* Eileen R. Kaufman, *The Lawyers Justice Corps: A Licensing Pathway to Enhance Access to Justice,* 18 U. ST. THOMAS L. J. 159 (2022), https://papers.ssrn.com/sol3/papers.cfm?abstract_id=3852313

56. *Or. Supp. Report, supra* note 37, at 13.

CHAPTER 13

1. *See Law Schools,* STATE BAR OF CALIFORNIA, https://www.calbar.ca.gov/Admissions/Law-School-Regulation/Law-Schools (last visited Jan. 21, 2022). California also licenses candidates who have attended unaccredited law schools, or no law school, but who have passed the first-year exam (often referred to as the baby bar) and the regular bar exam. *Id.*

2. Derek T. Muller, *Which Law Schools Have the Best and Worst Debt-to-Income Ratios Among Recent Graduates? 2020 Edition,* EXCESS OF DEMOCRACY (Dec. 20, 2020), https://excessofdemocracy.com/blog/2020/12/which-law-schools-have-the-best-and-worst-debt-to-income-ratios-among-recent-graduates-2020-edition

3. California-accredited Santa Barbara and Ventura Colleges of Law offer a hybrid JD program that is 70% online with four intensive weekends in person each semester. *See Hybrid Juris Doctor (JD),* SANTA BARBARA AND VENTURA COLLEGES OF LAW, https://www.collegesoflaw.edu/hybrid-juris-doctor-2/ (last visited Jan. 13, 2022). California-accredited Concord Law School offers an entirely online JD program. *See* CONCORD LAW SCHOOL, PURDUE UNIVERSITY GLOBAL, https://www.concordlawschool.edu/ (last visited Jan. 3, 2022).

4. Chapters 8 and 9 discuss problems and reforms related to character and fitness to practice law.

5. WILLIAM SULLIVAN, ANNE COLBY, JUDITH WELCH WEGNER, LLOYD BOND, & LEE S. SHULMAN, EDUCATING LAWYERS: PREPARATION FOR THE PROFESSION OF LAW 28, 128 (2007).

6. *See* Chapter 9 (proposing that a 1L professional formation course be required to promote character and fitness for practice); *see generally* NEIL W. HAMILTON & LOUIS D. BILIONIS, LAW STUDENT PROFESSIONAL DEVELOPMENT AND FORMATION: BRIDGING LAW SCHOOL, STUDENT, AND EMPLOYER GOALS (2022) (providing support for and guidance on such courses).

7. DEBORAH JONES MERRITT & LOGAN CORNETT, BUILDING A BETTER BAR: THE TWELVE BUILDING BLOCKS OF MINIMUM COMPETENCE 75 (2020), https:/

/iaals.du.edu/sites/default/files/documents/publications/building_a_better_bar
.pdf

8. *See, e.g.*, Robert R. Kuehn & David R. Moss, *A Study of the Relationship Between Law School Coursework and Bar Exam Outcomes*, 68 J. LEGAL EDUC. 62 (2019).

9. MERRITT & CORNETT, *supra* note 7.

10. *Id.* at 74.

11. Chapter 3 discusses the exclusionary purpose behind some decisions to withdraw the diploma privilege.

12. *See* Collaboratory on Legal Education & Licensing for Practice, *Diploma Privilege and the Constitution*, 73 SMU L. REV. F. 168 (2020); Beverly Moran, *The Wisconsin Diploma Privilege: Try It, You'll Like It*, 2000 WIS. L. REV. 645 (2000).

13. *See* Milan Markovic, *Protecting the Guild or Protecting the Public? Bar Exams and the Diploma Privilege*, 35 GEO. J. LEGAL ETHICS 163 (forthcoming 2022), (presenting evidence that bar exams do not reduce attorney misconduct compared to diploma privilege), https://ssrn.com/abstract=3789235

14. *See* Wis. Sup. Ct. R. 40.03 (diploma privilege).

15. *See* Collaboratory, *supra* note 12; *see also* Catherine Martin Christopher, *Modern Diploma Privilege: A Path Rather Than a Gate* (Oct. 5, 2021) (proposing adoption of a new version of the diploma privilege based on partnership between law schools and bar examiners), https://ssrn.com/abstract=3936649 or http://dx .doi.org/10.2139/ssrn.3936649

16. Chapter 12 describes clinical residencies more fully. *See also* MERRITT & CORNETT, *supra* note 7, at 63 (identifying weaknesses of bar exams for assessing minimum competence and noting that "Practice-based assessments, such as ones based on clinical performance, offer promising avenues for evaluating minimum competence").

17. *See, e.g.*, Richard R. Ranney & Ronald Hambleton, *Do Portfolio Assessments Have a Place in Dental Licensure: Point-Counterpoint*, 37 JOURNAL OF AMERICAN DENTAL ASSOCIATION 30, 30–42 (2006); Katherine Keane, *NCARB Announces Alternate Path to Licensure for Experienced Professionals*, ARCHITECT MAGAZINE (April 28, 2017); https://www.architectmagazine.com/practice/ncarb-announces -alternate-path-to-licensure-for-experienced-professionals_0; *AXP Portfolio*, NATIONAL COUNCIL OF ARCHITECTURAL REGISTRATION BOARDS (describing portfolio of ninety-six key tasks designed to demonstrate competency across six practice fields), https://www.ncarb.org/gain-axp-experience/start-axp/record -experience/axp-portfolio (last visited April 21, 2022); *Nurse Licensing FAQs*, NEBRASKA DEPARTMENT HEALTH AND HUMAN SERVICES, http://dhhs.ne.gov/ licensure/Pages/Nurse-Licensing-FAQs.aspx (last visited May 18, 2020); *Demonstrating Qualifying Engineering Experience for Licensure*, NATIONAL SOCIETY OF PROFESSIONAL ENGINEERS, https://www.nspe.org/resources/licensure/resources/

demonstrating-qualifying-engineering-experience-licensure (last visited May 18, 2020).

18. *General Information,* COMMISSION ON TEACHER CREDENTIALING, https://www.ctc.ca.gov/educator-prep/tpa (last visited May 18, 2021); *CalTPA Preparation Materials,* CALIFORNIA EDUCATOR CREDENTIALING ASSESSMENTS, https://www.ctcexams.nesinc.com/TestView.aspx?f=HTML_FRAG/CalTPA_PrepMaterials.html (last visited April 22, 2022).

19. John Burwell Garvey & Anne F. Zinkin, *Making Law Students Client-Ready: A New Model in Legal Education,* 1 DUKE F. LAW & SOC. CHANGE 101, 115–17 (2009), https://perma.cc/N7GN-FBT5

20. *See Daniel Webster Scholar Honors Program,* UNH FRANKLIN PIERCE SCHOOL OF LAW, https://perma.cc/C5FY-84DU

21. For descriptions of the program by its founding director, see John Burwell Garvey, *"Making Law Students Client-Ready"—The Daniel Webster Scholar Honors Program: A Performance-Based Variant of the Bar Exam,* N.Y. ST. BAR ASS'N. J. 44 (2013); Garvey & Zinkin, *supra* note 19, at 115–17.

22. *See Daniel Webster Scholar Honors Program, supra* note 20.

23. ALLI GERKMAN & ELENA HARMAN, AHEAD OF THE CURVE: TURNING LAW STUDENTS INTO LAWYERS 1 (2015), https://perma.cc/93K4-GRBA

24. *Id.*

25. *See Alternatives to the Exam (ATE),* OREGON STATE BAR TASK FORCE (June 18, 2021), https://taskforces.osbar.org/ate/ [hereinafter *Or. June 2021 Report*]; *Supplemental Report of Alternative to the Exam Taskforce,* OREGON STATE BAR TASK FORCE 16, 20–21, 23 (Nov. 29, 2021) [hereinafter *Or. Supp. Report*], https://taskforces.osbar.org/files/2021-11-29SupplementalReporttoJune182021ATERep ort.pdf; Brian Gallini, *Oregon Supreme Court Set to Examine Alternative Pathways to Attorney Licensure,* FACULTY LOUNGE, https://www.thefacultylounge.org/2021/07/oregon-supreme-court-set-to-examine-alternative-pathways-to-attorney-licensure.html#more (last visited Dec. 20, 2021).

26. *See Or. June 2021 Report, supra* note 25, at 8.

27. Chapter 15 presents the advantages of performance tests in a variety of licensing schemes.

28. In 2020 just 66% of Black law school graduates passed the bar exam on their first try, compared to 88% of white candidates, 80% of Asians candidates, and 76% of Hispanic candidates. *See* ABA: LEGAL EDUCATION AND ADMISSIONS TO THE BAR, SUMMARY BAR PASS DATA: RACE, ETHNICITY, AND GENDER: 2020 AND 2021 BAR PASSAGE QUESTIONNAIRE, https://www.americanbar.org/content/dam/aba/administrative/legal_education_and_admissions_to_the_bar/statistics/20210621-bpq-national-summary-data-race-ethnicity-gender.pdf (last visited April 22, 2022).

29. ABA data shows that 93% of white graduates passed a bar exam within

two years of graduation, compared to 79% of Blacks, 84% of Hispanics, 88% of Asians, and 86% of Native Americans. *See id.* A recent study that tracked individual test-takers over ten years of California bar exams showed disparate rates of ultimate passage. Minorities in California were most likely to never pass the California bar exam. For every 1,000 African American, Hispanic/Latinx, Asian and white examinees, the numbers of eventual passers were: 531 African Americans, 695 Hispanic/Latinx, 715 Asians and 805 whites. Mitchel L. Winick, Victor D. Quintanilla, Sam Erman, Christina Chong-Nakatsuchi, & Michael Frisby, *Examining the California Cut Score: An Empirical Analysis of Minimum Competency, Public Protection, Disparate Impact, and National Standards* (Oct. 15, 2020), https://papers.ssrn.com/sol3/papers.cfm?abstract_id=3707812

30. *See, e.g.,* Marlisse Silver Sweeney, *Discrimination and Power Imbalances Plague Canada's Lawyer Training Process,* LAW.COM (Dec. 20, 2019), https://perma.cc/6K68-8YJE

31. *See, e.g.,* Peggy Maisel, *The Education and Licensing of Attorneys and Advocates in South Africa,* 79 BAR EXAM'R 15, 21 (May 2010) ("Since it is the candidate attorney's responsibility to find the law firm or lawyer for articles, the practical effect of this requirement has been to make it more difficult for nonwhite law graduates to obtain admission as attorneys").

32. *See* Aidan Macnab, *Nova Scotia Scrapping Bar Exam in Overhaul of Bar Admission Process,* CANADIAN LAWYER MAGAZINE (Nov. 12, 2019), https://www.canadianlawyermag.com/resources/legal-education/nova-scotia-scrapping-bar-exam-in-overhaul-of-bar-admission-process/321822#:~:text=The%20bar%20exam%20will%20be,Readiness%20Education%20Program%2C%20or%20PREP; *Practice Readiness Education Program (PREP),* CANADIAN CENTRE FOR PROFESSIONAL LEGAL EDUCATION, https://cpled.ca/students/cpled-prep/ (last visited April 22, 2022).

33. *See About CPLED: Who We Are,* CANADIAN CENTRE FOR PROFESSIONAL LEGAL EDUCATION, https://cpled.ca/about-cpled/who-we-are/ (last visited March 26, 2022).

34. *See Practice Readiness Education Program (PREP), supra* note 32.

CHAPTER 14

1. *See, e.g.,* Dru Stevenson, *Costs of Codification,* U. ILL. L. REV. 1130, 1131–1133 (2014) (explaining that "between the Civil War and World War II, every State and the Federal Government shifted to codified versions of their statutes," and, as a result, the number of laws proliferated; further theorizing that the need for courts to interpret such laws increased (rather than decreased as is commonly assumed); and (at 1136) asserting that, "The legal system now faces the problem of too much law to know"); Corinna Coupette, Janis Beckedorf, Dirk Hartung, Michael Bommarito, & Daniel Martin Katz, *Measuring Law over Time: A Network Analytical*

Framework with an Application to Statutes and Regulations in the United States and Germany, FRONTIERS IN PHYSICS (2021) (estimating that between 1998 and 2019 the structural elements (chapters, parts, or sections) in the U.S. Code increased by 63% (322,600 added) and in the Code of Federal Regulations by 91% (1.3 million added)), https://www.frontiersin.org/articles/10.3389/fphy.2021.658463 /full

2. *See, e.g.,* DEBORAH JONES MERRITT & LOGAN CORNETT, BUILDING A BETTER BAR: THE TWELVE BUILDING BLOCKS OF MINIMUM COMPETENCE 39 (2020) (reporting that many surveyed lawyers "felt unprepared to interpret the statutes and regulations that formed a substantial part of their practice"), https://iaals.du.edu/ sites/default/files/documents/publications/building_a_better_bar.pdf

3. Deborah J. Merritt, *Growth of the Law*, LAW SCHOOL CAFÉ (Jan. 1, 2022) (based on case counts, finding the field of criminal procedure tested on the MBE to be five times larger now than when the MBE was introduced), https://www .lawschoolcafe.org/2022/01/01/growth-of-the-law/

4. The Florida Bar, *Supreme Court Removes Two Topics from Bar Exam Part A*, FLORIDA BAR NEWS (Jan. 29, 2020) (explaining reduction of bar subjects from 27 to 25 by eliminating Juvenile Law and Dependency), https://www.floridabar.org/ the-florida-bar-news/supreme-court-removes-two-topics-from-bar-exam-part-a/

5. *See FAQs About Recommendations*, NCBE: NEXTGEN BAR EXAM OF THE FUTURE (responding under the subheading, "What subjects tested in the current exam will no longer be tested in the next gen bar exam?"), https://nextgenbarexam .ncbex.org/faqs/ (last visited Dec. 22, 2021).

6. *See* ABA SECTION OF LEGAL EDUCATION AND ADMISSIONS TO THE BAR, LEGAL EDUCATION AND PROFESSIONAL DEVELOPMENT—AN EDUCATIONAL CONTINUUM: REPORT OF THE TASK FORCE ON LAW SCHOOLS AND THE PROFESSION: NARROWING THE GAP (1992); Bryant G. Garth & Joanne Martin, *Law Schools and the Construction of Competence*, 43 J. LEGAL EDUC. 469, 475, 477 (1993); Marjorie M. Shultz & Sheldon Zedeck, *Predicting Law Effectiveness: Broadening the Basis for Law School Admissions Decisions*, 36 LAW & SOC. INQUIRY 620 (2011); Neil Hamilton, *Empirical Research on the Core Competencies Needed to Practice Law: What Do Clients, New Lawyers, and Legal Employers Tell Us?*, 83 BAR EXAM'R 6 (Sept. 2014) (evaluating survey data from junior and senior lawyers in Minnesota, interviews, job analysis studies by the NCBE, and other studies); ALLI GERKMAN & LOGAN CORNETT, FOUNDATIONS FOR PRACTICE: THE WHOLE LAWYER AND THE CHARACTER QUOTIENT (2016), https://iaals.du.edu /sites/default/files/documents/publications/foundations_for_practice_whole_ lawyer_character_quotient.pdf

7. Chapter 7 discusses this research in detail, including MERRITT & CORNETT, *supra* note 2.

8. *See* MERRITT & CORNETT, *supra* note 2.

9. *See* Joan W. Howarth, *Teaching in the Shadow of the Bar,* 31 USF L. REV. 927, 929 (1997) ("The bar reinforces teaching that the law is fixed, neutral, and natural, rather than contingent, mutable, and often deeply flawed").

10. *See,* e.g., Jerome Frank, *Why Not a Clinical Lawyer-School?,* 81 U. PA. L. REV. 907, 913 (1933); *cf.* Lee S. Shulman, *Education of Professionals,* 98 ELEMENTARY SCHOOL JOURNAL 511, 519 (1998) ("the responsibility of the developing professional is not simply to apply what he or she has learned to practice but to transform, adapt, merge and synthesize, criticize, and invent in order to move from the theoretical and research-based knowledge of the academy to the kind of practical clinical knowledge needed to engage in professional work").

11. Susan L. Davis & Chad W. Buckendahl, *Incorporating Cognitive Demand in Credentialing Examinations, in* ASSESSMENT OF HIGHER ORDER THINKING SKILLS 304, 323 (Gregory Schraw & Daniel H. Robinson, eds. 2011). These researchers recommend that subject matter content and frameworks of differing levels of cognitive demand be addressed in licensing test development, in subject matter expert training, and in question analysis.

12. *See, e.g.,* Susan Bryant, Elliott S. Milstein, & Ann C. Shalleck, *Learning Goals for Clinical Programs, in* SUSAN BRYANT, ELLIOTT S. MILSTEIN, & ANN C. SHALLECK, TRANSFORMING THE EDUCATION OF LAWYERS: THEORY AND PRACTICE OF CLINICAL PEDAGOGY 13 (2014); Robert D. Dinerstein & Elliott S. Milstein, *Learning to Be a Lawyer: Embracing Indeterminacy and Uncertainty,* in BRYANT ET AL., *supra,* at 327; Deborah Jones Merritt, *Crossing the Divide,* in LINDA H. EDWARDS, THE DOCTRINE SKILLS DIVIDE: LEGAL EDUCATION'S SELF-INFLICTED WOUND 347 (2017).

13. *See* Davis & Buckendahl, *supra* note 11, at 26–27 (defining metacognition as "thinking about and regulating one's thinking" and arguing that metacognition is comprised of three sub-components: declarative knowledge, including knowledge of ourselves; procedural knowledge, including knowledge of strategies; and conditional knowledge, including insights about why and when to employ certain strategies).

14. *See, e.g.,* Bryant, Milstein & Shalleck, *supra* note 12, at 13, 25; Rosa Kim, *Lightening the Cognitive Load: Maximizing Learning in the Legal Writing Classroom,* 21 PERSPECTIVES: TEACHING LEGAL RESEARCH AND WRITING 101, 103 (2013); Patti Alleva & Jennifer A. Gundlach, *Learning Intentionally and the Metacognitive Task,* 65 J. LEGAL EDUC. 710, 714 (2016) (reflecting on the role of metacognition in teaching civil procedure).

15. *See* Joan W. Howarth, *What Law Must Lawyers Know?,* 19 CONN. PUB. INT. L. J. 1 (2019).

16. *See Licensing Examinations,* LAW SOCIETY OF ONTARIO, https://lso.ca/becoming-licensed/lawyer-licensing-process/licensing-examinations (last visited Dec. 27, 2021); Andrea A. Curcio, Carol Chomsky, & Eileen Kaufman, *How to*

Build a Better Bar Exam, N.Y. ST. B. ASS'N J., 37, 38–40 (Sept. 2018).

17. MERRITT & CORNETT, *supra* note 2, at 37.

18. Cognitive domains and knowledge are more complex than my simple distinction between familiarity and memorization suggests. *See, e.g.,* A TAXONOMY FOR LEARNING, TEACHING, AND ASSESSING: A REVISION OF BLOOM'S TAXONOMY OF EDUCATIONAL OBJECTIVES (Lorin W. Anderson & David R. Krathwohl, eds. 2001) (describing the cognitive process dimension (lower to higher order thinking skills of remembering, understanding, applying, analyzing, evaluating, and creating) and the knowledge dimension (factual, conceptual, procedural, and metacognitive)).

19. *E.g.,* Rebecca White Berch, *Letter from the Chair,* 87 BAR EXAM'R 1, 2 (Summer 2018) https://thebarexaminer.org/article/summer-2018/letter-from-the-chair/

20. Merritt and Cornett also recommend reducing or eliminating memorization on bar exams. *See* MERRITT & CORNETT, *supra* note 2, at 24–25, 37–38.

21. *See Licensing Examinations, supra* note 16; Curcio et al., *supra* note 16.

22. For example, New York supplements the Uniform Bar Exam with the New York Licensing Exam, a two-hour, open book multiple-choice test of New York law. *See Uniform Bar Exam, New York Law Course, and New York Law Exam,* NEW YORK STATE BOARD OF LAW EXAMINERS, https://www.nybarexam.org/UBE/UBE.html (last visited June 23, 2019).

23. For research showing experienced lawyers flunking the MBE, *see* Steven Foster, *Does the Multistate Bar Exam Validly Measure Attorney Competence?,* 82 OHIO ST. L. J. ONLINE 31 (2021).

24. James Bandler & Nathan Koppel, *Raising the Bar: Even Top Lawyers Fail California Exam,* WALL ST. J. (Dec. 5, 2005), https://www.wsj.com/articles/SB113374619258513723

25. Educational requirements are discussed in Chapter 13.

CHAPTER 15

1. *See generally Final Report of the Testing Task Force,* NCBE: NEXTGEN BAR EXAM OF THE FUTURE, (2021) [hereinafter *Testing Task Force Final Report*], https://nextgenbarexam.ncbex.org/reports/final-report-of-the-ttf/

2. *Facts About Recommendations: Content,* NCBE: NEXTGEN BAR EXAM OF THE FUTURE, https://nextgenbarexam.ncbex.org/faqs/ (last visited March 27, 2022).

3. *See Testing Task Force Final Report, supra* note 1, at 4, 21–23.

4. *See* DEBORAH JONES MERRITT & LOGAN CORNETT, BUILDING A BETTER BAR: THE TWELVE BUILDING BLOCKS OF MINIMUM COMPETENCE 72 (2020), https://iaals.du.edu/sites/default/files/documents/publications/building_a_better_bar.pdf

5. *See Snapshot of NextGen Bar Exam,* NCBE: NEXTGEN BAR EXAM OF THE

FUTURE, https://nextgenbarexam.ncbex.org/ (last visited Jan. 8, 2022).

6. *See* MERRITT & CORNETT, *supra* note 4, at 31.

7. Judge Cynthia Martin, Chair, NCBE Implementation Steering Committee, *Future Direction of the UBE*, addressing California Blue Ribbon Commission on the Future of the Bar Exam (July 6, 2021), https://www.youtube.com/watch?v= j3OyK7wlr-g (at 03:35:25, last visited Jan. 15, 2022).

8. See *Multistate Performance Test: Preparing for the MPT,* NCBE, https://www .ncbex.org/exams/mpt/preparing/ (last visited Jan. 16, 2022).

9. *See Jurisdictions Administering the MPT.* NCBE, https://www.ncbex.org/ exams/mpt/ (last visited March 27, 2022).

10. "The MPT is not a test of substantive knowledge. Rather, it is designed to evaluate certain fundamental skills lawyers are expected to demonstrate regardless of the area of law in which the skills are applied." *Id.* at *Purpose.* For an argument that performance tests should be reinvigorated and given increased importance, see Ben Bratman, *Improving the Performance of the Performance Test: The Key to Meaningful Bar Exam Reform,* 83 UMKC L. REV. 565 (2015). For the uses of performance tests in legal education, see Sara Berman, *Integrating Performance Tests into Doctrinal Courses, Skills Courses, and Institutional Benchmark Testing: A Simple Way to Enhance Student Engagement While Furthering Assessment, Bar Passage, and Other ABA Accreditation Objectives,* 42 J. OF LEGAL PROF. 147 (2018), https://ssrn.com/abstract=3206929

11. *See Uniform Bar Examination: UBE Scores,* NCBE, https://www.ncbex.org/ exams/ube/scores/ (last visited Jan. 13, 2022).

12. *See* NCBE TESTING TASK FORCE, YOUR VOICE: STAKEHOLDER THOUGHTS ABOUT THE BAR EXAM: PHASE 1 REPORT OF THE TESTING TASK FORCE 23 (Aug. 2019), https://nextgenbarexam.ncbex.org/wp-content/uploads/FINAL-Listening -Session-Executive-Summary-with-Appendices-2.pdf

13. MERRITT & CORNETT, *supra* note 4, at 66. "[F]ocus group members characterized the performance tests as 'valuable,' the 'most useful' part of the bar exam, and 'very practical.'" *Id.* at 67 (in-text citation numbers omitted).

14. *Id.* (citation omitted).

15. *Id.* (citation omitted).

16. *See* Joan W. Howarth & Judith Welch Wegner, *Ringing Changes: Systems Thinking About Legal Licensing,* 13 FIU L. REV. 383, 423–27 (2019) (benefits of staged licensing); *id.* at 454–58 (staged licensing enables testing of advanced competencies); Jayne W. Barnard & Mark Greenspan, *Incremental Bar Admissions: Lessons from the Medical Profession,* 53 J. LEGAL EDUC. 340 (2003) (advocating staged attorney licensing).

17. Nevada performance tests have used actual statutes, constitutional provisions, and cases since August 2020. *See Model Answers,* STATE BAR OF NEVADA, https://nvbar.org/licensing-compliance/admissions/bar-exam/model-answers/

(last visited Jan. 11. 2022).

18. The NCBE needs to undertake further research on the appropriate timing for MPTs. New lawyers in the *Building a Better Bar* study confirmed my experience that excessive time pressure on many MPTs undermines their ability to assess minimum competence. MERRITT & CORNETT, *supra* note 4, at 64.

19. *See 1L Skills Check Overview,* LAW SCHOOL ADMISSIONS COUNCIL, https://www.lsac.org/about/1l-skills-check (last visited Aug. 21, 2021). As a consultant with LSAC on the project, I am impressed by the methodological significance and promise of LSAC's expert work to make 1L Skills Check scores reliable.

20. *See* Joan W. Howarth, *The Case for a Uniform Cut Score,* 42 J. LEGAL PROF. 69 (2017).

21. *See* Johnna Gueorguieva, Sara Locatelli, & Amy Roedl, *Standard Setting,* in CERTIFICATION: THE ICE HANDBOOK (James Henderson, ed. 3d ed., 2019) at 339, 347.

22. *Id.*

23. MICHAEL J. ZIEKY, MARIANNE PERIE, & SAMUEL A. LIVINGSTON, CUT-SCORES: A MANUAL FOR SETTING STANDARDS OF PERFORMANCE ON EDUCATIONAL AND OCCUPATIONAL TESTS 52 (2008).

24. GREGORY J. CIZEK & MICHAEL B. BUNCH, STANDARD-SETTING: A GUIDE TO ESTABLISHING AND EVALUATING PERFORMANCE STANDARDS ON TESTS 52 (2006). Law professor Ilya Somin makes the entertaining suggestion that the quickest way to bar exam reform would be to make bar examiners take the exam every year. *See* Ilya Somin, *How to Make Bar Exams Great Again,* VOLOKH CONSPIRACY (July 9, 2019), https://reason.com/volokh/2019/07/09/how-to-make-bar-exams-great-again/

25. *See* MERRITT & CORNETT, *supra* note 4, at 64; *cf.* Ruth Colker, *Test Validity: Faster Is Not Necessarily Better,* 49 SETON HALL L. REV. 679, 689 (2019) (speeded tests should be prohibited unless validity with time pressure is established).

26. *See* William D. Henderson, *The LSAT, Law School Exams, and Meritocracy: The Surprising and Undertheorized Role of Test-Taking Speed,* 82 TEX. L. REV. 975 (2004).

27. *See* MERRITT & CORNETT, *supra* note 4, at 64.

28. *Id.* (citation omitted).

29. *See* MELISSA J. MARGOLIS & RICHARD A. FEINBERG, EDS., INTEGRATING TIMING CONSIDERATIONS TO IMPROVE TESTING PRACTICES (2020).

30. *See, e.g.,* Daniel P. Jurich, *A History of Test Speededness: Tracing the Evolution of Theory and Practice,* in MARGOLIS & FEINBERG, *supra* note 29, at 1, 14 ("the critical influence that speed can have on test validity necessitates empirical evidence defending the selected time limits"); Paul De Boeck & Frank Rijmen, *Response Times in Cognitive Tests: Interpretation and Importance,* in MARGOLIS & FEINBERG, *supra* note 29, at 142, 142 ("the stringency of a given time limit will

affect the validity of the inferences we make from exam scores").

31. "Practice in professions and occupations often changes over time. . . . Each profession or occupation should periodically reevaluate the knowledge and skills measured in its examination used to meet the requirements of the credential." AMERICAN EDUCATIONAL RESEARCH ASSOCIATION, AMERICAN PSYCHOLOGI-CAL ASSOCIATION, & NATIONAL COUNCIL ON MEASUREMENT IN EDUCATION, STANDARDS FOR EDUCATIONAL AND PSYCHOLOGICAL TESTING 176–77 (2014).

32. *Cf.* Deborah J. Merritt, *Growth of the Law,* LAW SCHOOL CAFÉ (Jan. 1, 2022) (body of criminal procedure law is now five times larger than when MBE was introduced in 1972), https://www.lawschoolcafe.org/

33. *See* 2022 California Rules of Court, *Rule 9.6. Supreme Court Approval of Bar Examination,* JUDICIAL COUNCIL OF CALIFORNIA, Rule 9.6(b) ("The State Bar must conduct an analysis of the validity of the bar examination at least once every seven years"), https://www.courts.ca.gov/cms/rules/index.cfm?title=nine&linkid =rule9_6 (last visited April 22, 2022).

INDEX

AALS. *See* Association of American Law Schools

ABA. *See* American Bar Association

Abel, Richard, 15, 28, 29, 35, 166n11

Accommodations for disabled persons, 7, 45–46

ADA (Americans with Disabilities Act of 1990), 88

African Americans. *See* Black Americans

Allen, Macon Bolling, 18

American Bar Association (ABA): on bar admission standards, 19, 26; on bar exam passage rates, 7; Black law schools, role in shutting down, 26, 41; on case method of legal education, 22; on character and fitness inquiries, 81, 87, 88; on clinical residencies, 113; Commission on the Future of Legal Education, 70; on diploma privilege, 21, 24, 164n59; law school accreditation by, 8, 25–26, 39–42, 53, 65, 118–120, 156n38; LGBTQ rights considered by, 86; *MacCrate Report*, 62–63, 65, 70, 71; on night schools, 24–26; on professional identity formation, 195n12; race discrimination and, 26, 41; on racial disparities in legal profession, 155n37; on state boards of bar examiners, 25, 164n49

Americans with Disabilities Act of 1990 (ADA), 88

Apprenticeships: clinical residencies vs., 110; diploma privilege vs., 121; discrimination and, 18, 37; history of, 16, 166n10; requirements for, 19, 21

Asian populations: bar exam passage rates for, 7, 210–211nn28–29; MBE scores among, 7; oral bar exams for, 19

Association of American Law Schools (AALS): on bar admission standards, 26; on case method of legal education, 22; diploma privilege opposed by, 21; on night schools, 24, 25; on state boards of bar examiners, 164n49